ESL
Grammar Workbook 1

for intermediate speakers and writers of english as a second language

LOW-INTERMEDIATE

ALLAN KENT DART

New York University

REGENTS/PRENTICE HALL, Englewood Cliffs, New Jersey 07632

Library of Congress Cataloging in Publication Data

DART, ALLAN KENT, 1937-
  ESL grammar workbook.

    CONTENTS: 1. Low-intermediate. —2. High-intermediate.
    1. English language   Text-books for foreigners.
2. English language—Grammar—1950-   I. Title.
PE1128.D345   428'.2'4076   77-25316
ISBN 0-13-283663-7 (v. 1)
ISBN 0-13-283671-8 (v. 2)

TO MY MOTHER,
AND
IN MEMORY OF MY FATHER

 © 1978 by Prentice-Hall, Inc.
A Simon & Schuster Company
Englewood Cliffs, New Jersey 07632

Printed in the United States of America.

19   18   17

ISBN   0-13-283663-7

Prentice-Hall International (UK) Limited, *London*
Prentice-Hall of Australia Pty. Limited, *Sydney*
Prentice-Hall Canada Inc., *Toronto*
Prentice-Hall Hispanoamericana, S. A., *Mexico*
Prentice-Hall of India Private Limited, *New Delhi*
Prentice-Hall of Japan, Inc., *Tokyo*
Simon & Schuster Asia Pte. Ltd., *Singapore*
Editora Prentice-Hall do Brasil, Ltda., *Rio de Janeiro*

CONTENTS

PREFACE

Books 1 and 2 of *ESL Grammar Woorkbook* constitute a survey of the English language for intermediate students of English as a second language. The material has been designed primarily for students in colleges, universities, and adult education programs.

Books 1 and 2 may be used as a complete course of study for an intensive one-semester program of approximately 175 hours, or the work may be divided for a two-semester program. However, Book 1 is not a prerequisite to Book 2, for the two books have been designed as separate textbooks.

The material in this text has been tested by me and other teachers at New York University over a period of three years. Book 2 (in a somewhat different form) was tested with three different pilot groups in a sixty-hour program designed for the New York Telephone Company. Thus, the material has been intensively tested both with students who were preparing for future university studies, and with non-academic students in an industrial setting who were studying English to improve their performance on the job.

There are many people I want to thank for the constructive criticism, encouragement, and interest they showed during the development of the manuscript. Unfortunately, space does not permit me to thank them all. For their many suggestions and the strong motivating force that they provided, I would particularly like to thank Clarice Wilkes Kaltinick, Rosalie Yarmus Lurie, Fred Malkemes, Jr., Linda Rooney Markstein, and my good neighbor, Anna M.

Halpin. I would also like to thank Milton G. Saltzer, Director of the American Language Institute, New York University, for permitting me to test the material in my classes.

To the following at Prentice-Hall, I wish to express my appreciation: Marylin Brauer, Ilene McGrath, and Teru Uyeyama.

I also want to express my special indebtedness to my friend Gary-Gabriel Gisondi, librarian at the Performing Arts Research Center of the New York Public Library at Lincoln Center. Without his assistance and inspiration, this book could not have been written.

My deepest gratitude must go to the hundreds of students I have had over the years who have made my teaching career so enjoyable and meaningful. An especially strong feeling of gratitude is felt toward those who participated in the shaping of the final draft of the manuscript: Alcira Derevizus (of Argentina); Jose Concepcion (of Cuba); Ronna Estrada and Martha Mejia (of Columbia); Ho-Foo Hui (of Curaçao); Josefina Rivera (of the Dominican Republic); Armelle Mathurin and Nicole Villejoint (of Haiti); Angelina Goldamez (of Honduras); Swandayati (Lin) Aliwarga (of Indonesia); Raymond Malkomian (of Iran); Abdel Jaber Tarik (of Palestine); Tazuko Hosaka (of Japan); Hae-Kyoung Cha (of Korea); Hilda Avalos (of Peru); Reinaldo Franqui (of Puerto Rico); Tull Syvanarat (of Thailand); Eddy Dieguez (of Uruguay); and Orlando Angarita, Nary Barrios, and Clemilde (Cleo) Beltran (of Venezuela).

Allan Kent Dart

INTRODUCTION

This textbook is for low-intermediate students of English as a second language who have completed an intensive beginners' course of approximately 175 hours or a few shorter courses over an extended period of time. The book would also be appropriate for intermediate students who have had no formal course work but have had some practical exposure to the language.

The explanations and exercises are carefully sequenced and graded, so I recommend that the order of the chapters be followed as closely as possible since past material is constantly being reviewed within the context of the new material that is being presented.

The exercises are usually preceded by grammatical explanations in which the paragraphs are numbered so that the various points of the explanation may be easily referred to by everyone in the class. As an effective introduction to the exercises that are to follow, I suggest that the instructor read the grammar explanations out loud to the students. This short period of reading descriptions and examples (the examples may be used for choral practice) will allow the students to practice the pronunciation of various grammatical terms, and it will also help ensure that everyone will have a clear understanding of the Focus that is to appear in the exercise.

Every Grammar Exercise in this book contains complete exercises which focus on a specific topic. For best results, it is essential that everyone keep his or her mind on the Focus that is stated at the top of each exercise. The Focus is there to give control to the lesson and direction to the group.

Most of the exercises are designed so that they may be used as a plan for a guided period of conversation by the group. For example, in a Grammar Exercise with the Focus of *yes-no* questions, the list of questions may be used as a script by the instructor for conducting a drill. Depending on the group and its teacher, during such drills it might be best for the students to keep their books closed.

The exercises can also be used as quizzes, as homework, or for writing assignments during a class. A particularly effective procedure is for the students not to use a pen or pencil while they are doing an exercise in class. Then the exercise may be given as a homework assignment. While the students are doing their homework, they will be testing themselves to see what they have remembered, or may have forgotten, from the previous meeting.

The pages are perforated and easy to tear out. If the students wish, at the end of this course they may remove all of the pages (including those not submitted to the teacher), and reassemble them in a binder or folder. By doing this, they will create their own presentation, which will add a personal touch to their book. Also, it will be a convenient way for them to review the corrections the teacher has made in their assignments.

Sometimes during an exercise, a student will find *s/he*, a "word" that can mean *she* or *he*—for example, *S/he lives in Boston* (she); or *S/he lives in Boston* (he).

Sentences like *S/he took his/her wife/husband out to dinner on his/her birthday* also sometimes occur. With such a sentence, one can say or write *S/he took his/her wife/husband out to dinner on his/her birthday;* or *S/he took his/her wife/husband out to dinner on his/her birthday*.

Note: Primarily the use of these devices is to help the students develop their skills in using pronouns and possessive adjectives. Secondarily, it reflects the author's attempt to create a nonsexist atmosphere for a group meeting.

Notes and reminders are some of the other learning devices used throughout this book. A Note supplies new information, and a Reminder helps a student remember something that has already been discussed.

The terms FORMAL and INFORMAL are frequently used in grammar explanations in this text. Formal usage is that style found in formal writing—for example, a letter to an ambassador, a scientific report, or a doctoral thesis. An informal style of writing would most likely be used in a letter to a school friend, a quick note to a neighbor, or an article in a newspaper about a football game.

Because the emphasis in this book is on spoken English, the material in the exercises most frequently represents an informal style of writing, and the model sentences reflect the style of speaking that is used by educated people in an informal situation. I hope that students and teachers will find their experience with this book interesting and enjoyable.

THE SIMPLE PRESENT TENSE AND INTRODUCTION TO PARTS OF SPEECH

1.1

THE VERB *BE*

1. *Am, are,* and *is* occur as the three forms of the verb *be* in the simple present tense. CONTRACTIONS of subject pronouns and *am, are,* and *is* appear in informal usage. A contraction always contains an APOSTROPHE ('), which represents the omitted (missing) letter.

	Singular	Plural		Singular	Plural
First person	I *am*	we		I'*m*	we
Second person	you *are*	you	*are*	you'*re*	you	'*re*
Third person	he	they		he	they
	she } *is*			she } '*s*	
	it			it	

2. In the negative form of the verb *be* in the simple present tense, the adverb *not* follows the verb. *Aren't* and *isn't* are the contracted form of *are not* and *is not.* There is no contracted form for *am not.*

I'*m not*	we
you *aren't*	you } *aren't*
he	they
she } *isn't*	
it	

3. In writing, a *yes-no* question with the verb *be* begins with the verb and ends with a QUESTION MARK (?): ***Are** you a teacher?* ***Is** he a student?*

4. In informal usage we may respond to a *yes-no* question with a simple *yes* (or *yeah*), *no,* a grunt, a sigh, or perhaps a nod or slight shake of the head. However, in formal (more polite) usage we respond to a *yes-no* question with a short *yes-no* answer. In writing, a COMMA (,) appears after the *yes* or *no,* and the answer ends with a PERIOD (.). Contractions usually occur with *no* answers, but contractions are never used with short *yes* answers, but they appear in long *yes* answers: *Yes, **I'm** a teacher.* Compare:

SHORT YES-NO ANSWERS WITH THE VERB BE

Yes,	{ I am. you are. he (she, it) is. we (you, they) are.	No,	{ I'm not. you aren't. he (she, it) isn't. we (you, they) aren't.	No,	{ I'm not. you're not. he (she, it)'s not. we (you, they)'re not.

Remember: Contractions never occur with short *yes* answers.
Note: *Ain't* is a nonstandard contracted form for *am not, are not,* and *is not;* it does not occur in educated speech and writing.

1.2

GRAMMAR EXERCISE   Name _____ Date _____

> Focus: The Verb *Be* in Statements

Fill in the blanks with appropriate forms of the verb *be*. Practice using contractions. Do this exercise aloud and/or in writing.

EXAMPLES: a. It 's a beautiful and warm day.
              b. I <u>am</u> a citizen of another country.
              c. They <u>aren't</u> very good friends of mine.

1. I _____ from Africa/Asia/Europe/Latin America/the Middle East/North America.

2. We _____ students of English as a second language.

3. It _____ bad for your health to smoke.

4. They _____ good friends of my parents.

5. She _____ a student of the Bible.

6. You _____ a new friend of mine.

7. We _____ at the beginning of this book.

8. I _____ a native speaker of Arabic/Bengali/Chinese/French/German/Greek/Hindi/Italian/Japanese/Korean/Persian/Portuguese/Russian/Spanish/Swahili/Swedish/Thai/Vietnamese.

9. I _____ a happy person.

10. He _____ a member of my class.

11. She _____ the director of the organization.

12. We _____ in an English class.

13. I _____ an African/a European/a Latin American/a Middle Easterner/a North American/an Oriental.

14. He _____ the teacher of my class.

15. You _____ a relative of mine.

16. They _____ a happy couple.

17. Fortunately, I _____ sick.

18. Unfortunately, it _____ a nice day.

19. I _____ in a good mood.

20. She _____ a good tennis player.

21. You _____ a native speaker of English.

22. Unfortunately, they _____ happy with their new house.

23. S/he _____ a married man/woman.

24. We _____ in a large room.

25. They _____ students at this school.

1.3

GRAMMAR EXERCISE   Name _____ Date _____

Focus: *Yes-No* Questions and Answers with the Verb *Be*

Do this exercise aloud and/or in writing. The questions may be used by the instructor as a script for an oral practice.

EXAMPLES: a. <u>Are</u> you an American?
            b. <u>Is</u> she a European?
            c. <u>Are</u> they a happy couple?

1. _____ you a student of English as a second language?

2. _____ you from Asia/Europe/Latin America/the Middle East/Africa?

3. _____ she from South America?

4. _____ I wrong/correct?

5. _____ we in a large/small/comfortable/dirty room?

6. _____ he your brother?

7. _____ you a native speaker of Spanish/French/Chinese?

8. _____ it cold in Alaska?

9. _____ you hungry/thirsty/tired?

10. _____ it cold/hot outside?

11. _____ it difficult to learn a second language?

12. _____ you married/single?

13. _____ you an American citizen?

14. _____ they worried about something?

15. _____ we in a large/small group?

Now complete the following *yes-no* answers.

EXAMPLES: d. Yes, she <u>is</u>.
            e. No, he <u>isn't</u>.

16. Yes, I _____.   26. No, I _____.

17. No, I _____.   27. Yes, they _____.

18. Yes, we _____.   28. No, they _____.

19. No, they_____.   29. No, she _____.

20. Yes, you _____.   30. Yes, I _____.

21. No, you _____.   31. No, we _____.

22. Yes, he _____.   32. No, he _____.

23. No, she _____.   33. No, you _____.

24. Yes, they _____.   34. No, I _____.

25. No, we _____.   35. Yes, I _____.

1.4

TYPES OF NOUNS

1. Nouns, like subject pronouns (*I, you*, etc.), may occupy the subject position of a sentence: **Life** *is wonderful;* **Food** *isn't cheap;* **China** *is a large country;* **Rice** *is an important food.*

2. A PROPER NOUN always begins with a capital letter in writing. Some kinds of proper nouns are (a) personal names: *George Washington, Betsy Ross;* (b) names connected to geography: *India, Tokyo, the Nile, the Pacific, the Grand Canyon;* (c) names of languages, nationalities, and religions: *English, a Mexican, Buddhism;* (d) names of state, national, and religious holidays: *Labor Day, Thanksgiving, Christmas, Easter, Ramadan;* and (e) the days and months of the year: *Saturday, April.*
   Note: The seasons of the year are not proper nouns and always begin with a small letter: *fall (autumn), winter, spring, summer.*

3. A CONCRETE NOUN describes some thing (a physical object) that we can see (*a movie, a painting*), touch (*a rock, a sculpture*), or smell (*a flower, an herb*).

4. An ABSTRACT NOUN describes a concept or idea, something that has no physical appearance: *justice, freedom, integrity, beauty, honor.*

5. A COLLECTIVE NOUN describes a group of people, animals, or objects that is considered a single unit: *class, group, family, flock, herd.*
   Note: When a collective noun is used as the subject of a sentence, it usually takes a singular form: *My family is not in this country; The group is excited about the new class.*

6. A COUNTABLE NOUN describes some thing that we can count: *one book, two books; one dollar, two dollars; one year, two years.*

7. An UNCOUNTABLE NOUN does not have a plural form (some end in *s*, however); it describes some thing that cannot be counted: *tea, steel, sugar.*

1.5

GRAMMAR EXERCISE   Name _____ Date _____

Focus: Noun Subjects with the Verb *Be*

Do this exercise aloud and/or in writing. Fill in the blanks with appropriate forms of the verb *be* in the simple present tense, and with appropriate nouns where called for.

EXAMPLES   a. English <u>is</u> an international language.
             b. Love <u>is</u> more important than money.
             c. Cigarettes <u>aren't</u> good for your health.

1. My family _____ in Europe/Asia/America/Africa/the Middle East.

2. English _____ my native language.

3. My first language _____ [supply] _____.

4. The formula for carbon monoxide _____ CO.

Name _____ Date _____

5. February _____ a nice month in Alaska/my hometown.

6. Butter _____ good for you.

7. The sun _____ approximately 93 million miles from the earth.

8. Coffee _____ an important product of Brazil/my native country.

9. Algebra _____ an easy subject.

10. Mr. and Mrs. [supply name] _____ _____ from [supply] _____.

11. The Pacific _____ the largest _____ in the world.

12. The Nile _____ the longest _____ in the world.

13. Christmas _____ my favorite holiday.

14. Christmas _____ an important holiday in many parts of the world. Christmas isn't an important holiday in _____.

15. Boys _____ very different from girls.

16. Coffee _____ an important product of _____.

17. A nice house _____ cheap.

18. The President and his wife _____ friends of mine.

19. December _____ cold in _____.

20. Washington, D.C., _____ the capital of _____.

21. London _____ the capital of _____.

22. _____ _____ the capital of _____.

23. Cigarettes _____ dangerous to your health.

24. _____ _____ dangerous to your health.

25. Paris _____ the most beautiful city in the world.

26. _____ _____ the most beautiful city in _____.

27. A good automobile _____ expensive.

28. _____ _____ expensive.

29. May and June _____ beautiful months in California.

30. _____ _____ beautiful months in _____.

31. Chemistry _____ an interesting subject.

32. _____ _____ an interesting subject.

1.6

Focus: Noun Subjects in *Yes-No* Questions

Pronunciation Note: A contraction of a noun subject and the verb *be* (e.g., *Love's wonderful.*) rarely occurs in written English; however, in spoken English we hear a contracted form: (a) *Elizabeth is* sounds like *Elizabeths;* (b) *Railroads are* sounds like *railroads-er;* (c) *Mr. and Mrs. Brown are* sounds like *Mr. and Mrs. Brown-er;* (d) *Cigarettes are* sounds like *cigarettes-er;* (e) *Washington, D.C., is* sounds like *Washington dee-sees;* (f) *Nouns are* sounds like *nouns-er.*

Supply *is* or *are* in the blanks of the following *yes-no* questions. Then supply *it* or *they* and an appropriate form of the verb *be* in the *yes-no* answer following each question.

EXAMPLES: a. <u>Is</u> Tokyo a large city? Yes, <u>it is</u>.
             b. <u>Are</u> diamonds expensive? Yes, <u>they are</u>.
             Note: Noun subjects do not occur in *yes-no* answers.

1. _____ friends necessary? Yes, _____.

2. _____ cigarettes bad for your health? Yes, _____.

3. _____ English an important language in international trade? Yes, _____.

4. _____ potatoes expensive now? No, _____.

5. _____ Christmas your favorite holiday? No, _____.

6. _____ the Mississippi the longest river in the world? No, _____.

7. _____ shoes expensive? Yes, _____.

8. _____ a language difficult to learn? Yes, _____.

9. _____ Mexico in North America? Yes, _____.

10. _____ records expensive? Yes, _____.

11. _____ apples good for you? Yes, _____.

12. _____ vacations in Europe expensive? Yes, _____.

13. _____ Costa Rica in North America? No, _____.

14. _____ life difficult? Yes, _____.

Now practice pronouncing the contracted forms of noun subjects with the verb *be.*

15. apples are = *apples-er*
16. books are = *books-er*
17. English is = *Englishiz*
18. diamonds are = *diamonds-er*
19. dogs are = *dogs-er*

20. phones are = *phones-er*
21. people are = *people-er*
22. money is = *moneys*
23. friends are = *friends-er*
24. cats are = *cats-er*

1.7

GRAMMAR EXERCISE   Name _____ Date _____

Focus: Noun Subjects

algebra	Buddhism	cigarettes	France	money	rice	vacations
bananas	butter	cotton	friends	movies	Saturday	wine
beef	Catholicism	democracy	life	potatoes	telephones	
books	chicken	diamonds	love	religion	tobacco	

Pick out appropriate nouns from the above list and use them as noun subjects in the blanks. The nouns that end in -s are plural, and the ones that do not end in -s are singular. **Reminder:** (a) An uncountable noun is singular: *Coffee is expensive;* (b) a proper noun (e.g., *France, Saturday, London*) begins with a capital letter; and (c) a sentence begins with a capital letter.

EXAMPLES: a. <u>Religion</u> isn't very important in his life.
                     b. <u>Diamonds</u> are an important natural resource of South Africa.

1. _____ are popular all over the world.

2. _____ is the most important food in Asia.

3. _____ is my favorite day of the week.

4. _____ are expensive almost everywhere.

5. _____ is an important part of French cooking.

6. _____ is an important product of France.

7. _____ are very bad for your health.

8. _____ is necessary for a happy life.

Now supply an appropriate form of the verb *be* as well.

9. _____ more important than money.

10. _____ the most important religion in the Orient.

11. _____ delicious with chicken.

12. _____ more important than money and success.

13. _____ an important product of Egypt.

14. _____ wonderful/terrible.

15. _____ my favorite kind of meat.

16. _____ an important product of Central America.

17. _____ a beautiful and prosperous (rich) country.

18. _____ a very interesting subject.

19. _____ expensive in my native country.

20. _____ sometimes difficult to understand.

21. _____ a big problem for many people.

22. _____ an important product of Virginia.

23. _____ good for you.

24. _____ easy/difficult.

1.8

RULES FOR SPELLING PLURAL NOUNS

Regular Spellings

1. We can make most countable nouns plural by simply adding *-s* to the singular form: *girl, girls; orange, oranges; tree, trees.*

Nouns Ending in -s, -z, -ch, -sh, or -x

2. (a) When a singular noun ends in the above letters, add *-es: class, classes; couch, couches; bush, bushes; tax, taxes.*

   (b) When a final *-ch* ending sounds like [K], add only *-s: stomach, stomachs; epoch, epochs; monarch, monarchs.*

Nouns Ending in -y

3. (a) When a noun ends in *-y* preceded by a consonant (all letters except the vowels *a, e, i, o,* and *u*), change the *y* to *i* and add *-es: lady, ladies; library, libraries; party, parties.*

   (b) When a noun ends in *-y* preceded by a vowel, do not make a change and add only *-s: valley, valleys; day, days; tray, trays.*

Nouns Ending in -f or fe

4. When a one-syllable noun ends in *-f* or *-fe*, drop the final letter or letters and add *-ves: knife, knives; life, lives; self, selves.*
   Exceptions: *gulf, gulfs; safe, safes; belief, beliefs; roof, roofs; chief, chiefs.*

Nouns Ending in -o

5. (a) Usually, when a noun ends in *-o* preceded by a consonant, we add *-es: mosquito, mosquitoes; Negro, Negroes; hero, heroes.*

   (b) If a vowel precedes the *-o*, add only *-s: zoo, zoos; radio, radios.*

   (c) When a noun that ends in *-o* is a musical term taken from the Italian, add *-s* only: *alto, altos; solo, solos; soprano, sopranos; piano, pianos.*

Some Irregular Spellings

6. (a) Some irregular plural forms are: *child, children; foot, feet; goose, geese; man, men; ox, oxen; woman, women; mouse, mice; tooth, teeth.*

   (b) Three nouns that have the same form in the singular and plural are: *sheep, sheep; fish, fish; deer, deer.*

   (c) *Series* and *means* have the same form in the singular and plural (e.g., *The series is . . . . The series are . . . .*)

Plural Forms of Latin and Greek Origin

7. A few nouns from Latin and Greek still retain their original plural form: *crisis, crises; analysis, analyses; axis, axes; datum, data; criterion, criteria; phenomenon, phenomena; radius, radii; stimulus, stimuli; thesis, theses; parenthesis, parentheses; hypothesis, hypotheses.*

1.9

Focus: Spelling Plural Forms of Countable Nouns

Supply the correct spellings of the plural forms of the following nouns. An asterisk (*) before a noun indicates that the word is of Latin or Greek origin. Carefully check the rules for spelling plural countable nouns. Use your dictionary for the words that you do not know.

EXAMPLES: a.   lady <u>ladies</u>   c.   class <u>classes</u>
               b.   *medium <u>media</u>   d.   potato <u>potatoes</u>

1.	mosquito _____		31.	deer _____
2.	child _____		32.	zoo _____
3.	*crisis _____		33.	leaf _____
4.	piano _____		34.	foot _____
5.	attorney _____		35.	series _____
6.	man _____		36.	*datum _____
7.	fish _____		37.	ox _____
8.	*parenthesis _____		38.	calf _____
9.	mouse _____		39.	handkerchief _____
10.	Negro _____		40.	tray _____
11.	country _____		41.	hero _____
12.	umbrella _____		42.	couch _____
13.	knife _____		43.	radio _____
14.	valley _____		44.	self _____
15.	*thesis _____		45.	stomach _____
16.	gentleman _____		46.	thief _____
17.	library _____		47.	*criterion _____
18.	*analysis _____		48.	bush _____
19.	woman _____		49.	*phenomenon _____
20.	soprano _____		50.	means _____
21.	tooth _____		51.	loaf _____
22.	party _____		52.	*stimulus _____
23.	roof _____		53.	half _____
24.	boy _____		54.	epoch _____
25.	*radius _____		55.	wolf _____
26.	goose _____		56.	day _____
27.	*axis _____		57.	shelf _____
28.	life _____		58.	party _____
29.	tax _____		59.	wife _____
30.	dictionary _____			

1.10

COUNTABLE AND UNCOUNTABLE NOUNS

1. A COUNTABLE NOUN describes something that we can count: (a) a concrete noun may be countable: *There are a **dozen flowers** in the vase; There are **twelve paintings** in the exhibition; There are **three apples** in the refrigerator* (we can count *flowers, paintings,* and *apples*); (b) a collective noun is countable: *There are **seven classes** at my institute; There are **many orchestras** in London; There are **three nations** in North America* (we can count *classes, orchestras,* and *nations*); and some proper nouns are countable: *I was in Mexico **five Christmases** ago; There are **many Greeks** in New York City* (we can count *Christmases* and *Greeks*).

2. An UNCOUNTABLE NOUN describes something that we cannot count: (a) an abstract noun is uncountable: ***Freedom** is not always easy; **Integrity** is necessary in business; Give me **liberty** or give me death* (*freedom, integrity,* and *liberty* as concepts [ideas] cannot be counted); (b) many concrete nouns are uncountable: ***Rice** is an important **food** in China; **Gold** is a soft metal; The cost of **oil** is high* (we cannot count *rice, food, gold,* or *oil*; however, we can count ***five grains** of rice, **two boxes** of food, **three ounces** of gold,* and ***ten barrels** of oil*).

3. Uncountable nouns do not have a plural form; however, many uncountable nouns may be made countable, but the meaning of the word changes. Compare:

Uncountable	Countable
Art is an imitation of life.	*The folk arts of Mexico are wonderful.*
Life is precious.	*A cat has nine lives.*
Beer is good on a hot day.	*I drank five beers last night.*
Religion is a strong force.	*There is only one important religion in Spain.*
She has beautiful skin.	*How many skins are there in your mink coat?*
I like Italian sculpture.	*We have two sculptures in our collection.*
Paper is very expensive now.	*Where are those important papers?*

1.11

GRAMMAR EXERCISE

Name _____ Date _____

Focus: Distinguishing Countable from Uncountable Nouns

In the parentheses indicate with a C or a U whether the italicized word in the sentence is countable or uncountable.

EXAMPLES: a. (C) *People* are interesting.
b. (U) *Coffee* is an important product of Brazil.

1. (   ) For me, a *cup* of coffee in the morning is necessary.

2. (   ) *Fruit* is very expensive in the winter.

Name _____ Date _____

3. (   ) *Religion* is an interesting subject.

4. (   ) There are many *religions* in the world.

5. (   ) *Rice* is the most important food in the world.

6. (   ) In one kilo of rice there are many *grains*.

7. (   ) *Life* is a mystery.

8. (   ) The **Lives** *of the Saints* is an interesting work to read.

9. (   ) *Milk* is good for babies.

10. (   ) A *glass* of milk is good with a sandwich.

11. (   ) *Honesty* is important in a good friendship.

12. (   ) *Love* is more important than money.

13. (   ) The *information* in this report is not accurate (correct).

14. (   ) *Money* is sometimes a problem.

15. (   ) A very good *friend* isn't easy to find.

16. (   ) *Sheep* are not independent animals.

17. (   ) *Wool* is very expensive.

18. (   ) *Cigarettes* are bad for your health.

19. (   ) A *leaf* of tobacco is quite (very) large.

20. (   ) *Tobacco* is an important product of many countries.

21. (   ) *Chocolate* is not good for the teeth.

22. (   ) There are some *chocolates* in my pocket.

23. (   ) I am a student of English as a second *language*.

24. (   ) *English* is an important language in world business and trade.

25. (   ) *Meat* is very expensive.

26. (   ) Cold *meats* are good for a picnic.

27. (   ) *Freedom* is a wonderful thing.

28. (   ) *Oil* is an important natural resource of the Middle East.

29. (   ) A *barrel* of oil isn't cheap.

30. (   ) *Exercise* in the morning is good for you.

31. (   ) There are many *exercises* in this book.

32. (   ) *Water* is necessary for life.

THE POSSESSIVE FORM OF NOUNS

1. It is possible to change a singular noun to a possessive form by adding an APOSTROPHE (') plus an *s* ('s) to the end of the word: *The **President's** secretary is here; One **man's** meat is another **man's** poison.* (old saying)

2. Only an apostrophe changes a regular plural noun to a possessive form: *Our **sons'** school is very good; Most of my **friends'** friends are friends of mine.*

3. When an irregular plural noun does not end in -*s*, use an apostrophe plus an *s*: *The **children's** teacher is Chinese; The **men's** room* (bathroom) *is over there.*

4. To make a possessive noun out of a proper noun that ends in -*s*, we may use only an apostrophe: *This is **Charles'** coat; Mr. and Mrs. **Williams'** house is lovely;* or we may use an apostrophe plus an *s: There is Betsy **Jones's** mother; **Charles's** pronunciation is excellent; **James's** wife is a lawyer.*
   Note: Today, *'s* after proper nouns ending is -*s* is more common.

5. A possessive noun may appear without a following noun when that noun is understood: *Men's problems are different from **women's*** (problems); *The children are at the **dentist's*** (office) *today: There is a sale today at **Bloomingdale's*** (store).

6. A possessive noun is most often used when it refers to a <u>person</u> or a <u>living</u> <u>being</u> (animals, insects, etc.): ***Mary's** problems are serious; My **dog's** bark is very loud; The **butterfly's** wings are beautiful.*

7. With <u>things</u>, we are more likely to use a phrase with *of: the color of the room, the sound of his voice, the size of the house, the cost of the shirt.* However, a possessive noun appears with (a) expressions of time: ***yesterday's** storm, a **week's** visit, **today's** class;* (b) words related to natural phenomena: *the **sun's** rays, the **ocean's** tides;* and (c) words related to political bodies or groups of people working together: *the **government's** decision, the **company's** product, the **city's** water supply, the **class's** homework.*

1.13

GRAMMAR EXERCISE   Name _____ Date _____

Focus: The Possessive Form of Nouns

car	definition	home	mother	problems	son
child	desk	husband	newspaper	product	streets
compositions	environment	jobs	parks	program	teacher
crew	father	lives	poison	rays	toys
daughter	friends	meat	president	secretary	wife

Choose singular or plural nouns from the above list and supply them in appropriate blanks. Transform the noun subjects of the following sentences into possessive nouns. Check the rules carefully.

EXAMPLES: a. One man's <u>meat</u> is another man's <u>poison</u>.
              b. A man's <u>home</u> is his castle. (old saying)

1. The sun _____ are very strong at the Equator.

2. The children _____ are in the garden.

3. Men _____ are very different from women's.

4. My uncle _____ is Japanese.

5. My dictionary _____ of a noun isn't very good.

6. My boss _____ is a member of my country club.

7. Most of my friends _____ are friends of mine.

8. My parents _____ is in the South.

9. The President _____ is not very good.

10. Is Betsy Jones _____ in the other room?

11. Our boys _____ is from the Far West.

12. Charles _____ is a famous lawyer.

13. Linda _____ is a lovely young girl.

14. Our daughter _____ is in the army.

15. My company _____ is very good.

16. Unfortunately, the city _____ are dangerous at night.

17. The ship _____ is excellent.

18. Today _____ is full of interesting news.

    Note: The noun *news* is always singular: *The news **is** bad*.

19. The earth _____ is in danger.

20. Their wives _____ are interesting.

21. The students _____ are on the teacher _____.

22. People _____ are interesting to a novelist.

    Note: The noun *people* is always plural: *People **are** strange*.

23. Girls _____ are usually different from boys'.

PERSONAL AND REFLEXIVE PRONOUNS

	Subject	Object	Possessive Adjective	Possessive Pronoun	Reflexive
Singular	I	me	my	mine	myself
	you	you	your	yours	yourself
	he	him	his	his	himself
	she	her	her	hers	herself
	it	it	its		itself
Plural	we	us	our	ours	ourselves
	you	you	your	yours	yourselves
	they	them	their	theirs	themselves

Personal Pronouns

1. (a) SUBJECT PRONOUNS occupy the subject position of a sentence: *He is a North American; You are at the beginning of this course; She is from southern Europe.*

(b) OBJECT PRONOUNS are used as the object of a verb: *I know him well; I see her every day;* or as the object of a preposition: *I live with them; I spoke to her.*

(c) POSSESSIVE ADJECTIVES are used to modify (describe) a noun: *This is my book; Is she your child? That is our problem.*

(d) POSSESSIVE PRONOUNS do not appear before nouns: *This is mine; This book is yours.* They often appear as subjects: *Mine is the best.*
Note: Reflexive pronouns will be discussed in Chapter 2.

Demonstrative Pronouns

2. Like personal subject pronouns (*I, you, she,* etc.), the DEMONSTRATIVE PRONOUNS, *this, that, these,* and *those,* occupy the subject position of a sentence: *This is a picture of my father; That is the formula for success.*

(a) *This* refers to a person or thing close to the speaker: *This (woman) is an old friend of mine; This (here in my hand) is a rare butterfly.*

(b) *That* refers to a person or thing at some distance from the speaker: *That is a picture of my mother on the wall; That (a bird up in a tree) is a nightingale.*

(c) *These* (the plural of *this*) refers to persons or things close to the speaker: *These are important examples; These are the best years of our lives.*

(d) *Those* (the plural of *that*) refers to persons or things at some distance from the speaker: *Those (books up on the top shelf) are very old; Those (apples up in the tree) are ready to pick.*

1.14 (Continued)

Demonstrative Adjectives

3. When *this, that, these,* and *those* precede a noun, they are called DEMONSTRATIVE ADJECTIVES because they modify the nouns that they precede: ***This food*** *is delicious;* ***That painting*** *is by Picasso;* ***These diamonds*** *here in my hand are very valuable;* ***Those chairs*** *are very beautiful.* Compare:

Demonstrative Pronouns	Demonstrative Adjectives
This is easy.	*This explanation* is easy.
That is heavy.	*That chair* is heavy.
These are good.	*These apples* are good.
Those are bad.	*Those oranges* are bad.

Note: (a) The place word (adverb of place) *here* is where the speaker is: *This diamond **here** in my hand is my mother's;* (b) the place word *there* is any other place that we can point to: *That person over **there** is my boss.*

Note: Demonstrative adjectives and pronouns are also called DETERMINERS.

1.15

GRAMMAR EXERCISE   Name _____ Date _____

Focus: Subject Pronouns

Fill in the blanks with appropriate subject pronouns.

EXAMPLES: a. <u>We</u> are human beings.
              b. <u>I</u>'m not a citizen of Canada.

1. _____ is a new student here.
2. _____'re not very good apples.
3. _____'s a hot and humid day.
4. _____'re not native speakers.
5. _____ is an old friend of mine.
6. _____ is a beautiful day.
7. _____'s a medical doctor.
8. _____'re Europeans.

9. _____'s an actor.
10. _____'m a student.
11. _____'re pilots.
12. _____'m not sick.
13. _____'s cold.
14. _____'re students.
15. _____'s late.
16. _____'m happy.

GRAMMAR EXERCISE   Name _____ Date _____

Focus: Possessive Adjectives

Pronunciation Note: In writing, contractions of demonstrative pronouns and *is* and *are* do not appear (with the exception of *that's* in informal usage); however, in speaking, contracted forms occur: (a) *this is* sounds like *thisiz;* (b) *that is* sounds like *thatz;* (c) *these are* sounds like *these-er;* and (d) *those are* sounds like *those-er.*

Note: The personel pronoun *it* refers to animals, insects, objects, or things: *It is a beautiful butterfly; Its name is not familiar to me. It's* (the contracted form of *it is*) and *its* (the possessive adjective) have the same pronunciation.

Fill in the blanks with *is* or *are* plus an appropriate possessive adjective. The subject pronouns given in the parentheses will indicate which possessive adjective to use.

EXAMPLES: a. This <u>is my</u> diamond. (I)
              b. These <u>are his</u> letters. (he)
              c. This <u>is its</u> name. (it)

1. That _____ nature. (it)   9. That _____ desire. (I)

2. This _____ life. (you)   10. This _____ home. (we)

3. These _____ fish. (we)   11. These _____ materials. (you)

4. This _____ idea. (I)   12. This _____ sentence. (I)

5. That _____ car. (we)   13. That _____ car. (we)

6. Those _____ geese. (they)   14. Those _____ mistakes. (they)

7. This _____ name. (it)   15. These _____ knives. (I)

8. Those _____ glasses. (I)   16. That _____ purse. (she)

Now supply appropriate possessive adjectives in the blanks.

17. This is _____ typewriter.   20. This is _____ pencil.

18. These are _____ children.   21. That is _____ name.

19. That is _____ home.   22. Those are _____ books.

Now complete the sentences.

21. This _____.

22. These _____.

23. That _____.

24. Those _____.

1.17

Name _____ Date _____

Focus: Possessive Pronouns

We use possessive pronouns to avoid (get away from) needless repetition; for example, in the sentence *This is my idea*, the phrase *is my idea* is repetitious. By replacing *is my idea* with *mine*, we avoid unnecessary repetition: *This idea is **mine**.*

Change the possessive adjectives given in the parentheses to possessive pronouns. Then, along with the nouns also given in the parentheses and appropriate forms of the verb *be*, complete the sentences. When doing the exercise out loud (aloud), use contracted forms of noun subjects and the verb *be*. Practice questions and answers.

EXAMPLES: a. This <u>book is mine.</u>   (my book)
            b. Those <u>books are ours.</u>   (our books)

1. That _____. (your book)
2. Those _____. (his papers)
3. These _____. (their presents)
4. This _____. (my raincoat)
5. These _____. (my responsibilities)
6. That _____. (her hat)
7. These _____. (my cigarettes)
8. Those _____. (our packages)
9. That _____. (my money)
10. Those _____. (your materials)
11. This _____. (my sentence)
12. That _____. (their car)
13. This _____. (your umbrella)
14. That _____. (his problem)
15. This _____. (my drink)
16. These _____. (our children)
17. These _____. (their clothes)
18. This _____. (my idea)
19. Those _____. (our tickets)

Now complete the following.

EXAMPLES: a. <u>This book isn't</u> yours.
            b. <u>That book isn't (is)</u> mine.

20. _____ mine.
21. _____ his/hers/yours.
22. _____ theirs/ours.

1.18

Name _____ Date _____

Focus: Demonstrative Pronouns

Pronunciation Note: In spoken English, (a) *this is not* sounds like *thisiz-not* or *thisizint*; (b) *that is not* sounds like *thatz-not* or *thatizint*; (c) *these are not* sounds like *these-er-not* (or *these aren't*); and (d) *those are not* sounds like *those-er-not* (or *those aren't*).

Reminder: In informal writing, only *that's,* the contraction of *that is,* occurs.

Fill in the blanks with appropriate demonstrative pronouns and forms of the verb *be*.

EXAMPLES: a. <u>That is</u> a beautiful painting.
             b. <u>These aren't</u> difficult sentences.
             c. <u>Those are not</u> good apples.

1. _____ the first sentence of the exercise.

2. _____ diamonds here in my hand.

3. _____ an Italian car across the street.

4. _____ my books over there on the desk.

5. _____ English cigarettes here in my pocket.

6. _____ the best years of our lives.

7. _____ the seventh sentence.

8. _____ my shoes under the bed.

9. _____ French cheese in this package.

10. _____ an English class.

11. _____ your pencil there in your pocket.

12. _____ my desk on the other side of the room.

13. _____ important papers here on my desk.

14. _____ a very large class.

15. _____ good ideas in this proposal.

16. _____ a grammar exercise.

Now complete the sentences with your own words.

17. This isn't _____.

18. That is not (*thatz-not*) _____.

19. These are _____.

20. These aren't _____.

21. These are not (*these-er-not*) _____.

22. Those aren't _____.

23. Those are not (*those-er-not*) _____.

24. This/that is _____.

25. These/those are _____.

1.19

INFORMATION QUESTIONS WITH WHOSE

Like a declarative sentence and a *yes-no* question, an INFORMATION QUESTION always has a subject and a verb. An INFORMATION WORD (e.g., *whose, where,* etc.) occurs at the beginning of a question and, in writing, a question mark appears at the end: *Whose book is this?*

A. Model Exchange

q. Is this book yours?
a. No, it's not.
q. Whose is it?
a. John's.

B. Model Exchange

q. Whose pencil is this?
a. It's not mine.
q. Whose is it?
a. It's his.

C. Model Exchange

q. Is this yours?
a. No, that's Bill's.
q. Whose is this pen?
a. It's mine.

D. Model Exchange

q. Are those papers yours?
a. No, they're not.
q. Whose are they?
a. They're nobody's.

Note: *Whose* may appear alone at the beginning of an information question or be accompanied by a noun: ***Whose** are these?* ***Whose shoes** are these?*

Suggestion: Practice changing everyone's name in the group to possessive nouns; for example, Carlos = Carlos's, Tazuko = Tazuko's, Abdel = Abdel's, Nahid = Nahid's, Tull = Tull's, etc.

Pronunciation Note: (a) *Whose* sounds like *hooze;* (b) *Whose are* sounds like *hooze-er;* (c) *Whose is* sounds like *hooziz.*

Practice asking and answering the following information questions.

1. Whose book is this/that?
2. Whose hair in this group is brown/black/blond?
3. Whose pen/jacket/coat/dictionary/briefcase/watch is this/that?
4. Whose parents are in this country?
5. Whose book is in your hands?
6. Whose native country is Japan/France/Korea?
7. Whose is this/that?
8. Whose books/papers/glasses/pencils are these/those?
9. Whose are these/those?
10. Whose classroom is this?

1.20

PREPOSITIONS

1. A PREPOSITION connects one part of speech with another: *That book **on** the table is mine; The women **with** the big hat is beautiful.*

2. When a preposition combines with a noun or pronoun, the combination is called a PREPOSITIONAL PHRASE: *We are **in a classroom**; John is **at the dentist's**; Her son is **with her**.*

3. A PLACE PREPOSITION is used in a prepositional phrase to indicate where a person, place, or thing is. Some place prepositions are *in, at, on,* and *between.*

   (a) *In* gives the idea of a place that is an enclosure (a box, a container, a pocket, a closet): *My money is **in a little box in the closet**; My keys are **in my pocket**. In* is also used to refer to a "system," "organization," or "formula": *The earth is **in a solar system**; They are **in a social club**; There is a mistake **in this formula**.*

   (b) *At* refers to an area or place (a school, a home, an office): *He is **at the National University of Mexico**; They aren't **at home**; There is a serious problem **at the office**.*

   (c) *On* suggests a surface of some *thing* (a floor, the earth, a street): *Your pencil is **on the floor**; We are **on the earth**; Many people are **on the street** today.*

   (d) *Between* is for a person or thing that appears in the middle of a unit of three: *She is **between him and me**; During a solar eclipse the **moon is between the earth and the sun**; Albany is **between New York and Montreal**; The patient is **between life and death**.*
   Note: Sometimes *in, on,* and *at* are interchangeable; in other words, we have a choice: *They are **at the beach*** or *They are **on the beach***. The prepositional phrase *at the beach* suggests a place; the phrase *on the beach* suggests the surface (the sand of the beach). In the sentence *He is at the library, at the library* suggests a place; in *He is in the library, in the library* suggests an enclosure (building).

1.21

GRAMMAR EXERCISE   Name _____ Date _____

    Focus: Prepositions of Place

Fill in each blank with *in, on, at,* or *between.* First do this exercise as a quiz.

EXAMPLES: a. A period is at the end of a sentence.
            b. The Empire State Building is in New York City.
            c. Mary's doll is on the floor.
            d. Hawaii is between California and Japan.

1. The children aren't _____ school today. They're sick _____ bed.

2. This exercise is _____ a page. This page is _____ a book.

3. Your book is _____ your desk. This book is _____ my hands. My eyes are _____ this page.

4. Their summer house is _____ a mountain. The mountain is _____ the Alps. The Alps are _____ Switzerland.

1.21 (Continued)

Name _____ Date _____

5. Istanbul is _____ Europe and Asia. Half of the city is _____ Asia and half is _____ Europe.

6. No one is _____ the moon. We are _____ the earth. There are nine planets _____ the system.

7. The earth is _____ space.

8. The Atlantic Ocean is _____ Europe and North America.

9. The United States is _____ Canada and Mexico.

10. The Hawaiian Islands are _____ the Pacific. England is _____ an island. It is _____ the North Atlantic.

11. The baby is _____ her bed. The dog is _____ the bed.

12. My dictionary isn't _____ the shelf. He is a librarian _____ the Los Angeles Public Library. He is _____ work today.

13. They are _____ the beach today. There are many umbrellas _____ the beach. Many of the children are _____ the water.

14. It is very hot _____ the Equator. It is very cold _____ the North Pole. There is now pollution _____ the world's oceans.

15. We are _____ a school. This school is _____ a city.

16. Your eyes are _____ your head. Your tongue is _____ your mouth. Your head is _____ your shoulders. Your brain is _____ your head. Your hat is _____ your head. Your glasses are _____ your nose. Your shoes are _____ your feet. Your feet are _____ the floor. Your hands are _____ your lap. We are _____ a room.

17. California is _____ the west coast of the United States.

18. There are flowers _____ the table. My boss is _____ his desk.

19. My money is _____ the drawer. There are aspirins _____ the medicine cabinet. They are _____ the top shelf.

EXPRESSIONS OF PLACE

1. A prepositional phrase that is an EXPRESSION OF PLACE may contain more than one preposition: *The Eiffel Tower is **in the middle of Paris**; We are **in a small room in a big building**; The sun is **in the center of our solar system***.

2. An expression of place usually contains a preposition + *the* + noun + *of*: *The North Pole is **at the top of the world**; We are **in the middle of a conversation***.

   Some Expressions of Place with *The* and *Of*:

   (a) A large sign is **on the side of** my office building.
   (b) I am **in the front of** the bus.
   (c) The best seats are **in the back of** the theater.
   (d) The S.S. Titanic is **at [on] the bottom of** the Atlantic Ocean.
   (e) Her name is **at the bottom of** the list.
   (f) The label is **on the bottom of** the box.
   (g) Her name is **at the top of** the list.
   (h) The Appendix is **at the back of** this book.
   (i) The Introduction is **at the front of** this book.
   (j) A young man is **at the beginning of** his life.
   (k) An old man is **at the end of** his life.
   (l) It is hot **in the middle of** the earth.

3. *In the front of* and *in the back of* sometimes appear without *the*. When this occurs, the meaning is completely different; for example, *We are **in the front of** the theater* means *We are inside the theater in the front part*, but *We are **in front of** the theater* means *We are outside the theater in the front*; *We are **in the back of** the car* means *We are inside the car in the back part*; but *We are **in back of** the car* means *We are outside the car in the back*.

4. Object and possessive pronouns frequently follow *in front of* and *in back of*: *She is **in front of me**; I am **in back of him**; His desk is **in back of mine**; My car is **in back of theirs***.

5. The preposition *to* occurs after the adjectives *close* and *next*, and the preposition *from* occurs after the adjective *far*: *The moon is relatively **close to us**; Spain is **next to France**, The sun is very **far from us***.

1.23

GRAMMAR EXERCISE

Name _____ Date _____

Focus: Expressions of Place

Supply appropriate prepositions in the blanks. Use the prepositions *at*, *from*, *in*, *of*, or *to*. First do this exercise as a quiz.

EXAMPLES: a. Picadilly Circus is <u>in</u> the center <u>of</u> London.
          b. The title is <u>on</u> the cover <u>of</u> this book.

1. Our summer house is _____ the side _____ a mountain.

2. The earth is far _____ the sun.

3. The sun is _____ the center _____ our solar system.

4. The patient is close _____ death.

5. A list of irregular verbs is _____ the back _____ this book.

6. My boss's desk is _____ back _____ mine.

7. We are almost _____ the end _____ the twentieth century.

8. Hawaii is _____ the middle _____ the Pacific Ocean.

9. The Ural Mountains are _____ the middle _____ Europe.

10. Paris is close _____ Brussels.

11. The stars are far _____ the earth.

12. Your head is _____ the top _____ your body.

13. The *S. S. Titanic* is _____ the bottom _____ the Atlantic Ocean.

14. There is a big sign _____ the side _____ the building.

15. My best friend's house is next _____ mine.

16. The teacher's desk is _____ the front _____ the classroom.

17. This sentence is _____ the middle _____ this page.

18. The North Pole is _____ the top _____ the world.

19. The South Pole is _____ the bottom _____ the world.

20. Los Angeles is far _____ New York.

21. She is _____ the middle _____ her pregnancy.

22. China is next _____ the Soviet Union.

23. Boston isn't far _____ New York.

24. Her desk is _____ back _____ her boyfriend's.

25. Unfortunately, I'm not close _____ my family.

26. We are far _____ the beginning _____ this exercise.

27. My office is next _____ my boss's.

28. Your name is _____ the top _____ this page.

29. We are close _____ the end _____ this exercise.

30. Their garden is _____ back _____ their house.

1.24

INFORMATION QUESTIONS WITH *WHERE*, AND MORE ABOUT PREPOSITIONS

1. To find out (discover) where a person, a place, or thing is, we ask an information question that begins with *where*, the information word: ***Where is the sun? Where are the children's toys?***
   Pronunciation Note: (a) *Where is* sounds like *wears*; and (b) *where are* sounds like *wear-er*.
   Reminder: Object pronouns may appear as objects of prepositions: *My son is next **to me;** Our daughter is very far **from us**.* Possessive pronouns also occur as objects of prepositions: *Their apartment is **between mine and yours;** The Williams's house is next **to ours;** My age is close **to yours.***

2. The preposition *around* refers to the surroundings (or encirclement) of a person, place, or thing: *There is a beautiful garden **around their house;** Your belt is **around your waist;** That is a diamond necklace **around that woman's neck**.*

3. Some preposition + noun combinations that are confusing to students are (a) *We are **in** (not on) the first row of seats;* (b) *They are **at** (not in) a party;* (c) *The flowers are **in** (not on) the middle of the table;* (d) *Your head is **on** (not at) your shoulders;* (e) *Your name is **at** (not on) the top of this page.*

Supply appropriate prepositions in the blanks.

1. He is _____ the second row of seats.

2. _____ the World in Eighty-Days is an old but good movie.

3. Is your name _____ the top _____ this page?

4. This is a secret _____ you and me.

5. Your books are _____ the top _____ my desk. Your dictionary is _____ the drawer. This page is _____ a book.

6. There are many islands _____ the South Pacific.

7. My parents are _____ a dinner party tonight.

8. Our children's school is next _____ a large factory.

9. Your shoes are _____ your feet. Your feet are _____ the floor.

10. There is a wonderful playground _____ our children's school.

11. A teenager (thirteen to nineteen) is a young person _____ childhood and adulthood.

12. My coat is _____ the hook near the door.

13. The teacher's desk is _____ the front _____ the classroom.

14. We are now _____ the end _____ this exercise.

1.25

INFORMATION QUESTIONS WITH *WHERE*

The teacher may use the following questions as a script for conducting a drill. Practice answering the questions with complete sentences or just prepositional phrases.

A. Model Exchange

q. Where are your keys?
a. They're in my pocket.
q. Where is your dictionary?
a. It's on my desk.

B. Model Exchange

q. Where are your keys?
a. . . . in my pocket.
q. Where is your dictionary?
a. . . . on my desk.

Suggestion: A large map may prove very helpful for this exercise.

1. Where is the Appendix/Introduction of this book?
2. Where is the United States/Hawaii/Istanbul/the Pacific Ocean?
3. Where are the Canary Islands/the Azores/Puerto Rico/Tahiti?
4. Where is the North Pole/the South Pole/Santa Claus?
5. Where is the Atlantic Ocean/Lake Titicaca/the Amazon/the Nile?
6. Where is San Francisco? Is it *on* the west coast *of* the United States? Where is New York City?
7. Is Paris *on* the coast or *in* the interior of France? Where is it?
8. Where is Rio de Janeiro? Is it *in* the interior of Brazil?
9. Where is Brasilia?
10. Are Buenos Aires and Montivideo *on* a river?
11. Where are the Ural Mountains? Where is Mt. (Mount) Everest?
12. Where is Bogota/Mexico City/La Paz? Is La Paz *in* the Andes?
13. Is New York close *to* Boston? Are we far *from* Tokyo?
14. Is Cairo *at* the mouth or *at* the source of the Nile? Where is it?
15. Is New Delhi *in* the middle of India or *on* the coast of the Arabian Sea? Where is Bombay? Is Chile next *to* Argentina and Bolivia? Is it a very long and thin country?
16. Where is Moscow/Washington, D.C./London/Brussels/Berlin/Stockholm/Saigon/Seoul/ Rome/Dublin/Lisbon/Madrid/Prague/Warsaw/Peking/Athens/Jerusalem/Tehran/ Bangkok/Rangoon/Singapore/Manila/Djakarta/Canberra/Rabat/Johannesburg/ Caracas/Lima/Quito/Santiago/Asunción/Managua/Tegucigalpa/Ottawa/Port-au- Prince/Santo Domingo/Havana/the most beautiful city in the world?
17. Where are my shoes/my watch/my ring?
18. Where is your bracelet/your glasses/your belt/your watch?
19. Where is my desk/book/pencil/coat/tie?
20. Where is the sun/the earth/our solar system?
21. Are you *in* front *of* or *in* back *of* me? Is your desk *between* [name] _____ and [name] _____? Is your desk next *to* [name] _____? Where are we?
22. Where are we *in* this book? Are we far *from* the end?
23. Where are we *in* this exercise now?

1.26

A AND AN

1. *A* is the INDEFINITE ARTICLE and appears before a singular noun or an adjective that begins with a consonant sound: *She is **a scientist**; Life is **a mystery**; It is **a wonderful** day; That is **a beautiful** story.*

2. *An,* the alternate form of *a,* is used before a singular noun that begins with a vowel sound: *This is **an apple**; **An ostrich** is a large bird.*

3. When a singular noun or an adjective begins with a consonant letter but has a vowel sound, *an* is used to modify the word; for example, the words *hour, honor,* and *heir* begin with a consonant letter but have a vowel sound: *My grandfather has **an hour** of exercise every afternoon; It is **an honor** to meet you; He is **an heir** to a great fortune.*
   Note: The use of *an* before the words *hotel* and *historical* is old-fashioned; *a* is preferred: *That is **a hotel** for the very rich; This is **a historical** moment.*

4. Certain adjectives and nouns that begin with the vowel *u* have a consonant sound (*you*): *This is **a university**; The people of the nation are **a united** people; That is **a universal** truth; A marriage is **a union** of two people; This is **a useful** procedure.* However, most nouns and adjectives beginning with the vowel *u* have a vowel sound (*a*): *That is **an ugly** painting; This is **an unusual** antique; That is **an unnecessary** question; That area is **an undeveloped** part of the country.*

5. *A* or (*an*) does not precede a plural countable noun or an uncountable noun: *Men are different from women; Nature is an interesting subject to study.* When an article does not precede a noun, we refer to the absent article as ZERO ARTICLE (no article): *They are <u>0</u> children of mine; <u>0</u> Elephants are large; <u>0</u> Money is necessary for a good life.*

6. Idiomatically, *a* may replace the word *per: They go to Europe twice a (per) year; He makes a thousand dollars a (per) month.*

7. *A* may also have the meaning of *one: That is a beautiful horse; There is a mosquito in this room.*
   Note: We rarely use *one* to modify a singular noun; *a* is customary.

1.27

GRAMMAR EXERCISE   Name _____ Date _____

Focus: The Indefinite Article A (An)

Fill in the blanks with *a* or *an*. First do this exercise as a quiz.

EXAMPLES: a. <u>A</u> house is not <u>a</u> home. (old saying)
          b. <u>An</u> ounce of prevention is worth <u>a</u> pound of cure. (old saying)

1. _____ happy baby is _____ wonderful thing to see.

2. This flower is _____ orchid. This one is _____ rose.

3. _____ apple _____ day keeps the doctor away. (old saying)

4. One of my teachers is _____ European. This is _____ English class.

5. This is _____ historical moment.

6. That is _____ unusual story.

Name _____ Date _____

7. _____ university is _____ place of learning.

8. The United States is _____ union of fifty states.

9. His father is _____ honorable man.

10. That is _____ hotel for people with money.

11. _____ half hour of prayer or meditation every afternoon is good for you.

12. Half _____ hour of physical exercises every morning is good for everyone.

13. It is _____ honor to meet you.

14. A bullfight is _____ exciting thing to see.

15. _____ education in _____ university can be expensive.

16. England, Wales, Scotland, and Northern Ireland are _____ United Kingdom.

17. _____ apple is _____ fruit. _____ potato is _____ vegetable.

18. _____ elephant is very large. _____ giraffe is very tall.

19. She is _____ honest woman.

20. I am _____ human being.

21. He is _____ honorable person.

22. That is _____ historical fact.

23. _____ united world is necessary.

24. This is _____ unnecessary problem.

25. She has _____ headache. I have _____ aspirin for her.

26. _____ hotel room in Paris isn't cheap.

27. _____ hour is only _____ small part of _____ day.

28. _____ house is expensive.

29. This is _____ unique piece of sculpture.

30. This is _____ unusual example of African art.

31. Love is _____ universal thing.

32. _____ umbrella is necessary on a rainy day.

33. A horse is _____ useful animal.

34. _____ hippopotamus is _____ ugly animal.

35. _____ hour of relaxation after a meal is good for your health.

36. This is _____ article about the Indians of New Mexico.

37. _____ half hour is only thirty minutes.

38. A movie is usually _____ hour and _____ half.

39. She is _____ heiress.

40. _____ operation in _____ hospital is very expensive.

41. _____ ocean is larger than _____ sea.

1.28

GRAMMAR EXERCISE   Name _____ Date _____

Focus: The Indefinite Article A (An) or Zero Article

When necessary, supply *a* or *an* in the blanks. When *a* or *an* is not necessary, place a *0* (zero). First do this exercise as a quiz.

EXAMPLES: a. That painting is <u>a</u> good example of Chinese art.
            b. <u>0</u> English is an international language.

1. _____ love is blind. (old saying)

2. _____ grapefruit is bigger than _____ orange.

3. _____ geese are birds. _____ goose is good for _____ Christmas dinner. _____ goose is _____ female, but _____ gander is _____ male.

4. _____ deer is fast. _____ deer are beautiful animals.

5. _____ inch is longer than _____ centimeter. _____ kilogram is lighter than _____ pound. _____ mile is longer than _____ kilometer. _____ miles are longer than _____ kilometers.

6. _____ children are young adults. _____ baby is a wonderful creation. _____ babies are always hungry.

7. There is _____ mouse in the kitchen. _____ mice are very little.

8. _____ dog is man's best friend. (old saying)

9. _____ cigarettes are _____ bad habit. Tobacco is _____ important product of Virginia.

10. _____ sheep are not very intelligent animals. _____ fish live in water.

11. _____ children are more honest than _____ adults.

12. _____ people are interesting. _____ person in love is sometimes foolish. _____ men are very different from _____ women.

13. _____ potatoes are cheap now. _____ carrot is orange.

14. _____ period appears at the end of _____ sentence.

15. These are examples of _____ sentences with and without _____ articles.

16. That is _____ English car. Those are _____ Japanese cameras.

17. _____ hour with a psychiatrist is expensive.

18. _____ flowers are beautiful. That is _____ beautiful rose.

19. Is this _____ example of _____ interrogative sentence?

20. _____ sentence begins with _____ capital letter.

21. That is _____ hotel for retired people.

22. This is _____ English grammar book. _____ English is my second language.

23. His teacher is _____ American. Those people are _____ Americans.

24. _____ lemons are sour. _____ lemon is yellow.

1. *The* is the DEFINITE ARTICLE and, like *a* or *an*, it is also called a determiner. The pronunciation of *the* when it precedes a word that begins with a vowel sound rhymes with *pea* or *sea*: **The air** *is polluted today;* The Ugly Duckling *is a wonderful story.*

2. *The* modifies a noun that describes a *particular* person, place, or thing: *Elizabeth II is the* **Queen** *of the* **United Kingdom** (there is only <u>one</u> Queen of England, and there is only <u>one</u> United Kingdom); **The sun** *is in the* **center** *of our solar system* (there is only <u>one</u> sun, and there is only <u>one</u> center).

3. *The* is used to modify a noun that describes a *particularity,* but the indefinite article *a* or *an* modifies a noun that describes a *generality.* Compare:

   (a) **An apple** *a day is good for you* (general); versus **The apple** *in my hand is from the state of Washington* (particular).

   (b) *This is* **a formula** *for success* (general, there are many formulas for success); versus H_2O *is* **the formula** *for water* (particular, there is only <u>one</u> formula for water).

4. *The* does not precede an uncountable noun when the noun describes some thing in general. However, *the* appears with an uncountable noun when the noun describes a particularity. Compare:

   (a) <u>0</u> *Honesty is an important quality* (general); versus **The honesty** *of a politician is often questioned* (particular).

   (b) <u>0</u> *Coffee is good in the morning* (general); versus **The coffee** *in this can is from Brazil* (particular).

5. *The* precedes a concrete countable noun that represents a class or group (e.g., *a kind of animal, a kind of flower, a kind of insect*): **The male lion** *is lazy;* **The orchid** *is a beautiful flower;* **The bee** *is always very busy.*
   Note: *A* or *an* is also used in this manner: **A shark** *has big jaws;* **A rose** *smells sweet;* **A butterfly** *has a short life.* However, *the* emphasizes the class or group, but *a* emphasizes an individual member of a class. *A* has the meaning of *any* in this case.

6. *The* always precedes an adjective in the superlative degree: *French wine is* **the best** *in the world; His wife is* **the most beautiful** *woman in town.*

1.29 (Continued)

7. Zero article usually occurs with the names of countries: _0 England is on an island; 0_ Chile is a long and narrow country; _0 China has a very large population; 0 Hungary is a socialist country._
    Exception: _The_ precedes _Netherlands; The Netherlands is a low country._

8. _The_ occurs with names of countries when the name refers to a political union: _The United States of America is in North America; The Soviet Union is the largest country in the world; The Union of South Africa is at the tip of a continent._

9. Zero article occurs with the names of cities (except _the Hague_): _0 Cairo is at the mouth of the Nile; 0 Tokyo is the largest city in the world; 0 Paris is called the city of light._

10. _The_ accompanies the names of rivers, oceans, and seas: _the Nile, the Amazon, the Ganges, the Atlantic Ocean, the Indian Ocean, the Arabian Sea, the Mediterranean Sea._

11. Zero article occurs with the names of lakes and bays: _0 Lake Titicaca, 0 Lake Baikal, 0 Hudson Bay_ (but _the Bay of Biscay_). _The_ appears with groups of lakes: _the Great Lakes, the Finger Lakes._

12. _The_ accompanies the names of ranges of mountains: _the Andes, the Rockies, the Himalayas, the Alps, the Sierra Nevada._ Zero article occurs with the name of a single mountain (except _the Matterhorn_): _0 Mount Everest, 0 Mount Kilimanjaro, 0 Mount Whitney._

13. _The_ is used with points on the globe (the earth): _the Equator, the South Pole, the North Pole._

14. _The_ is used with the names of geographic areas: _the Middle East, the Far East, the Far West, the Orient, the Occident._

15. Zero article occurs with the names of continents: _0 Europe, 0 North America, 0 Africa, 0 Asia._

16. _The_ precedes the name of an archipelago, a desert, a forest, a gulf, or a peninsula: _the Malay Archipelago, the Sahara Desert, the Black Forest, the Persian Gulf, the Italian Peninsula._

1.30

GRAMMAR EXERCISE   Name _____ Date _____

Focus: The Definite Article *The* or Zero Article

Supply *the* or zero article in the blanks. First do this exercise as a quiz.

EXAMPLES: a. Buckingham Palace is <u>the</u> Queen of England's home.
  b. The sun is in <u>the</u> center of our solar system.
  c. <u>0</u> nature is an interesting subject to study.

1. _____ moon is close to _____ earth.

2. Our solar system is in _____ universe. The sun is in _____ center of this system.

3. _____ history is an interesting subject. _____ history of religion is a long story.

4. _____ Bible is an interesting and inspirational book.

5. Catholicism is _____ major religion of Italy, France, and Spain.

6. _____ religion is an important subject at a Catholic university. _____ center of
   _____ Catholic Church is in _____ Rome.

7. _____ formula for _____ water is H_2O. _____ water in this glass is dirty.

8. _____ refrigerator in my apartment is old.

9. _____ telephones are expensive in many countries. _____ telephone in my bedroom is white.

10. _____ milk is good for babies. _____ milk in _____ refrigerator is bad.

11. _____ elephant is _____ largest animal in Africa.

12. Anthropology is the study of _____ man. _____ man in the other office is my
    boss.

13. _____ nature is very often difficult to understand. _____ nature of a cat is to be
    independent. _____ nature of a mother is to protect her children.

14. _____ cheese is originally milk. _____ cheese in this sandwich is delicious.
    _____ cheese is high in calories.

15. _____ United States is in North America.

16. _____ France is a beautiful and prosperous country.

17. _____ language is a form of communication. English is _____ language of
    _____ Australia. _____ Russian is _____ language of _____ Soviet
    Union.

18. _____ air is composed of nitrogen (approximately 78 percent), oxygen (approximately
    21 percent), small amounts of argon, carbon dioxide, neon, helium, and other gases.

19. _____ air in Tokyo is polluted. _____ air at _____ Lake Kashmir is
    wonderful. _____ air in Los Angeles is smoggy.

20. _____ Hague is a city in _____ Netherlands.

21. _____ Mt. (Mount) Everest is in _____ Nepal.

22. _____ Matterhorn is in _____ Switzerland.

23. _____ water is a solvent. _____ water in _____ Lake Baikal is very clear.

24. _____ gold is a soft metal. _____ gold in my wedding ring is eighteen carats.

25. _____ life is wonderful. _____ life of a mosquito is short.

26. Spain and Portugal are on _____ Iberian Peninsula.

27. _____ Mediterranean Sea is between _____ Europe and _____ Africa.

28. _____ steel is strong. _____ steel in that building is from Germany.

29. _____ Saudi Arabia is in _____ Middle East.

30. _____ love is more important than _____ money.

31. _____ love of Romeo and Juliet was innocent.

32. I drink _____ water with my meals. _____ water in _____ Mediterranean Sea is saline (salty).

33. _____ Pretoria is _____ capital of _____ Union of South Africa.

34. _____ Mount Kilimanjaro is in _____ Africa.

35. _____ Andes are in _____ South America.

36. _____ English is an international language. _____ English of Shakespeare is often difficult to understand.

37. _____ tobacco is an important agricultural product of _____ Turkey. _____ tobacco in these cigarettes is from Virginia.

38. _____ oil is an important natural resource of Venezuela.

39. _____ exercise in the morning is good for you. _____ exercise on the first page of this book is easy.

40. _____ Pacific Ocean is between _____ Japan and _____ United States. _____ Nile is in _____ Egypt. _____ Lake Titicaca is in _____ South America.

41. _____ formula for carbon monoxide is CO.

42. _____ hair is a part of _____ human body.

43. _____ hair of a Persian cat is long and very soft.

1.31

ADJECTIVES

1. An ADJECTIVE is a modifier; for example, in *Paris is a **beautiful city***, the adjective *beautiful* modifies (describes) the noun *city*; in *He is a **happy person***, the adjective *happy* modifies the noun *person*.

2. In English, unlike many other Indo-European languages, an adjective does not have a plural form. It can modify a singular noun (*She is a **nice person***), and without a change in form, it can modify a plural noun (*They are **nice people***).

3. Usually, an adjective in a sentence precedes the noun that it modifies: *This is **delicious food**; They are **beautiful children***.

4. However, in certain types of sentences, adjectives may follow the nouns that they modify. This usually occurs with the verbs *be, feel, seem, appear,* and *look: Wanda is Hungarian; I feel comfortable; Barbara seems unhappy; John appears happy; The dog looks sick.* When adjectives follow nouns, they are called PREDICATE ADJECTIVES.

Some Kinds of Adjectives

5. (a) Like proper nouns, a PROPER ADJECTIVE always begins with a capital letter: *This is an **English** poem; She is a **Protestant** minister; We ate our **Thanksgiving** dinner.*

(b) *-Ing adjectives* are derived from present participles: *That is an **interesting** idea; It's a **boring** movie; They are **working** people.*

(c) *-Ed adjectives* are derived from regular past participles: *I am **tired**; She is **bored**; We are **encouraged**; He is an **educated** man.*

(d) Some adjectives are also derived from irregular past participles: *My watch is **broken**; That man is **drunk**; Their children are **grown**.*

1.32

GRAMMAR EXERCISE   Name _____ Date _____

Focus: Adjectives Preceding Singular Nouns

Fill in each blank with an appropriate form of the verb *be*, the indefinite article *a* or *an*, and an appropriate adjective.

bad	developed	foolish	interesting	quiet	timid
beautiful	developing	funny	large	rich	ugly
big	excellent	good	magnificent	sad	unhappy
boring	expensive	handsome	naughty	small	wonderful
cheap	fabulous	happy	old	smart	young
clever	famous	important	poor	spoiled	
curious	fascinating	intelligent	prosperous	terrible	

EXAMPLES: a. *Romeo and Juliet* <u>is a sad</u> story about young love.
b. Switzerland <u>isn't a large</u> country.

1. Cervantes' *Don Quixote* _____ book.

2. *The Bible* _____ book.

1.32 *(Continued)*

3. The Netherlands _____ country in Europe.

4. Shakespeare's *Hamlet* _____ play.

5. Movies _____ product of Hollywood.

6. Sweden _____ country in Scandinavia.

7. Catholicism _____ religion in Italy.

8. My mother and father _____ couple.

9. My sister/brother _____ student in mathematics.

10. Mexico/Iran/the Soviet Union _____ country.

11. Nature _____ subject to study.

12. I _____ person.

13. My father/mother _____ man/woman.

14. Ms./Miss/Mrs. [supply name] _____ woman.

15. [supply name] _____ girl/boy/man/woman.

16. General Motors _____ international company.

17. My wife/husband and I _____ couple.

18. An elephant/a lion/a fox _____ animal.

19. A lion in a cage _____ animal.

20. That _____ idea/theory/formula.

21. S/he _____ child.

22. Love/hate _____ thing.

23. Mr. [supply name] _____ man.

24. This _____ exercise/class/room.

25. My girlfriend/boyfriend _____ person.

26. S/he _____ friend of mine.

27. A cat _____ animal.

28. This/that _____ [supply a noun].

GRAMMAR EXERCISE   Name _____ Date _____

Focus: Adjectives Preceding Singular and Plural Nouns

Fill in each blank with an appropriate form of the verb *be*, plus *a*, *an*, or zero article, and an appropriate adjective.

American	Chinese	excellent	good	naughty	Protestant	unusual
automatic	clever	exciting	industrious	new	religious	wonderful
bad	complicated	foreign	Japanese	old	social	
Buddhist	depressing	French	lazy	plastic	sophisticated	
careful	electric	fresh	loving	pornographic	spoiled	
careless	elegant	German	manual	poor	Swiss	
Catholic	English	glamorous	mechanical	primitive	terrible	

EXAMPLES: a. Bill and Grace are sophisticated people.
              b. Their daughter is a mechanical engineer.

1. That_____ typewriter.

2. S/he _____ minister/priest/rabbi.

3. He _____ monk.

4. [supply name] _____ actor/actress/singer.

5. They_____ children/students.

6. Christmas _____ holiday.

7. [supply names] _____ people.

8. This _____ magazine/book.

9. That_____ fruit/vegetable.

10. That_____ method/formula/system.

11. [supply name] _____ teacher.

12. This _____ cheese/wine/beer.

13. That_____ camera/watch/car.

14. I _____ person.

15. [supply name] _____ president/politician.

16. Those _____ dishes/knives/glasses.

17. [supply a (an) + name] _____car/motorcycle.

18. [supply name] _____ man/woman.

19. They_____ technicians/engineers.

20. [supply names] _____ men/women.

Now complete the sentences with your own words.

21. This _____.

22. That _____.

23. These _____.

1.34

GRAMMAR EXERCISE   Name _____ Date _____

Focus: Adjective Following Singular Nouns

Fill in the first blank with *am*, *are*, or *is* and an appropriate adjective. Then fill in the second blank with *am*, *are*, or *is* and the ANTONYM of the adjective in the first blank. **Note:** An antonym expresses the opposite meaning of another word.

beautiful — ugly	happy — unhappy	ordinary — unusual	thin — heavy (or fat for people)
cold — hot	hard — soft	relaxed — nervous	thin — thick (for things)
correct — wrong	healthy — unhealthy	rich — poor	warm — cool
dry — humid	honest — dishonest	selfish — generous	weak — strong
easy — difficult	large — small	sweet — sour (*dry* for	wonderful — terrible (or awful)
expensive — cheap	light — heavy (weight)	wine, *bitter* for	young — old
fast — slow	narrow — wide	chocolate	
good — bad	near — far	tall — short	

EXAMPLES: a. Love <u>is wonderful</u>, but hate <u>is terrible</u>.
　　　　　　 b. His hair <u>is thick</u>, but mine <u>is thin</u>.

1. An elephant _____, but a donkey (burro) _____.

2. The moon_____, but the sun _____.

3. Arithmetic _____, but calculus _____.

4. A desert _____, but a jungle _____.

5. This painting _____, but that one _____.

6. My sister _____, but my brother _____.

7. We_____, but they _____.

8. I _____, but (supply name) _____.

9. The United States _____, but India _____.

10. A rabbit (hare)_____, but a turtle_____.

11. Diamonds_____, but pearls _____.

12. Silver_____, but gold _____.

13. This orange _____, but that one _____.

14. This candy _____, but that candy _____.

15. Electricity_____, but water _____.

16. My father _____, but my grandfather _____.

17. My mother _____, but my grandmother_____.

18. A plane_____, but a train _____.

19. American culture _____, but European culture _____.

20. My wife/husband _____, but I _____.

21. This wine _____, but that wine _____.

22. S/he _____, but s/he _____.

23. The kitchen _____, but the bedroom _____.

1.35

Focus: Noun Modifiers

Nouns may be used to modify other nouns in much the same way that adjectives modify nouns: *Where are my **opera** glasses? This is a **diamond** necklace.* Like adjectives, noun modifiers do not have a plural form, and they always precede the noun they modify. Compare:

Correct	Wrong
That is a book store.	*That is a (store book).*
These are coffee spoons.	*These are (spoons coffees).*

Fill in the blanks with appropriate nouns selected from the following list.

algebra	can	foot	heart	nylon	salad	strawberry	wine
baby	cancer	furniture	history	opera	silk	tennis	winter
Bible	car	gas	insurance	paper	silver	water	
biology	coffee	gold	leather	phone	skin	wedding	
book	cotton	grammar	milk	rayon	spring		

EXAMPLES: a. This is <u>strawberry</u> jam.
               b. She is a <u>grammar</u> teacher.

1. That is a _____ book.
2. He's an _____ singer.
3. I'm a _____ salesperson.
4. My doctor is a _____ specialist.
5. He's a _____ teacher.
6. This is my _____ ring.
7. These are _____ spoons.
8. This is a _____ blouse.
9. Where's my _____ bill?
10. Is this a _____ opener?
11. These are _____ cups.
12. Where's the _____ bucket.
13. That's a _____ bowl.
14. That's a _____ bottle.
15. These are _____ shoes.
16. This is a _____ coat.
17. These are _____ glasses.
18. This is a _____ exercise.

Now supply an appropriate noun (singular or plural) of your own choice in the blanks.

EXAMPLES: c. He's an automobile <u>mechanic</u>.
               d. They're computer <u>engineers</u>.

19. She's a science _____.
20. Is that ice _____?
21. This is my wedding _____.
22. They're chemistry _____.
23. She's a music _____.
24. This is my winter _____.
25. These are my graduation _____.
26. Where are the opera _____.
27. These are dinner _____.
28. This is a bottle _____.
29. This is a baby _____.
30. Those are grammar _____.
31. These are water _____.
32. This is a cotton _____.
33. This is a diamond _____.
34. They're music _____.
35. He's a car _____.
36. That's a phone _____.

1.36

THE EXPLETIVE *THERE*

1. The word *there* is called an EXPLETIVE when it helps to introduce a verb (usually *be*) to the subject of a sentence: ***There are people*** *in the other room;* ***There is a bottle of milk*** *on the table.*

2. A determiner usually precedes the subject, followed by a prepositional phrase: *There is **a beautiful child** in the garden; There is **no water** on the moon; There are **some children** on the roof of the house.*

Some Adjectives and Expressions Following Expletive *There*

3. (a) *Some–any*

Some and *any* modify both countable and uncountable nouns. *Some* appears in affirmative statements and questions: *There are some Mexicans in the group; Is there some water on the floor? Any* occurs in negative statements: *There isn't any money in her family; There aren't any aspirins in the medicine cabinet.*

(b) *Much–many*

Much can modify only uncountable nouns: *There isn't much time in a day. Much* does not usually appear in affirmative statements, but it often appears in negative statements and *yes-no* questions: *There isn't much luck in his life; Is there much milk in the refrigerator?*

Many may modify only plural countable nouns and, unlike *much*, occurs in both negative and affirmative statement: *There are many people in the store today; There aren't many Americans in China.*

(c) *A lot of–lots of*

A lot of and *lots of* are informal substitutes for *much* (*many*) and may be used with both countable and uncountable nouns: *There are a lot of children in the park today; They have lots of money in the bank.*

(d) *Little–few*

Little may modify only uncountable nouns: *There is little food in many Indian homes; There is little oil in western Europe. Few* can modify only countable nouns: *There are few students at that school; There are few doctors in that village.*

(e) *A little–a few*

A little and *a few* occur more frequently than *little* and *few. A little* precedes only uncountable nouns: *There is a little money in my bank account. A few* may precede only countable nouns: *There are a few bad people in the world; There are a few Japanese in the group. A little* and *a few* show greater quantity than *little* and *few: There is **little** time left* (almost none); *There is **a little** time left* (about an hour); *There are **few** Americans in the class* (only two); *There are **a few** Americans in the class* (about five).
Important Note: (*A*) *little* and (*a*) *few* do not occur in negative statements.

(f) *A little bit of*

A little bit of is an expression that occurs in informal usage. It usually precedes an uncountable noun: *There is a little bit of alcohol in this drink; There is a little bit of pepper in this soup.*

(g) *Enough*

Enough suggests a sufficient (adequate) amount. It can be used with both countable and uncountable nouns: *There is enough money to buy a car; There isn't enough milk for the children.*

1.36 (*Continued*)

(h) *Plenty of*

Plenty of suggests more than a sufficient amount (more than enough) and occurs only in affirmative statements: *There is plenty of money in their bank account* (they are millionaires).

(i) *No*

The adverb *no* may occur as an adjective and modify both countable and uncountable nouns: *There is no time for fun in my life; There are no fish in that lake*.
Special Note: *No* cannot modify a noun when a preceding verb is in its negative form. Compare:

Correct	Wrong
*There **isn't any** money in the bank.*	*There **isn't no** money in the bank.*

Isn't no is called a double negative and does not occur in educated speech and writing.
Pronunciation Note: *There is* sounds like *therz; there are* sounds like *there-er; there are not* sounds like *there-er-not*.

Questions with *There*

4. In *yes-no* questions with expletive *there* and the verb *be*, the verb precedes the expletive: ***Are there** any people in the other room?* In *yes-no* answers the verb follows the expletive: *Yes, there are; No, there aren't*.

5. In information questions the information word *how* combined with *much* or *many* plus a noun is used. *How much* precedes uncountable nouns: ***How much money** is there in your savings account? How many* precedes countable nouns: ***How many students** are there in your English class?*

1.37

Name _____ Date _____

Focus: The Expletive *There*

Supply *some, any, much, many, lots of, a lot of,* or *no* in the blanks. Do not use *much* in affirmative statements.

EXAMPLES: a. There isn't <u>much</u> water in the Middle East.
          b. There are <u>a lot of</u> vegetables in the refrigerator.

1. There isn't _____ milk in the refrigerator.

2. There isn't _____ oil in Japan.

3. There is _____ money in their bank account.

4. There is _____ salt in this soup.

5. There are _____ Japanese students in the class.

6. There is _____ wine in this dish (a dish of food).

7. There isn't _____ love in her life.

8. There is _____ sugar in my coffee.

9. There are _____ rich people in India.

10. There isn't _____ water on the moon.

11. There is _____ snow in the northern part of Canada.

12. There aren't _____ children in the playground today.

Now supply an appropriate form of the verb *be* as well.

EXAMPLES: c. There <u>isn't much</u> water in the Sahara.
          d. There <u>isn't any</u> fruit in the refrigerator.

13. There _____ rich people in mainland China.

14. There _____ oil in Texas.

15. There _____ pictures in this book.

16. There _____ people on the moon.

17. There _____ people at the South Pole.

18. There _____ South Americans in the class.

19. There _____ coal in South America.

20. There _____ vegetation in the Sahara.

21. There _____ money in my bank account.

22. There _____ oil in Saudi Arabia.

23. There _____ sugar in Cuba.

24. There _____ water at a desert oasis.

25. There _____ people in China.

26. There _____ bad people in the world.

27. There _____ chemicals in the human body.

28. There _____ problems in my life.

1.38

GRAMMAR EXERCISE

Name _____ Date _____

Focus: The Expletive *There*

Supply *little, a little, few, a few,* or *no* in the blanks.

EXAMPLES: a. There is <u>a little</u> milk in the refrigerator.
b. There are <u>no</u> people on the moon.

1. There are _____ people in the Sahara.

2. There are _____ vegetables in the refrigerator.

3. There is _____ happiness in a criminal's life.

4. There are _____ apples in the fruit basket.

5. There is _____ ice in the refrigerator.

6. There are _____ sheep on my father's farm.

7. There are _____ dollars in my wallet.

8. There is _____ money in my bank account.

9. There are _____ boys in my daughter's class.

10. There is _____ rain in the Sahara.

Now use *lots of, a lot of, some, any, much,* or *many*.

11. There is _____ rain in London.

12. There is _____ coffee in Brazil.

13. There is _____ spice in this food.

14. There is _____ rice in China.

15. There is _____ gold in South Africa.

16. There are _____ students in that school.

17. There are _____ sentences in this exercise.

18. There isn't _____ salt in this soup.

Now supply an appropriate form of the verb *be* as well.

19. There _____ buildings in New York.

20. There _____ ice at the North Pole.

21. There _____ problems in the world.

22. There _____ orange groves in Florida.

23. There _____ Chinese students in my class.

24. There _____ birds in the sky.

25. There _____ water on the floor.

26. There _____ people in Tokyo.

27. There _____ problems in my life.

28. There _____ love in his life.

1.39

GRAMMAR EXERCISE   Name _____ Date _____

Focus: *Yes-No* Questions with Expletive *There*

Fill in the first blank with *is* or *are*, and in the second blank supply *some, any, a little, a little bit of, a few, a lot of, lots of, no, much,* or *many.*

EXAMPLES: a. Is there any furniture in their new house?
              b. Are there a lot of workers at that factory?

1. _____ there _____ fun in your life?

2. _____ there _____ people in your family?

3. _____ there _____ coal in South America?

4. _____ there _____ irregular verbs in English?

5. _____ there _____ alcohol in this drink?

6. _____ there _____ peaches and apples in the stores now?

7. _____ there _____ water on the moon?

8. _____ there _____ children in the playground?

9. _____ there _____ oil in France?

10. _____ there _____ flower farms in the Netherlands?

11. _____ there _____ North Americans in your hometown?

1.40

GRAMMAR EXERCISE   Name _____ Date _____

Focus: Information Questions with *There*

Supply *how much* or *how many* in the first blank and *is* or *are* in the second.

EXAMPLES: a. How many people are there in China?
              b. How much milk is there in the refrigerator?

1. _____ ounces _____ there in a pound?

2. _____ gold _____ there in your ring?

3. _____ deer _____ there in the park?

4. _____ women _____ there in your English class?

5. _____ pounds _____ there in a ton?

6. _____ teeth _____ there in a horse's mouth?

7. _____ legs _____ there on a spider?

8. _____ degrees _____ there in a circle/a right angle?

9. _____ nitrogen _____ there in water?

10. _____ fish _____ there in the fishbowl?

1.41

THE VERB *HAVE*

1. We use the verb *have* (a) to show possession: *You **have** a good reason to be here;* and (b) to express a habitual activity or occurrence: *I **have** a birthday party only once a year.*

2. *Have* and *has* are the two forms that appear in the conjugation of the verb *have* in the simple present tense. *Has* is called an *-s* form and is used in the third-person singular only.

		Singular		Plural	
First person	I	} have	we	} have
Second person	you		you	
	he		they	
Third person	she	} has		
	it			

3. In the simple present tense, the AUXILIARY (helping) verb *do* and the adverb *not* are used to make a negative verb phrase with the verb *have*. We use the *-s* form *does* in the third-person singular.

		Singular		Plural	
First person	I	} do not have	we	} do not have
Second person	you		you	
	he		they	
Third person	she	} does not have		
	it			

4. *Don't* and *doesn't*, the contractions of *do not* and *does not*, are used in informal usage: *I **don't have** a car; She **doesn't have** any time.*

   Special Note: The verb *have* also appears in a negative form without the help of the auxiliary verb *do: I haven't any money; She hasn't a car.* This form is chiefly British; however, it sometimes occurs in American usage. The forms *do not (don't) have* and *does not (doesn't) have* are preferred in this textbook.

5. In *yes-no* questions with the verb *have, do* or *does* is used at the beginning of the question, immediately followed by the subject.

YES-NO QUESTIONS WITH THE VERB *HAVE*

Auxiliary	Subject	Verb	Object	Prepositional Phrase
Do	you	have	a pen	with you?
Does	she	have	a radio	in her bedroom?
Do	we	have	time	for another drink?
Does	he	have	a bike?	

6. The contractions *don't* and *doesn't* usually appear in *no-* answers; however, for emphasis, the noncontracted forms sometimes occur: *Do you have my wallet? No, I do **not**. Does she have the answer? No, she does **not**.* Note that the stress is on the adverb *not*.

YES-NO ANSWERS WITH THE AUXILIARY DO

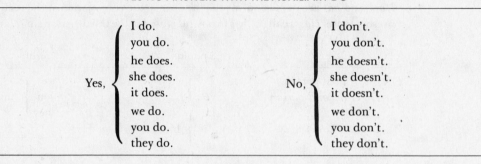

Yes,		No,	
	I do.		I don't.
	you do.		you don't.
	he does.		he doesn't.
	she does.		she doesn't.
	it does.		it doesn't.
	we do.		we don't.
	you do.		you don't.
	they do.		they don't.

7. In information questions, information words like *how, what,* and *where* (often combined with adjectives and nouns) are placed at the beginning of the question, immediately followed by *do* or *does*.

INFORMATION QUESTIONS WITH THE VERB *HAVE*

Information Words	Object	Auxiliary	Subject	Verb	Prepositional Phrase
What	time	do	you	have?	
How	much money	do	you	have	in the bank?
What	color eyes	does	she	have?	
What		do	you	have?	
What	kind of chairs	do	they	have	in their kitchen?
How	many students	does	he	have	in his class?
What	color kitchen	do	you	have?	

Pronunciation Note: *What kind of* sometimes sounds like *what kind-a*.
Note: No preposition follows *what color: What color car do you have?*
Special Note: The verb *have* also appears in questions without the help of the auxiliary *do;* the form is chiefly British, however: *Has she any money? How much time have you?*

1.42

Focus: Affirmative Statements with *Have*

Supply *have* or *has* in the blanks.

EXAMPLES: a. The Soviet Union <u>has</u> a multinational population.
                b. I <u>have</u> a strong desire to speak English well.

1. Italy _____ the shape of a boot.

2. People _____ strange ideas sometimes.

3. The world _____ a serious pollution problem.

4. Everyone in the class _____ a dictionary.

5. We _____ a vacation once a year.

6. His family _____ a small summer house at the beach.

7. Sheep _____ little intelligence.

8. A lion _____ a long tail, paws, and very sharp teeth.

9. The United States _____ a long border (frontier) with both Canada and Mexico.

10. China _____ the largest population in the world.

11. You _____ a beautiful smile.

12. This wine _____ a bitter taste.

13. S/he _____ a date (appointment) with his/her girlfriend/boyfriend tonight.

14. I _____ a big/little appetite in the morning.

15. They _____ a very serious problem with their son.

16. My cat _____ a beautiful fur coat and a long fluffy tail.

Now supply a subject + *have* or *has*.

EXAMPLES: c. I <u>have</u> a secret.
                d. Spanish <u>has</u> many irregular verbs.

17. _____ a beautiful new car.

18. _____ a terrible stomach ache.

19. _____ a serious problem at the office.

20. _____ a very powerful engine.

21. _____ a very big appetite.

22. _____ a beautiful little house in the forest.

23. _____ a wonderful taste.

24. _____ a lot of fun with their children.

25. _____ no papers on my desk.

26. _____ a lot of good ideas.

27. _____ many social and economic problems.

1.43

Focus: Negative Declarative Statements with the Verb *Have*

Supply appropriate negative forms of the verb *have* in the blanks. Practice using both contracted and noncontracted forms. **Reminder:** Contractions appear most frequently in spoken English and informal writing, such as a letter to a friend. Contractions occur less frequently in formal writing, such as a letter to the president of a university, or a thesis for a Ph.D.

EXAMPLES: a. Many countries <u>do not have</u> much industrial development.
              b. She <u>doesn't have</u> enough money to go out with her friends.

1. February _____ thirty days.

2. Mexico City _____ a good water supply.

3. I _____ enough paper to finish my composition.

4. A fish _____ a large brain.

5. English _____ a very logical system of phonetics.

6. England _____ many natural resources.

7. This food _____ enough salt in it.

8. A mosquito _____ a long life.

9. They _____ enough money to buy a car.

10. The government _____ good social programs.

11. The Queen of England _____ much political power.

12. Switzerland _____ any borders on the sea.

13. We _____ the formula for the chemical.

14. The Catholic Church _____ many members in Asia.

15. I _____ an appetite today.

16. The United States _____ any diamond deposits.

17. Many countries in the Middle East _____ much plant life.

18. I _____ that person's phone number, unfortunately.

19. Fortunately, my hometown _____ much pollution.

20. I _____ enough time for a vacation.

21. Sheep _____ much intelligence.

22. This report _____ accurate (correct) information.

23. They _____ any money in the bank.

24. The president of this university _____ good ideas.

25. S/he _____ much luck in love.

26. Religion _____ the answer for many people.

27. The Ambassador _____ permission from the government to negotiate with the enemy leaders.

28. People in many countries _____ the right to vote.

1.44

GRAMMAR EXERCISE   Name _____ Date _____

Supply *do* **or** *does* **in the blanks. Note:** To the question *Does everyone have problems?* we may answer *Yes, he does* (formal) or *Yes, they do* (informal). **Reminder:** *Have* without *do* in questions is chiefly British.

EXAMPLES: a. <u>Does</u> England have an empire now?
              b. <u>Do</u> you have a good reason to be here?

1. _____ the world have a lot of inflation now?

2. _____ everyone have a dictionary?

3. _____ your friends have much free time at school?

4. _____ deer have a lot of problems with hunters?

5. _____ water have any nitrogen in it?

6. _____ the United States have much oil?

7. _____ your parents have a good relationship with each other?

8. _____ an elephant have a large appetite?

9. _____ people have strange ideas sometimes?

10. _____ the moon have any air?

11. _____ sheep have much intelligence? _____ fish have lungs?

12. _____ India have enough food for its people?

13. _____ women have equality with men in your native country?

14. _____ she have a British/American/foreign accent?

15. _____ our solar system have a center?

16. _____ a giraffe have a long neck?

17. _____ your parents have a car?

18. _____ you have any interest in religion?

19. _____ cheese have much protein in it?

20. _____ the Soviet Union have a good relationship with your native country?

Now complete the sentences.

21. Does your father _____ ?

22. Does the President _____?

23. Do you_____?

24. Do we _____?

25. Does this school _____?

26. Does China/Japan/Mexico _____?

27. Do the children/students _____?

1.45

GRAMMAR EXERCISE   Name _____ Date _____

Focus: Information Questions with the Verb *Have*

Supply *how much, how many, what kind of,* or *what color* in the first blank and *do* or *does* in the second.

EXAMPLES: a. <u>What kind</u> of car <u>does</u> your wife have?
            b. <u>What color</u> shirt <u>does</u> Jack have on?
            c. <u>How much</u> money <u>do</u> you have in your pocket?
            d. <u>How many</u> kids do your neighbors have?
            Note: *Kids* is slang for *children*, chiefly American. It does not usually appear in writing.

1. _____ dictionary _____ everyone have?

2. _____ coat _____ sheep have?

3. _____ weather _____ your hometown have?

4. _____ perfume _____ you have on?

5. _____ accent _____ you have?

6. _____ irregular verbs _____ English have?

7. _____ hands _____ a clock have?

8. _____ job _____ your mother have?

9. _____ apartment _____ you have?

10. _____ nicotine _____ a cigarette have in it?

11. _____ jewelry _____ you have on?

12. _____ lives _____ people have in your hometown?

13. _____ neck _____ a giraffe have?

14. _____ days _____ February/March/June/August have?

15. _____ eyes _____ your girlfriend/boyfriend have?

16. _____ house _____ your neighbors have?

17. _____ water _____ an oasis have?

18. _____ days _____ a year (leap year) have?

19. _____ political power _____ the Queen have?

Now complete the sentences.

20. What kind of TV/radio/amplifier _____?

21. How much money _____?

22. How many cousins/nephews/nieces _____?

23. What kind of house/apartment/car_____?

24. What color _____?

25. How much/how many/what kind of _____?

1.46

FORMS

1. The BASE FORM (simple form) of a verb appears in all persons in the simple present tense except in the third-person singular.

	Singular	Plural
First	I		we	
Second person	you } live	you } live
Third person	he		they	
	she } lives	
	it		

2. A base form + an -s is called an -S FORM and occurs in the third-person singular in the simple present tense only: *Everyone **needs** food; She **goes** to the dentist twice a year.*
Remember: -*S* forms occur only in the simple present tense.

Rules for Spelling -s Forms

3. (a) We can change most base forms into -s forms by simply adding an -s: (want) *Everyone **wants** peace;* (wear) *She **wears** beautiful clothes;* (drive) *He **drives** to work every day.*

(b) When a base form ends in -o, -s, -sh, -x, or -z, add -es: (go) *He **goes** to Europe twice a year;* (miss) *Orlando **misses** his family in Venezuela very much;* (brush) *Nicole **brushes** her hair a hundred times a day;* (tax) *The government **taxes** the people a lot.*

(c) When a base form ends in -y preceded by a consonant, change the -y to -i and add -es: (carry) *Jane **carries** a briefcase to work every day;* (bury) *My dog always **buries** his bones;* (cry) *Our baby **cries** all night long.*

(d) When a base form ends in -y preceded by a vowel, do not make a change, but add only -s: (play) *He **plays** the guitar beautifully;* (buy) *She **buys** all her clothes at Macy's;* (stay) *He always **stays** with his family in Toronto.*

(e) Only the verbs *have* and *be* are irregular in their spellings: *The Mona Lisa* (La Giaconda) ***has** a beautiful smile; Good health **is** our most precious possession.*

1.47

GRAMMAR EXERCISE   Name _____ Date _____

Focus: -S Forms in Affirmative Statements

Change the base forms given in the parentheses into -s forms and place them in the blanks. Carefully check the rules for spelling -s forms.

EXAMPLES: a. (need) Everyone <u>needs</u> money.
b. (water) The gardener <u>waters</u> the rose plants three times a week.

1. (travel) Light _____ at 186,000 miles a second.

2. (circle) The earth _____ the sun.

1.47 (Continued)

3. (tax) The government _____ our income.

4. (worry) My best friend's illness _____ me a lot.

5. (drink) Dad [informal for father] _____ two cocktails before dinner every night.

6. (fix) Mom [informal for mother] _____ a special breakfast for the family every Sunday morning after church.

7. (keep) Jack _____ his cigarettes in the refrigerator.

8. (smoke) His wife _____ a pack of cigarettes a day.

9. (speak) My algebra teacher _____ with a French accent.

10. (grow) Rice _____ in a few places in the United States.

11. (miss) Sigfried is unhappy and _____ his family in Germany.

12. (play) Our daughter _____ both the piano and the guitar.

13. (watch) Our child _____ TV every afternoon after school.

14. (work) His father _____ for an important company in Athens.

15. (do) Betty _____ her homework every afternoon.

16. (operate) The surgeon _____ at the hospital in the mornings.

17. (ring) My alarm clock _____ at 6:30 every morning.

18. (do) My brother _____ physical exercises every morning.

19. (take) My grandmother _____ a little nap every afternoon.

20. (get) Our little girl _____ up at seven o'clock every day.

21. (listen) My roommate _____ to the news on the radio every morning at breakfast.

22. (rise/set) The sun _____ in the east and _____ in the west.

23. (go) My lawyer _____ to court every day.

24. (have) My neighbor _____ a lot of trouble with his young son.

25. (be) Money _____ the root of all evil. (old saying)

26. (carry) The President _____ many heavy responsibilities.

27. (precede) Usually, an adjective _____ a noun.

28. (follow) Sometimes, an adjective _____ a noun.

29. (wear) Our daughter _____ a uniform to school every day.

1.48

GRAMMAR EXERCISE   Name _____ Date _____

Focus: Base Forms versus -s forms

Supply base forms or -s forms in the blanks. **Reminder**: -s forms appear only in the third-person singular in the simple present tense.

EXAMPLES: a. (speak) I speak two languages.
            b. (give) The sun gives us life.

1.48 (Continued)

Name _____ Date _____

1. (have) Everyone _____ the desire to learn English well.

2. (live) Our French teacher _____ in the middle of Paris.

3. (occur) Many car accidents _____ on the nation's highways during the holiday weekends.

4. (fall) The leaves _____ from the trees in October.

5. (serve) That restaurant _____ excellent food.

6. (love) John _____ Mary. My parents _____ me.

7. (grow) Apples _____ best in a cool climate.

8. (do) We _____ the exercises in this book for homework.

9. (have) People _____ strange ideas, sometimes.

10. (like) Mice _____ cheese.

11. (live) A mouse _____ in our kitchen.

12. (have) Air _____ a lot of nitrogen in it.

13. (grow) Good grapes for wine _____ in California.

14. (cost) Good wine _____ a lot of money.

15. (provide) Sheep _____ us with wool.

16. (pay) His company _____ him a very high salary.

17. (give) Money _____ us security.

18. (make) A friend of mine _____ very good cookies.

19. (subscribe) My parents _____ to the *London Times*.

20. (taste) Cheese _____ good with wine.

21. (go) My family _____ to the beach often in the summer.

22. (take) The class _____ a break for fifteen minutes every day.

23. (have) Geese _____ very long necks.

24. (wear) Mr. Jackson _____ a shirt and tie to work every day.

25. (revolve) The earth _____ around the sun.

26. (need) Children _____ a lot of love and protection.

27. (love) Our little boy _____ his dog very much.

28. (live) Deer _____ in the forest behind our house.

29. (provide) A cow _____ us with milk.

30. (occur) *-S* forms _____ in the third-person singular only.

31. (contain) Water _____ hydrogen.

32. (cost) Paper _____ a lot of money nowadays.

33. (have) Men _____ different problems than women.

GRAMMAR EXERCISE   Name _____ Date _____

Focus: *Don't versus Doesn't*

In the negative form of the simple present tense, all verbs except the verb *be* are preceded by *do* or *does* + *not* in contracted or noncontracted form: *I **do not** like it;* or *I **don't** like it. Does not* or *doesn't* occurs in the third-person singular only.
Special Reminder: The verb in the negative form is always a base form: *She doesn't **like** it.*

Supply *don't* or *doesn't* + a base form in the blanks. Remember: *Do* or *does* never occurs with the verb *be* in the simple present tense in negatives and questions: *Is she a teacher? No, she isn't a teacher.*

EXAMPLES: a. (do) That student <u>doesn't do</u> any homework.
            b. (like) I <u>don't like</u> jealous or selfish people.

1. (have) Water _____ any nitrogen in it.

2. (play) The children _____ in the garden in the winter.

3. (grow) Apples _____ well in a hot climate.

4. (obey) That spoiled child _____ her parents.

5. (taste) This food _____ very good.

6. (appear) My favorite actor _____ in the movies very often.

7. (live) People _____ at the South Pole.

8. (provide) The earth _____ enough food for its people.

9. (make) My company _____ very good products, unfortunately.

10. (mean) This word _____ anything.

11. (have) My dictionary _____ a definition of that word.

12. (spell) Many children in my son's class _____ well.

13. (give) Money _____ us everything.

14. (drive) My parents _____ a car.

15. (grow) Cotton _____ in the northern part of the country.

16. (like) Many people _____ animal pets.

17. (exist) A perfect person _____.

18. (talk) Our neighbors _____ to us.

19. (understand) I _____ the meaning of that word.

20. (need) Fortunately, my grandmother _____ any money.

21. (write) My parents _____ to me very often.

22. (produce) Our cow _____ very much milk.

23. (know) People _____ the reason for the government's decision.

24. (mean) Life _____ much for that unhappy person.

25. (understand) His parents _____ his problems.

1.50

GRAMMAR EXERCISE   Name _____ Date _____

Focus: *Yes-No* Questions

Except with the verb *be,* the subject of a *yes-no* question in the simple present tense is always preceded by the auxiliary *do* or *does:* **Do you** *feel tired?* **Does time** *go fast?*
Reminder: The verb *have* without *do (does)* in questions is chiefly British usage.

Fill in the blanks with *do* or *does*.

EXAMPLES: a.   <u>Do</u> yellow and red make orange?
              b.   <u>Does</u> salty fish make you thirsty?

1.   _____ you do your homework at the library or at home?

2.   _____ coffee grow in many parts of your native country?

3.   _____ your father play tennis? _____ your parents play cards?

4.   _____ electricity cost very much in your hometown?

5.   _____ your father's cows produce much milk?

6.   _____ fresh vegetables have a lot of vitamins?

7.   _____ everyone in the room want to learn English well?

8.   _____ an ostrich bury its head in the sand?

9.   _____ light travel at 186,000 miles a second?

10.   _____ you need a passport to travel to China?

11.   _____ a child understand the problems of life?

12.   _____ your dog know its name? _____ you feed him every day?

Now supply appropriate base forms in the second blank as well.

13.   _____ yellow and blue _____ green?

14.   _____ the students _____ all of the new words?

15.   _____ your company _____ you a good salary?

16.   _____ you _____ to the radio very much?

17.   _____ a good English dictionary _____ very much?

18.   _____ men/women _____ the problems of women/men?

19.   _____ your grandmother _____ a nap after lunch?

20.   _____ you _____ bridge or canasta?

Now complete the sentences with your own words.

21.   Does your mother/father/wife/husband _____?

22.   Does a vacation in Greece _____?

23.   Do you_____?

1.51

Focus: Information Questions

Except with the verb *be*, the auxiliary *do* or *does* is always put between the information word(s) and subject of an information question in the simple present tense: ***Where do you live? What does that word** mean? **What kind of food do you** like?*
Note: Exceptions to this general rule will be discussed in Chapter 2.

Supply *do* or *does* in the blanks.

EXAMPLES: a. How <u>do</u> you do? (*How do you do?* is asked only at a first meeting.)
            b. What color eyes <u>does</u> your new girlfriend have?

1. How _____ you spell your name? How _____ your mother spell hers?

2. What _____ that word mean? What _____ your name mean?

3. How much rent _____ you pay for your apartment?

4. What kind of car _____ your father drive?

5. About how much time _____ you spend on homework every day?

6. Where _____ your best friend work?

7. How much _____ a good car cost?

8. About how much electricity _____ you use every month?

9. How many cars _____ General Motors produce every day?

10. What _____ the word "beautiful" mean?

Now supply appropriate base forms in the second blank as well.

11. What kind of work _____ your father/mother _____?

12. How much milk _____ your cow _____ every day?

13. How _____ your best friend _____ his/her name?

14. What kind of food _____ an elephant _____?

Now complete the sentences with your own words.

15. Where does your girlfriend/boyfriend _____?

16. What color car/house/bike _____?

17. How much money _____?

18. Where _____?

19. What kind of food _____?

20. _____ on the weekends?

21. _____ your car/your money?

22. _____ to school?

23. _____ in your store?

1.52

INFINITIVES

1. An INFINITIVE is a unit comprised of *to* + a base form: *to live, to be, to do*. An infinitive does not indicate person, number, or tense. It may occur as the object of a verb: *She **likes to cook***; *Everyone **wants to learn** English; Jimmy **tries to be** good*.

2. An infinitive combined with its complement is called an INFINITIVE PHRASE: *We want **to go on a trip around the world**; She wants **to take a course at the university***.

Some Verbs Followed by Infinitives

3.

agree	decide	like*	prefer*	try*
attempt*	expect	love*	promise	want
begin*	hope	need	remember*	
continue*	learn	plan*	start*	

Note: Verbs marked with an asterisk (*) may also be followed by gerunds (e.g., *I like dancing*.). Gerunds are discussed in the chapter on *-ing* forms and infinitives in Book 2 of this work.

4. Besides verbs, infinitives may follow adjectives or nouns combined with *it* and a form of the verb *be*: *It is **difficult to learn** a language; It's not **a good day to go** to the beach*. When *it* is used in this manner, it is called ANTICIPATORY IT because it anticipates (introduces) what is to follow.

5. Frequently, *for* + a noun or pronoun are inserted between the adjective and the infinitive in sentences that begin with anticipatory *it*; the noun or pronoun is the subject of the infinitive: *It is difficult for **my grandfather** to walk without assistance; It's easy **for us** to talk about other people's mistakes*.
   Note: *It* may also be called IMPERSONAL IT when it is used in statements about distance, identification, time, and weather:

   (a) Distance: *It is five miles to the next gas station; It is 93 million miles to the sun; It's a long way to the moon.*

   (b) Identification: *It is a secret formula; It is a French chair.*

   (c) Time: *It is five o'clock; What time is it?*

   (d) Weather: *It's cold outside; It's a beautiful day.*

1.53

GRAMMAR EXERCISE   Name _____ Date _____

Focus: Infinitives after Verbs

Fill in the blanks with appropriate infinitives made out of the base forms in the list below.

be	do	go	live	sew	talk
buy	earn	have	make	swim	wear
cook	eat	learn	play	take	work

1.53 (Continued)

EXAMPLES: a. My dog doesn't want <u>to eat</u> its food.
  b. I love <u>to go</u> to the movies.
     Note: *Love* is sometimes used to mean *like: I love (like) to eat; I love (like) to travel. Love,* meaning *like,* does not occur in negative statements: *I don't like (never love) to be alone.*

1. I like _____ physical exercises every morning.

2. We plan _____ to Europe on our next summer vacation.

3. Jack and Jane prefer _____ in the country; they don't like city life. They don't want _____ in an apartment.

4. I promise _____ my homework.

5. My father expects _____ a lot of money in his new business.

6. The patient needs _____ medicine three times a day.

7. We all hope _____ a lot in this course.

8. A friend of mine doesn't like _____ on the phone.

9. Many children don't like _____ to school.

10. Does your wife like _____? Does she like _____ clothes?

11. My mother loves _____ in the garden.

12. I want _____ a small house up in the mountains.

13. Cats don't like _____ in water. Birds don't like _____ in a cold place. My dog doesn't like _____ in the same room with my cat.

14. I love _____ in mountain rivers.

15. We prefer _____ our dinner in the garden in the summertime.

16. Most people don't like _____ alone.

17. I plan _____ another course after this one.

18. Children love _____ candy. They love _____ with animals.

Now complete the sentences with your own words.

  c. I love <u>to go for long walks in the forest.</u>
  d. He hopes <u>to enter the university next semester.</u>

19. I love _____.

20. I like/don't like _____.

21. I plan _____.

22. I want/don't want _____.

23. I need/don't need _____.

24. My mother/father likes _____.

25. [supply name] _____ likes/doesn't like _____.

1.54

GRAMMAR EXERCISE   Name _____ Date _____

Focus: Infinitives after Adjectives and Nouns

Fill in the blanks with appropriate infinitives made out of the base forms in the list below.

be	drink	go	pay	see	spend	walk
dance	eat	have	put	smoke	take	work
do	find	like	read	speak	talk	worry
			save			

EXAMPLES: a. It's difficult for my grandmother <u>to read</u> the newspaper.
　　　　　　b. It's foolish <u>to spend</u> all your money on expensive clothes.
　　　　　　c. It's not nice <u>to talk</u> about people behind their backs.

1. It's not good for you _____ a lot of butter.

2. It's easy for us _____ about other people's mistakes.

3. It's difficult for a two-year-old child _____.

4. It's impossible for me _____ cruel to animals.

5. It's foolish _____ about our past mistakes.

6. It's necessary _____ money for the future.

7. It's necessary for me _____ eight hours of sleep every night.

8. I have a good book _____.

9. It's not good for you _____ a lot of coffee.

10. It's difficult for me _____ English on the phone.

11. It isn't easy _____ an interesting job with good pay.

12. It's a lot of fun _____ the tango.

13. It's exciting _____ a bullfight.

14. She has a lot of things _____ today.

15. It's good for you _____ a lot of fresh vegetables.

16. It's important for children _____ milk every day.

17. It isn't smart (intelligent) _____ cigarettes.

18. It's not good for you _____ a lot of alcohol.

19. It's impossible for me _____ that terrible person.

20. It's difficult _____ a taxi on a rainy day.

21. It's foolish _____ about things that may never happen.

22. Is it necessary _____ a lot of homework for your class?

23. August is a good month _____ a vacation in Sweden.

24. It isn't much fun _____ income taxes.

25. It's difficult for me _____ thread through the eye of a needle.

26. It's exciting and educational _____ a trip around the world.

1.55

ADVERBS

1. An ADVERB modifies (a) a verb: *She **dances beautifully**;* (b) an adjective: *I am **very happy**;* (c) another adverb: *The students write **very well**;* or (d) an entire (complete) sentence: ***Fortunately, he's happy; Unfortunately, he's unhappy**.*

2. We make an ADVERB OF MANNER by adding an *-ly* ending to an adjective: *(beautiful) Their child sings **beautifully**; (correct) He answered the question **correctly**.*

3. The adverbs of manner *hard* and *fast* are exceptions: they do not end in *-ly.* They may occur as adjectives or adverbs: *(adj.) He is a **fast worker**;* or *(adv.) He **works fast**; (adj.) She is a **hard worker**;* or *(adv.) She **works hard**.*
   Note: The adverb *hardly* means *scarcely* or *barely*: *She hardly understands English. Hard* and *hardly* are completely different in meaning.

4. Another adverb of manner that is an exception is *well,* the adverbial form of *good: He speaks French **well*** (never *goodly*); *She always does her assignments **well*** (never *goodly*).

5. The ADVERBS OF TIME, *early, late, daily, weekly, monthly,* and *yearly,* also occur as adjectives: *The San Francisco Chronicle is a **daily newspaper**; The **early bird** gets the worm.* (old saying)
   Note: Like *hard* and *fast,* the above adverbs of time have the same form as adjectives or adverbs: *He is always a **late student**; He always **comes** to school **late**; I **pay** my phone bill **monthly**; This is my **monthly payment**.*

6. INTENSIFYING ADVERBS serve as emphasizers: *He works **too hard**; An artist often has a **very lonely** life; She is an **extremely nice** person; That man is **quite** (very) **handsome**; Their child always **acts rather** (very) foolishly; She is **more intelligent** than I.*

7. SENTENCE ADVERBS (sentence modifiers) modify an entire sentence: ***Fortunately, my health is good; Obviously, that young man is in love; Actually, they are not very happy together; Presumably, she is an honest woman**.*
   Special Note: Unlike in some other languages, *actually* in English means *really* (not *now* as in Spanish, French, and Italian).

8. Sentence adverbs like *perhaps, possibly, probably, maybe, hopefully, certainly,* and *absolutely* occur as one-word answers to a *yes-no* question: *Are we in love? Perhaps; Absolutely; Hopefully;* etc.

9. ADVERBS OF DEGREE suggest an amount of completion: *He is **almost** twenty-five years old; My refrigerator is **completely** empty; Our new house is **partially** finished; The project is **entirely** completed; I don't have **enough** money to take a vacation; I'm **almost** finished.*

10. ADVERBS OF FREQUENCY describe the frequency of an event: *She is **sometimes** homesick; The President is almost **never** alone.*

11. ADVERBS OF PLACE AND DIRECTION tell where some person, place, or thing is: *Poland is **east** of Germany; Turn **left** at the corner; Your father is **here**; My desk is **there**.*

1.55 (Continued)

Rules for Spelling Adverbs Derived from Adjectives

12. (a) When an adjective ends in a final -*y* preceded by a consonant, change the -*y* to -*i* and add -*ly*: (*happy*) They are **happily** married; (*easy*) She does all her work **easily**; (*crazy*) He often acts **crazily**.

(b) When adjectives end in -*ble*, -*ple*, -*tle*, and -*dle*, the -*le* is dropped before adding -*ly*: (*possible*) **Possibly**, we will take a vacation next month; (*humble*) I **humbly** beg your pardon; (*terrible*) She is a **terribly** nice person; (*simple*) I **simply** don't know the answer.

(c) When an adjective ends in -*l*, keep the -*l* and add -*ly*: (*beautiful*) That soprano sings **beautifully**; (*accidental*) I **accidentally** made a mistake.

(d) When an adjective ends in a silent -*e*, keep the -*e* and add -*ly*: (*sincere*) I am **sincerely** sorry to hear about your bad luck; (*complete*) The glass is **completely** full; (*extreme*) She is an **extremely** clever artist; (*divine*) That ballerina dances **divinely**.

1.56

GRAMMAR EXERCISE   Name _____ Date _____

  Focus: Adverbs

Make adverbs out of the adjectives given in the parentheses and supply them in the blanks. Carefully check the rules for spelling adverbs.

EXAMPLES: a. (beautiful) His sister plays the piano <u>beautifully</u>.
  b. (late) He always gets to work <u>late</u>.

1. (good) That lazy person never does a job _____.

2. (careful) My boss always looks at my work _____.

3. (clever) A fox behaves very _____.

4. (slow) A turtle crawls _____. (quick) A cockroach crawls _____.

5. (hard) A female lion works _____. (lazy) A male lion always behaves very

  _____.

6. (good) This calculator doesn't work _____.

7. (late) My teacher never gets to the class _____. (early) In fact, s/he usually

  arrives _____.

8. (hard) Ants and bees work very _____.

9. (fast) A leopard runs _____. (slow) The water of the Nile flows _____.

10. (good) Apples grow _____ in a cool climate.

11. (hard) The poor usually work very _____.

12. (slow) My grandfather always drives his car very _____.

13. (foolish) Children sometimes act and behave _____.

14. (smooth) Bill and his wife dance together very _____.

15. (good) S/he always dresses _____.

16. (clear) Unfortunately, the patient doesn't think _____.

17. (diligent) He always does his work _____.

18. (beautiful/intelligent) S/he speaks _____ and _____.

19. (terrible/good) S/he cooks _____, but s/he always washes the dishes _____.

20. (proper) Their young boy always acts very _____.

21. (easy/successful) S/he's lucky; s/he does everything _____ and _____.

22. (sincere) S/he always speaks _____.

23. (crazy) S/he sometimes acts _____.

24. (hard/fast) My boss works _____ and _____.

25. (late) That customer sometimes pays his bills _____.

26. (good) Their child always does every project at school _____.

27. (correct/beautiful) S/he speaks _____ and _____.

1.57

Focus: Frequency Adverbs Preceding Verbs

Except with the verb *be*, frequency adverbs always precede the verbs they modify in the simple present tense: *The sun **always sets** in the west; It **hardly ever rains** in the Sahara.* **Note:** *Hardly ever* means *seldom* or *rarely. Ever* never appears alone in affirmative statements.

Fill in the blanks with appropriate frequency adverbs.

| always | hardly ever | occasionally | rarely | sometimes |
| frequently | never | often | seldom | usually |

EXAMPLES: a. Most people in India <u>never</u> eat meat.
               b. Cats and dogs <u>seldom</u> become good friends.

   1. Water _____ mixes with oil.

   2. The sun _____ rises in the east.

   3. Our little boy _____ watches the special programs for children on TV. He _____ watches the political or news programs.

   4. A subject and a verb _____ appear in a sentence.

   5. We _____ do a grammar exercise in about fifteen minutes.

   6. Our children _____ set the table before dinner.

   7. I _____ enjoy a few glasses of wine with my dinner.

   8. My phone _____ rings early on Sunday mornings.

   9. My parents _____ go to church on Sundays.

Now supply appropriate base forms or -s forms in the blanks.

   10. My secretary is excellent and seldom _____ a mistake.

   11. Adults usually _____ more problems than children.

   12. Cats usually _____ to be alone. A dog usually _____ the company of people.

   13. The people at my office always _____ nice-looking clothes.

Now supply an appropriate frequency adverb as well.

   14. Most of the students _____ their homework.

   15. I _____ to school on the bus/train.

   16. My father _____ to the radio in the mornings.

   17. My parents _____ to the beach on their vacations.

   18. My phone _____ after midnight.

   19. My boss _____ a lot of work for me to do.

   20. Our children _____ to school on Saturdays.

1.58

Focus: Frequency Adverbs with the Verb *Be*

Frequency adverbs more often follow the verb *be: He is **sometimes** late to class.*

Fill in the blanks with appropriate frequency adverbs selected from the list below. Reminder: *Hardly ever* means *seldom* or *rarely*. *Ever* never appears alone in affirmative statements.

| always | hardly ever | occasionally | rarely | sometimes |
| frequently | never | often | seldom | usually |

EXAMPLES: a. Life for the poor is <u>usually</u> very hard.
   b. Cats and dogs are <u>seldom</u> friendly with each other.

 1. Children are _____ more honest than adults.

 2. A woman is _____ the president of a large company.

 3. It is _____ very cold at the North Pole.

 4. It is _____ cold in the Sahara at night, but during the day it is _____ hot and dry.

 5. Life on a tropical island is _____ quite (very) slow.

 6. Life is _____ difficult for a happy child.

 7. People are _____ good. People are _____ perfect.

 8. Children are _____ good. Children are _____ difficult.

 9. Meat is _____ cheap. Potatoes are _____ expensive.

10. There are _____ many dangers in a big city.

Now supply an appropriate form of the verb *be* as well.

11. A cat _____ very independent.

12. The weather in the Caribbean _____ nice in the winter.

13. February in Moscow _____ cold.

14. My dentist _____ very busy all day long.

15. Life for the very rich _____ difficult.

16. It _____ difficult to meet people in a big city.

17. There _____ a lot of people at an airport.

18. Children _____ afraid of the dark.

19. The life of a student _____ wonderful but busy.

20. My parents _____ worried about me.

21. Our teacher _____ late to class.

22. She _____ a happy person.

23. Peter's appetite _____ good in the mornings.

1.59

Focus: Frequency Adverbs in Negative Verb Phrases with the Verb *Be*

The frequency adverbs *ever, always, usually,* and *often* may appear in negative verb phrases. They follow the verb *be* + *not* in a phrase: *It **isn't usually** cold in Los Angeles; His students **aren't ever** late.*

Note: *Isn't ever* means *never is, isn't always* means *usually is,* and *isn't usually (often)* means *rarely is* or *seldom is;* for example, *It isn't ever (never is) hot in Alaska; Our children aren't always (usually are) good; He isn't usually (rarely is) sick.*

Supply appropriate negative verb phrases with the verb *be* **and** *ever, always, usually,* **or** *often.*

EXAMPLES: a. It isn't ever warm at the North Pole.
              b. The weather in Los Angeles isn't always nice.

1. Cats and dogs _____ enemies.

2. Fortunately, he _____ sick.

3. It _____ hot in the Sahara.

4. I _____ in a good mood.

5. The weather in London _____ hot.

6. People _____ honest.

7. They _____ at church on Sundays.

8. Sally _____ a happy person.

9. Cats and dogs _____ friendly with each other.

10. Life for the rich _____ easy.

11. My boss _____ in a good mood on Monday mornings.

12. The weatherman _____ correct.

13. It _____ easy to find a husband/wife.

14. I _____ satisfied with my situation in life.

15. It _____ easy for her to speak English on the phone.

16. Our children _____ naughty (bad).

17. The exercises in this book _____ easy.

18. Potatoes _____ cheap.

19. It _____ easy to find a well-paying job.

20. John's parents _____ happy with his progress in school.

21. The weather in my hometown _____ nice.

22. Life _____ easy for the poor.

23. Fortunately, I _____ afraid of the future.

24. Her friends _____ willing to help her.

25. My car looks good, but it _____ dependable.

1.60

Focus: Frequency Adverbs in Negative Verb Phrases

Except with the verb *be*, a frequency adverb precedes a base form in a negative verb phrase in the simple present tense: *A male lion doesn't ever hunt (never hunts) for food; I don't always watch (usually watch) TV in the evening; My secretary doesn't often make (seldom makes) a mistake; I don't usually drink (seldom drink) alcohol.*

Supply appropriate base forms in the blanks. Do not use *be*.

EXAMPLES: a. I don't always <u>drink</u> coffee in the morning.
             b. She doesn't usually <u>work</u> on Sundays.
             c. They don't ever <u>go</u> to church.

1. I don't ever _____ between meals.

2. My car doesn't always _____ well.

3. My mother doesn't usually _____ breakfast for the family.

4. I don't always _____ out with my friends on Saturday night.

5. Our teacher doesn't always _____ us homework, fortunately.

Now supply an adverb + base form.

6. Vegetarians don't _____ meat.

7. My phone doesn't _____ early on Sunday mornings.

8. I don't _____ to the radio at breakfast.

9. He doesn't _____ problems with his boss.

10. I don't _____ shopping on a rainy day.

Now supply *don't/doesn't* + adverb + base form.

11. My grandfather _____ salt on his food.

12. Our young daughter _____ lipstick.

13. He _____ a jacket and tie to work.

14. John _____ the bus to school.

15. Her husband _____ her out to dinner.

16. My cat _____ with my dog.

Now complete the sentences with your own words.

17. My teacher/doctor/dentist _____.

18. Her neighbors_____.

19. The government_____.

20. Our family/team/church _____.

1.61

Focus: _Get_

The verb _get_ appears in many idiomatic expressions that cannot be easily translated into other languages. The following expressions occur most often in informal usage:

(a) _To get to a place_ means _to arrive at a place: Do you often get to school late?_

(b) _To get_ can mean _to become: Do you ever get hungry in the middle of the night?_
Note: _To get_ can mean _to become_ only when it precedes an adjective.

(c) _To get_ can mean _to receive: She always gets a lot of Christmas cards._

(d) _To get out of_ means _to leave_ a room or place: _I usually get out of work around five o'clock._

(e) _To get up_ can mean _to arise: I usually get up early._

(f) _To get on_ can mean _to board: I usually get on the train at Grand Central Station._

(g) _To get off_ can mean _to descend: I get off the train at the last stop._

(h) _To get into_ can mean _to enter: How do you get into the best university?_

(i) _To get into_ can also mean _to become involved with: He often gets into trouble with the teacher._

Supply the verb _get_ (base form or -s form) in the blanks.

EXAMPLES: a. Fortunately, our children seldom get sick.
              b. Our new baby always gets hungry in the middle of the night.

1. That lucky guy never _____ sick. (_Guy_ is slang for _man_.)

2. That poor woman never _____ good jobs.

3. I usually _____ out of bed early in the morning.

4. She always _____ up at 7:30 in the morning.

5. That fellow never _____ into trouble. (_Fellow_ is informal for _man_.)

6. How do you usually _____ on a horse?

7. How do we _____ into the best club in town?

8. A farmer usually _____ up with the cows.

9. We usually _____ out of our class around one o'clock.

10. That poor fellow never _____ good grades in school.

11. What time do you usually _____ to school?

12. How many Christmas cards does she usually _____?

13. My roommate usually _____ up around seven o'clock in the morning.

14. At what station do you usually _____ off the train?

15. That lucky girl always _____ good grades in her examinations.

16. Everyone usually _____ out of the office around five o'clock.

17. Do you ever _____ angry at your boss?

18. I usually _____ a little nervous at the doctor's office.

1.62

Focus: Yes-No Questions with the Verb Be and Frequency Adverbs

In a *yes-no* question in the simple present tense, a frequency adverb follows the subject: *Are* **you always** *in a good mood? Are* **you usually** *a happy person? Are* **you ever** *late for work? Is* **that selfish person never** *satisfied? Is* **it ever** *hot in London?*
Note: For emphasis, *never* occasionally occurs in *yes-no* questions: *Is an elephant's appetite* **never** *satisfied? Are people* **never** *perfect?* However, *rarely, hardly ever,* and *seldom* never appear in such questions.

Supply an appropriate form of the verb *be* in the first blank and an appropriate frequency adverb in the second blank.

EXAMPLES:
   a. <u>Is</u> the weather during the day <u>always</u> hot in the Sahara?
   b. <u>Are</u> you <u>usually</u> satisfied with your position in life?
   c. <u>Are</u> people <u>ever</u> perfect?

1. _____ life _____ easy for the rich/poor?

2. _____ it _____ cold at the North Pole?

3. _____ people _____ afraid of snakes?

4. _____ you _____ hungry late at night?

5. _____ the weather in a jungle _____ hot and humid?

6. _____ children _____ bad/good/naughty?

7. _____ your parents _____ angry at you?

8. _____ the weather in your hometown _____ nice in March?

9. _____ your mother and father _____ happy together?

10. _____ your homework _____ difficult/easy?

11. _____ your children _____ at school on Saturdays?

12. _____ the formula for water _____ the same?

13. _____ Monday _____ a difficult day for you?

14. _____ pigs _____ dirty animals?

15. _____ your cat _____ friendly with your dog?

16. _____ you _____ afraid of the future?

17. _____ the nights in the Sahara _____ cold?

18. _____ people _____ good?

19. _____ your boss _____ in a bad mood?

20. _____ everyone in your office _____ busy?

21. _____ a cat _____ a clean animal?

22. _____ Christmas _____ on December 25?

23. _____ Easter _____ in March?

1.63

Name _____ Date _____

Focus: *Yes-No Questions and Frequency Adverbs*

Reminder: Frequency adverbs always follow the subject of a question: *Does **a male lion always** depend on the female for food? Do **you usually** get home early or late?*
Note: There is no preposition in the expression *to get home: I always get home late* (but *I always get **to** school early*).
Reminder: *To get **to** a place* means *to arrive **at** a place*.

Supply *do* or *does* in the first blank and an appropriate frequency adverb + a base form in the second blank.

EXAMPLES: a. Does your neighbor's son <u>ever get</u> into trouble at school?
b. Do your parents <u>always understand</u> your problems?

1. _____ you _____ a good appetite in the mornings?

2. _____ your brother _____ to church on Sundays?

3. _____ you _____ into a silly (little foolish) mood?

4. _____ you _____ any mistakes during an exercise?

5. _____ your grandfather _____ well?

6. _____ everyone at work _____ a coffee break?

7. _____ you _____ up late on Sunday mornings?

8. _____ the students _____ their homework in ink?

9. _____ your baby _____ a nap after her lunch?

10. _____ the rich _____ an easy/difficult life?

11. _____ you _____ wine with your dinner?

12. _____ your roommate _____ lunch in the cafeteria?

13. _____ you _____ food with chopsticks?

Now supply your own subjects.

14. _____ a lot of birthday cards?

15. _____ TV in the evenings?

16. _____ to the radio at breakfast?

17. _____ the train to work?

18. _____ a good grade in a test?

19. _____ your mother in the kitchen?

20. _____ English at home?

21. _____ on Saturday night?

22. _____ bad dreams?

23. _____ exercises in the morning?

1.64

GRAMMAR EXERCISE   Name _____ Date _____

Focus: Information Questions with *How Often*

Except with the verb *be,* the auxiliary *do* or *does* occurs after the information words *how often* in the simple present tense: *How often **does** leap year come? How often **do** you shave?*

Supply *do* or *does* in the first blank and an appropriate base form in the second blank. **Pronunciation Note**: *Often* sounds like *ah-fen.*

EXAMPLES: a. How often <u>do</u> you <u>watch</u> TV?
              b. How often <u>does</u> the earth <u>revolve</u> around the sun?

1. How often _____ it _____ in the Sahara?

2. How often _____ you _____ to the radio?

3. How often _____ you _____ physical exercises?

4. How often _____ your mother/father _____ the house?

5. How often _____ your roommate _____ homework for school?

6. How often _____ she _____ her house plants?

7. How often _____ your son _____ nightmares? (*Nightmares* are bad dreams.)

8. How often _____ your Dad _____ the car to the garage for repairs?

9. How often _____ you _____ a cigarette?

10. How often _____ you _____ your hair?

11. How often _____ your family _____ on a vacation?

12. How often _____ your father _____ a business trip?

13. How often _____ you _____ alcohol/coffee/tea/milk?

14. How often _____ you _____ your neighbors to your house?

15. How often _____ you _____ a newspaper/a novel?

16. How often _____ your parents _____ a letter to you?

17. How often _____ you _____ taxes?

18. How often _____ leap year _____?

19. How often _____ you _____ a telegram?

20. How often _____ your brother _____ out with his girlfriend?

Now complete the sentences with your own words.

21. How often do your parents _____?

22. How often _____?

23. _____basketball/cards?

24. _____ a car/a bike?

1.65

GRAMMAR EXERCISE   Name _____ Date _____

Focus: Prepositions of Time

Fill in each blank with *at, during, from, in, on,* or *to.*

EXAMPLES: a. We usually go shopping on Saturday.
(*On* used with a day of the week)
b. The cherry trees in Washington, D.C., blossom in April.
(*In* used with a month)
c. Christmas is on December 25.
(*On* used with a month plus a date)
d. The class always begins at ten o'clock.
(*At* used with an hour of the day)
e. My grandparents always have lunch at noon (12 o'clock).
f. We were in Canada in 1976 on our vacation.
(*In* used with a year)
g. My neighbor's son goes to school at night.
(*At* used with a part of the day that is considered a point of time)
Note: But we say *in the morning, in the afternoon,* and *in the evening. In the night* rarely occurs in conversation and has an added connotation of darkness, perhaps in the poetic sense.
h. We had a lot of fun during the game.
(*During* used to express duration)
i. I always have about three cups of coffee in/during the morning.
(*In/during* with a part of the day [week, month, year, season] that is considered a period of time)
j. We are usually in class from ten to one o'clock.
(*From* used to express the beginning point, and *to* used to express the end point)

1. The leaves fall from the trees _____ October.

2. The spring semester at the university begins _____ January 31.

3. I always have a lot of homework to do _____ the evening.

4. The new year begins _____ midnight.

5. He's always very busy _____ the beginning _____ the end of the week.

6. I always swim a lot _____ the summer.

7. My father usually gets up _____ 6:30 _____ the morning.

8. Do you usually sleep well _____ night?

9. People in France usually take their vacations _____ August.

10. Many people don't like to travel _____ Friday the thirteenth.

11. Our baby usually wakes up _____ seven o'clock _____ the morning.

12. His father was born _____ August 20, 1937.

13. I sometimes take a nap _____ the afternoon.

14. Graduation ceremonies at the University are always _____ June.

1.66

GRAMMAR EXERCISE   Name _____ Date _____

Focus: Reviewing Place Prepositions and Expressions of Place

Supply in each blank an appropriate preposition from the following list. Do this exercise as a quiz.

around   *at*   *between*   *from*   *in*   *of*   *on*   *to*

EXAMPLES:
   a. A thirty-five-year old man is, more or less, in the middle of his life.
   b. He lives at 300 Park Avenue. His brother also lives on Park Avenue.
      Note: *At* is used when a house number precedes the name of a street, but *on* is used before the name of a street without a house number.
   c. There is a good drugstore on/at the corner of Park and Miller.
      Note: *At* or *on* is used with *the corner of*.
   d. I usually sit between Carlos and Anna during a class.
      Reminder: *Between* is used when we want to point out a person or thing that appears in the middle of a unit of three.

1. The Museum of Modern Art _____ New York City is _____ West 53rd Street _____ Fifth and Sixth Avenues.

2. My favorite grocery store is _____ the corner _____ Broadway and Park.

3. I always keep milk _____ the top shelf of the refrigerator.

4. We are _____ the beginning _____ this exercise.

5. The Ten Commandments are _____ the Bible.

6. A table of contents is usually _____ the beginning _____ a book.

7. There is some very bad news _____ this letter (or telegram).

8. There is a lot of good music _____ the radio. (Use *on*)

9. Aaron's name is always _____ the top _____ an alphabetical listing of names, but Zeno's is always _____ the bottom.

10. What are your favorite programs _____ TV? (Use *on*)

11. We are far _____ the sun. The sun is _____ the center _____ our solar system.

12. There is a big neon sign _____ the side _____ my office building.

13. I don't like to sit _____ the back _____ a theater.

14. I want to take a trip _____ the world.

15. A large part of China is next _____ the Soviet Union.

16. I don't like to sit _____ the first row of seats in a movie theater.

17. Do you usually have dancing _____ your parties?

18. We are close _____ the end of this exercise.

19. Most children don't like to sit _____ front _____ the teacher's desk.

20. We are far _____ the end _____ this book.

21. Please put that bouquet of flowers _____ the middle _____ the table.

22. This sentence is _____ the bottom _____ the page.

1.67

GRAMMAR EXERCISE   Name _____ Date _____

Focus: Prepositions of Direction

Supply in each blank an appropriate preposition from the following list.

at   down   from   in   into   out of   through   to   up

EXAMPLES: a. My father always goes <u>to</u> work at around eight in the morning.
           b. He usually returns <u>from</u> his office at five in the afternoon.
           c. A thief very often enters a house <u>through</u> a window.
           d. I live on the sixth floor of an apartment building. Every morning I walk <u>down</u> six flights of stairs. Every evening I walk <u>up</u> six flights of stairs.
              Note: A flight of stairs connects one floor of a building to another.
           e. What time do you usually get <u>to</u> work? When do you arrive <u>at</u> your office?
              Reminder: We *get to* a place, but we *arrive at* a place.
           f. When do we arrive <u>in</u> Munich?
              Note: We arrive *in* a city or a country, but we arrive *at* an office, airport, or a similar type place. However, we *get to* a city.
           g. What time do you get <u>into</u> bed every night? When do you usually get <u>out of</u> bed in the morning?
              Reminder: The examples above using *get* are idiomatic.

1. I usually get _____ my office at five o'clock.

2. Our son wants to get _____ the University of Ohio.

3. I don't want to take an umbrella _____ work today.

4. Do you usually bring a lot of work home _____ the office?

5. I usually enter my house _____ the back door.

6. It's difficult for me to put thread _____ the eye of a needle.

7. Where do you come _____?

8. When do we get _____ the end of the book?

9. Many words in English come _____ Latin and Greek.

10. News travels fast _____ the medium of radio.

11. It's more difficult to climb _____ a mountain than it is to climb _____.

12. Blood flows _____ the heart of an animal's body.

13. Many children think we get milk _____ a bottle.

14. Radio waves travel _____ the air.

15. The water in my town comes _____ the mountains.

16. We get gold _____ the earth. We get milk _____ a cow.

17. What time do you usually get _____ your house in the morning?

18. What time do we arrive _____ Athens? When do we get _____ Athens?

19. When do we arrive _____ Cairo? When do we arrive _____ the airport?

GRAMMAR EXERCISE Name _____ Date _____

Focus: *To/Two/Too*

1. *To, two,* and *too* understandably confuse many students. *To* is a preposition: *How often do you go to the store?* And, as we have discussed earlier, *to* is also combined with a base form to make an infinitive: *I love to travel.* *Two* is an adjective and modifies nouns: *I have **two dollars** in my pocket.* *Too* is an adverb and modifies adjectives or other adverbs: *That child has **too much** money; She speaks **too quickly**.*

2. When the adverb *too* modifies an adjective or adverb, a strong negative connotation is expressed. There is the suggestion of an excess of some thing or factor that is not needed or that we do not like or want: *He is **too selfish;** We have **too much inflation**.*

3. *Too* usually precedes an adjective that is followed by an infinitive: *This package is **too heavy to lift;** Our little girl is **too young to cross** the street alone.*

Fill in the blanks with *to, two,* or *too*.

EXAMPLES: a. <u>Two</u> and <u>two</u> make four.
  b. Do you ever go <u>to</u> church on Sunday.
  c. Life is <u>too</u> short to worry about foolish things.

1. Our son is _____ young to go into the army.

2. His _____ main problems are money and love.

3. How often do you speak _____ your neighbor next door?

4. It's _____ cold to go outside.

5. _____ is a more interesting number than one.

6. Do you usually drive _____ work?

7. Unfortunately, the athlete is now _____ old to play well.

8. It takes _____ to tango. (saying)

9. Who do you usually walk _____ school with?

10. That spoiled child has _____ much money to spend.

Now fill in the blanks with appropriate infinitives.

11. It's too cold _____ a walk in the park today.

12. I'm too tired _____ to the party tonight.

13. Obviously, you have too much work _____ at the office.

14. This package is too heavy _____ home.

15. I'm sorry, but this food is too spicy _____.

16. This coffee is too hot _____.

17. This book is too long _____ in one day.

1.69

Name _____ Date _____

Focus: *Too*

Phrases occur that contain *too* + adjective + *for* + (pro)noun object + infinitive: *That book is **too sad for me to read***; *This exercise isn't **too difficult for the students to do***.

Supply in each blank an appropriate adjective from the following list.

big	crowded	expensive	late	pornographic	short	sweet
bitter	dangerous	heavy	long	rainy	sour	violent
boring	depressing	hot	old	rotten	spicy	wet
cold	difficult	large	polluted	sad	spoiled	young

EXAMPLES: a. The water in the lake today is too <u>cold</u> for us to swim in.

b. It is too <u>late</u> for us to go to the football game.

1. This candy is too _____ for me to eat.

2. The air in this city is too _____ for us to breathe.

3. Today is too _____ and _____ for me to go shopping.

4. Chinese is too _____ for me to learn.

5. Our little girl is too _____ for us to leave home alone.

6. The weather today is too _____ for me to take my family to the park.

7. New York is too _____ for me to live in.

Now complete the sentences with *too* + adjective + *for* + (pro)noun object + infinitive.

8. This orange/tea is _____.

9. This package is _____.

10. That suit is _____.

11. Shakespeare is_____.

12. A Rolls-Royce is _____.

13. This book/magazine is _____.

14. These eggs are_____.

15. Mexican food is _____.

Now supply appropriate subjects in the blanks.

16. _____ is too fantastic for me to believe.

17. _____ is too tough for me to cut (*Tough* means *not tender*.)

18. _____ are too old for me to wear.

19. _____ is too soft for me to sleep on.

20. _____ is too small for my family to live in.

1.70

VERY, TOO, AND ENOUGH

1. *Very* is called an intensifier because it intensifies (makes stronger) the word that it precedes: *She is **very nice;** An elephant is **very large;** A giraffe is **very tall;** A fox is **very clever.***

2. *Too* weakens (makes weak) the adjective or adverb that it precedes; it has a completely different meaning from *very*. Compare:

Wrong	Correct
She is (too) beautiful. (No one is too beautiful).	*She is **very** beautiful.*
Moscow is (too) cold. (It's possible for millions of people to live there, isn't it?)	*Moscow is **very** cold.*
French food is (too) good. (Is any food too good?)	*French food is **very** good.*

3. When *too* precedes an adjective or adverb, it is almost always accompanied by an infinitive. *Too* + adjective (adverb) + infinitive can mean impossibility; for example: *This coffee is too hot to drink* (it is impossible to drink); *That book is too difficult to read* (it is impossible to read).

4. Whereas *too* means impossibility, an adjective + *enough* + infinitive means possibility: *He is young enough to get* (it is possible for him to get) *into the movies at half price;* however, a negative statement has the opposite meaning: *He isn't young enough to get* (he is too old to get) *into the movies at half price.*

5. *Enough* always follows the adjective that it modifies: *Our little boy isn't **old enough** to go to school; She is **beautiful enough** to be in the movies.*

6. When *enough* is used to modify a noun, it may precede or follow the word without any change in meaning: *There isn't enough food* (or *food enough*) *in the refrigerator for us to make dinner.*

1.71

GRAMMAR EXERCISE   Name _____ Date _____

Focus: *Very, Too,* and *Enough*

Supply *very, too,* or *enough* in the blanks.

EXAMPLES: a. That woman is a <u>very</u> good friend of my mother's.
             b. They are <u>too</u> poor to buy food for their children.
             c. Their daughter isn't old <u>enough</u> to wear lipstick.

1. Food is _____ expensive for us to waste.

2. There isn't _____ food in the large cities of India for the people to eat. The country

   has _____ many people.

3. I don't like cats. They're _____ independent.

4. Paris is a _____ beautiful city, but the weather in the winter is _____ cold and damp for me to live in.

5. Chinese is _____ difficult for me to learn.

6. English is _____ difficult, but I'm going to learn it.

7. There isn't _____ time in a day.

8. This exercise isn't _____ difficult for us to do.

9. She is a _____ beautiful woman, but she wears _____ much perfume.

10. He is a _____ handsome man.

11. Life is _____ short to worry about unimportant things.

12. The earth is _____ small for the size of its population.

13. We are _____ happy about our daughter's recent success.

14. I am _____ sorry to hear about your friend's death.

15. Rich people's children often have _____ much money to spend.

16. I am _____ glad (happy) to meet you.

17. They are rich _____ to travel all the time.

18. There isn't _____ fresh water in the world.

19. They are _____ happy with their new house.

20. That story is _____ fantastic to believe.

21. Do you have _____ money to go to the movies with me?

22. I know _____ many selfish people.

23. This jacket is _____ cheap, but it looks _____ cheap for me to wear.

24. It isn't warm _____ to go swimming today.

25. He is a _____ happy person.

26. That man is _____ unhappy to think clearly.

27. Our son is _____ young to enter the university.

Very, Too, and Enough   **75**

THE PRESENT CONTINUOUS TENSE

2

2.1

EVENTS NOW

1. The PRESENT CONTINUOUS TENSE is used to express an event or action that is happening now or temporarily: *We **are beginning** a new chapter of this book now; A lot of things **are happening** in school today; It's late in March and the days **are getting** longer.*

2. We form the present continuous tense with the verb *be* (as an auxiliary) + a PRESENT PARTICIPLE as the main verb of a verb phrase.

	Singular	Plural
First person	I am living	we
Second person	you are living	you } are living
Third person	he	they
	she } is living	
	it	

3. In informal usage contractions of subject pronouns and the verb *be* occur: ***She's*** *expecting a child;* ***It's*** *beginning to snow;* ***He's*** *listening to our conversation on the extension phone.*

Rules for Spelling Present Participles (*-ing* Forms)

4. (a) Usually, we need only to add *-ing* to a base form to make a present participle: (*bring*) *They're **bringing** home the new car today;* (*fall*) *A lot of rocks are **falling** on the highway;* (*eat*) *Our baby is **eating** with a spoon now.*

(b) When a base form ends in silent *e*, we drop the *e* and add *-ing*: (*change*) *They are **changing** my schedule today;* (*take*) *She is **taking** a few courses in anthropology this semester;* (*live*) *Nobody is **living** on the moon;* (*save*) *We're **saving** money for a rainy day;* (*drive*) *They're **driving** a beautiful new car.*

(c) When a one-syllable base form ends in *-ie*, the *-ie* is dropped and we add *-y* + *-ing*: (*lie*) *The dog is **lying** in front of the fireplace;* (*die*) *Unfortunately, the patient is **dying**.*

(d) There is no change when *-ing* is added to a word already ending in *-y*: (*carry*) *He is **carrying** all of the responsibilities;* (*copy*) *The students are **copying** sentences out of their workbooks;* (*stay*) *My grandfather is **staying** with us temporarily.*

(e) When a base form ends with a single consonant preceded by a single stressed vowel, double the final consonant before adding *-ing*: (*begin*) *I am **beginning** to get hungry;* (*get*) *The world's population is **getting** larger and larger;* (*run*) *Look! The dog is **running** away;* (*stop*) *Fortunately, the firemen are **stopping** the fire;* (*swim*) *Nobody is **swimming** in the pool;* (*hit*) *That terrible child is **hitting** the dog with a stick;* (*plan*) *We're **planning** to go away.*

2.1 (Continued)

5. Words called ACTION VERBS may appear in both the simple present and present continuous tenses.

SOME ACTION VERBS

answer	get	kill	operate	save
cook	help	leave	repeat	travel
do	jump	make	run	work

6. Words called NONACTION VERBS usually occur in the simple present tense; however, there are some exceptions.

SOME NONACTION VERBS

admire	appear	cost	hate	look
appreciate	be	feel	have	love

(a) The verb *be* is never used in the present continuous tense as a main verb except when it is followed by an adjective: *You're **being foolish**; You're **being selfish**; The children are **being good** today.*

(b) When we wish to express a temporary feeling or action, certain nonaction verbs occur in the present continuous tense: *He's admiring that beautiful girl's figure* (but *I admire French art*); *This operation is costing a lot* (but *Operations cost a lot*); *I'm feeling better today* (but *I feel lazy on weekends*); *I am loving these moments with you* (but *I love you*).

(c) To show possession, the verb *have* is usually used in the simple present tense: *I have a car; She has a wonderful personality.* However, the verb *have* occurs idiomatically in the present tense preceding certain nouns: (*difficulty*) *One of the students is having difficulty with the homework;* (*lesson*) *She is having a private lesson tomorrow;* (*operation*) *The patient is having an operation;* (*party*) *We are having a party for our children;* (*problem*) *The engineers are having a problem with the new computer;* (*time*) *I'm having a good/bad time on this vacation;* (*trouble*) *They're having trouble with their new car;* (*weather*) *We're having beautiful weather this month.*

2.2

Focus: Affirmative Statements in the Present Continuous Tense

Fill in the blanks with appropriate verb phrases in the present continuous tense. Make present participles out of the base forms in the parentheses. Carefully check the rules for spelling present participles.

EXAMPLES: a. (begin) We <u>are beginning</u> this exercise now.

               b. (learn) We <u>are learning</u> English step by step (gradually).

1. (do) I _____ the first sentence of this exercise now.

2. (revolve) The earth _____ around the sun.

3. (happen) A lot of things _____ right now (at exactly this moment). (look) I _____ at this page right now.

4. (set) The sun _____ in Paris/New York/Tokyo right now.

5. (melt) The ice in Antartica _____ slowly.

6. (die) All my house plants _____ from some disease.

7. (hold) I _____ this book in my hands.

8. (change) Fortunately, they _____ my schedule today.

9. (leave) Some friends of mine _____ for France at this very moment (right now).

10. (make) The maid _____ the bed right now.

11. (listen) Sh! Someone _____ to our conversation.

12. (run) Look! Your dog _____ away. Catch him!

13. (think) Everyone _____ about the present continuous tense.

14. (sit) We _____ in a circle of seats.

15. (learn/begin/grow) Our baby _____ to walk; also, he _____ to talk, and a new tooth _____ in his mouth. (become) He _____ a young man fast.

16. (use) I _____ his typewriter for the time being. (*For the time being* means *temporarily*.)

17. (get) It's April/October, and the days _____ longer/shorter.

18. (get) All of us _____ older day by day (gradually).

19. (live) They _____ in a hotel for the time being.

20. (work) She _____ in a factory temporarily.

21. (wait) He _____ for a phone call from his girlfriend.

22. (get) Everyone's English _____ better.

23. (carry) I _____ an umbrella to school today.

24. (plan) We _____ to go to a movie today.

25. (speak) She _____ English with a foreign accent.

26. (do) I _____ the last sentence of this exercise now.

2.3

GRAMMAR EXERCISE

Name _____ Date _____

Focus: Contrasting the Simple Present and Present Continuous Tenses

Occasionally, we may use either the simple present tense or the present continuous tense in the same sentence, but the meaning is different; for example, *The earth is circling the sun* (action now); or *The earth circles the sun* (fact). The present tense expresses a fact or a habitual action; the present continuous expresses action now.

Fill in the blanks with verbs in the simple present or present continuous tenses, whichever is correct.

EXAMPLES: a. (go) I go to the movies once in a while (occasionally).
b. (go) Our son is going to a private school for the time being.

1. (go) My whole family _____ to church once a week.

2. (listen) Sh! Someone _____ to our conversation.

3. (go) My wife and I _____ to the beach in the summer.

4. (ring) Listen! The phone _____ in the other room.

5. (fall) Rain seldom _____ in the Sahara.

6. (change) He is thirteen years old, and his voice _____.

7. (get) Let's change the conversation. It _____ too serious.

8. (come) Leap year _____ every four years.

9. (grow) My grandfather _____ tomatoes in his garden this summer.

   (grow) He _____ them every summer.

10. (leave) The children _____ for school right now.

11. (leave) The children _____ at 8:30 every morning of the week.

12. (take) Sh! The baby _____ her nap.

13. (change) In the north the season _____ four times a year.

14. (die) Unfortunately, the patient _____.

15. (come) The monsoon _____ once or twice a year.

16. (get) It's spring and the days _____ longer.

17. (get) The weather _____ very cold in Moscow in the winter.

18. (rain) It _____ hard, and I don't have an umbrella.

19. (fly) It's November and the birds _____ south.

20. (fly) Many birds of Europe _____ south to Africa every winter.

21. (happen) A lot of things _____ right now.

22. (change) That movie theater _____ its program once a week.

23. (play) Look! Some dogs _____ in our vegetable garden.

24. (happen) Nothing _____ in my hometown on Sundays.

25. (come) Look at those dark clouds. A rainstorm _____.

GRAMMAR EXERCISE   Name _____ Date _____

Focus: Adverbs in the Present Continuous Tense

The adverbs *now*, *gradually*, *slowly*, *quickly*, and *rapidly* are some of the few adverbs that occur in verb phrases containing the present continuous. They are inserted between the auxiliary and the main verb: *The weather is gradually getting better.*

Supply an appropriate form of the verb *be* in the first blank and a present participle made out of the base form given in the parentheses in the second.

EXAMPLES: a. (evaporate) The water in the world's oceans is quickly evaporating.
　　　　　　 b. (come) The patient is rapidly coming to the end of his life. (*To come to the end of* means *to arrive at the end of*.)

1. (deteriorate) Their marriage _____ slowly _____.

2. (get) Her hair _____ slowly _____ longer.

3. (turn) My mother's hair _____ gradually _____ gray.

4. (improve) His English _____ now _____ a lot.

5. (lose) My grandfather _____ rapidly _____ his teeth.

6. (become) Their sixteen-year-old daughter _____ gradually _____ a beautiful young woman.

7. (turn) My hometown _____ quickly _____ into a big city.

8. (get) The earth _____ slowly _____ closer to the sun.

9. (change) Their thirteen-year-old son's voice _____ rapidly _____. (become)
    He _____ gradually _____ a man.

10. (get) All of us _____ gradually _____ older.

11. (fall) Steve and Linda _____ gradually _____ in love.

12. (fall) After ten years of marriage, Peter and Laura _____ slowly _____ out of love. (*To fall in love* is the idiom used for the beginning of a romance, and *to fall out of love* is used for the end of one.)

13. (melt) The ice on the streets _____ now _____.

14. (grow) The world's population _____ rapidly _____ larger.

15. (improve) The patient's condition _____ now _____.

16. (get) The material in this book _____ gradually _____ more difficult.

17. (do) We _____ now _____ an exercise.

18. (come) It _____ quickly _____ to an end.

19. (come) We _____ gradually _____ to the end of the twentieth century.

20. (change) The world _____ quickly _____.

21. (fall) S/he _____ gradually _____ in (out of) love with him/her. (turn)
    Their love _____ now _____ into hate.

2.5

GRAMMAR EXERCISE   Name _____ Date _____

Focus: *Always* in the Present Continuous Tense

The frequency adverb *always* most often occurs in the simple present tense to express the frequency of a habitual activity: *That student **is always** on time; He **always does** his homework well.* To emphasize the frequency of a habitual activity, *always* occurs in a verb phrase containing the present continuous tense: *She **is always worrying** about her beautiful face; He **is always worrying** about his bank account.*

Supply the appropriate form of the verb *be*, *always*, and an appropriate present participle in the blanks.

EXAMPLES: a. Their little boy is always chewing gum.
           b. They are always bragging about the size of their house.
           c. My dog is always chasing cars.

1. My parents _____ about me.

2. S/he _____ gum/a cigarette.

3. My old dog _____ in front of the fire.

4. That foolish young man _____ dangerous drugs.

5. A cat _____ itself.

6. The wind at the top of that mountain _____.

7. A doctor _____ his or her hands.

8. A farmer _____ about the weather.

9. The phone in my office _____.

10. Our young son _____ baseball or football.

11. A good student _____ homework.

12. Mailmen _____ about dogs.

13. My cat and dog _____.

14. A banker _____ about money.

15. Egotistical people _____ about themselves.

16. Their new baby _____.

17. An animal in the jungle _____ for food.

18. The earth _____. (Use *revolving*.)

19. The sun in the desert _____.

20. The teacher _____ us a lot of homework.

21. Actors _____ about their fans (public).

22. A concert pianist _____.

23. A scientist _____ for new ways to improve our world.

24. My old cat _____ a nap in front of the fire.

25. They _____ about their beautiful daughter.

2.6

Focus: Expressing a Future Event with the Present Continuous Tense

When the present continuous tense is accompanied by a future time expression (e.g., *next week, tomorrow,* we may signal an action in future time: *The astronauts **are leaving** for outer space **tomorrow**; **I'm taking** a final examination **next week**.* When a time expression does not occur, we often use the adverb *soon: The twentieth century is coming to an end soon.*

Supply appropriate present participles in the blanks. Pay attention to the use of prepositions.

EXAMPLES: a. They're <u>serving</u> champagne during the intermission at the concert tomorrow night.
             b. We're <u>taking</u> our boat to Lake Tahoe on our next vacation.

1. The professor is _____ about evolution at the next meeting.

2. Our daughter is _____ from the university soon.

3. Our plane is _____ off in a few minutes.

4. I'm _____ a nap between lunch and dinner this afternoon.

5. Carlos is _____ to his native country soon.

6. Better days are _____ for all of us soon.

7. They're _____ for their trip around the world two weeks from today. They're _____ back at the end of the year. They're _____ their children with them.

Now supply appropriate prepositions in the blanks

8. They're serving champagne _____ the wedding reception _____ Saturday.

9. We are leaving _____ the south _____ France tomorrow.

10. His father is retiring _____ his job _____ a couple _____ years.

11. I'm watching a special science program _____ TV tonight.

12. They're getting married _____ the end _____ June.

13. We're doing another exercise _____ a couple _____ minutes.

14. Pierre is returning _____ France soon.

15. John is taking his girlfriend _____ him _____ the party tomorrow night. They're going _____ the party _____ his father's car.

16. I'm working _____ the beginning _____ the end _____ next week.

17. We're taking a vacation in Haiti _____ the beginning _____ the year.

18. We're beginning our tour _____ Europe _____ April 10.

19. The sun is setting _____ 5:33 this afternoon.

20. The new semester is beginning two weeks _____ today.

21. I'm not wearing anything special _____ the party _____ Sunday.

22. The world is not coming _____ an end soon.

2.7

THE NEGATIVE FORM, COMPOUND PRONOUNS, AND COMPOUND ADVERBS

1. The negative form of the present continuous tense is formed by inserting *not* between the auxiliary and the main verb of a verb phrase.

	Singular	Plural
First person	I am not going	we
Second person	you are not going	you ⎫ are not going
Third person	he ⎫ she ⎬ is not going it ⎭	they ⎭

Compound Pronouns

2. (a) COMPOUND PRONOUNS refer to indefinite <u>persons</u> or <u>things</u>, or indefinite quantities. They are:

	-body	*-one*	*-thing*
some-	somebody	someone	something
any-	anybody	anyone	anything
no-	nobody	no one	nothing
every-	everybody	everyone	everything

(b) Compound pronouns may serve as subjects or objects in a sentence: ***Someone** is talking about me behind my back;* or *I know **someone** in Toronto; **Anybody** can enter the contest;* or *I don't live with **anyone**; **Nothing** is happening today;* or *I want **nothing**; **Everybody** likes me;* or *I like **everybody**.*

Compound Adverbs

3. The COMPOUND ADVERBS *somewhere, anywhere, everywhere,* and *nowhere* function as modifiers of verbs; *She's living **somewhere** in Africa; No one is living **anywhere** on the moon; We're going **nowhere** tonight; We're going **everywhere** on our next vacation.*

4. (a) Compounds with *some-* occur in affirmative statements and questions: *I have something to tell you; Do you know someone in Athens? Someone* never follows a negative verb phrase (never *I don't know someone*); however, a negative verb phrase may follow *someone* when the compound is the subject of a sentence: *Someone (somebody) isn't doing the right thing.*

6. Compounds with *any-* occur in negative (never affirmative) statements and questions: *I'm not doing **anything** special today; Do you know **anything** about physics?* Negative verb phrases do not follow *any-* (never *Anything isn't happening*).
Special Note: Double negatives like *He isn't doing nothing* and *I don't know nobody* do not appear in educated speech and writing.

2.8

Name _____ Date _____

Focus: Negative versus Affirmative Verb Phrases

Fill in the blanks with negative or affirmative verb phrases in the present continuous tense.

EXAMPLES: a. (wear) I'm not wearing anything special to school tomorrow.
　　　　　　b. (wait) Somebody is waiting for you outside in the hall.

1. (do) I _____ anything about the problem.

2. (go) We _____ anywhere special on our vacation.

3. (happen) Nothing much _____ in town today.

4. (take) I _____ anyone to the dance on Saturday night.

5. (listen) Someone _____ to our conversation.

6. (cook) Mom _____ anything special for dinner tonight.

7. (pay) You _____ any attention to my explanation. (*To pay attention to* means *to listen carefully to*.)

8. (take) Nobody _____ care of those poor children. (*To take care of* means *to attend to, to protect,* or *to watch*.)

9. (live) He _____ somewhere in the middle of Africa.

10. (take) The patient _____ any medicine now.

11. (try) Watch out (be careful)! Somebody _____ to get your job. (tell) He _____ a lot of lies about you.

12. (wear) She _____ a little bit of perfume.

13. (do) That lazy person _____ anything with his/her life.

14. (try) Somebody _____ to steal that car.

15. (pay) They _____ any income taxes this year.

16. (sing) Listen! Some birds _____ in the apple tree.

17. (wear) Not everyone _____ a costume to the party.

18. (send) I _____ any Christmas cards this year.

19. (spend) My company _____ little money on this project.

20. (go) We _____ nowhere special for the holidays.

21. (lie) Somebody in the government _____ about the scandal in the tax office.

Now complete the sentences with your own words.

22. Everyone/nobody/somebody _____.

23. The doctor/nurse/lawyer/teacher _____.

24. The government _____.

25. The team/class _____.

2.9

GRAMMAR EXERCISE   Name _____ Date _____

Focus: *Yes-No Questions and Answers*

Yes-no questions in the present continuous tense are formed by inserting the subject of a sentence between the auxiliary and the main verb: ***Are you living*** *in the country?* Only the auxiliary (never the verb) appears in *yes-no* answers: *Yes, **I am;** No, **I'm** not.*

Note: In informal usage, a *yes-no* answer to *Is everyone coming tomorrow?* can be *Yes,* ***they*** *are; or No,* ***they*** *aren't.*

Supply an appropriate form of the verb *be* in the first blank and an appropriate present participle in the second.

EXAMPLES: a. <u>Is</u> everyone <u>coming</u> to the party tomorrow night?
            b. <u>Are</u> you <u>thinking</u> about anything special right now?

1. _____ she _____ in a hotel for the time being?

2. _____ they _____ about financial problems at this time?

3. _____ it _____ outside now?

4. _____ your boss _____ ___ care of the problem today?

5. _____ everyone _____ a vacation soon?

6. _____ she _____ English at an institute this fall?

7. _____ the baby _____ a nap in the other room?

8. _____ you _____ about your future studies?

9. _____ the wind _____ very hard?

10. _____ the patient _____ better today?

Now supply your own subjects.

11. _____ from the university soon?

12. _____ his girlfriend to the party?

13. _____ a course in French next semester?

14. _____ a mistake?

15. _____ care of anyone?

16. _____ your homework tonight?

Now complete the sentences with appropriate words.

17. Is the world _____?

18. Is the doctor/the teacher _____?

19. Is your husband/wife _____?

20. Are your neighbors_____?

21. Is everyone in this class _____?

GRAMMAR EXERCISE   Name _____ Date _____

Focus: The Expletive *There* in the Present Continuous Tense

Expletive *there* also occurs in sentences containing the present continuous tense: ***There is something burning on the stove; There** are some children playing in the garden*. The usual pattern of such a sentence is *there* + *be* + subject + verb + prepositional phrase.
Note: Compound pronouns frequently occur as subjects in this pattern.

Supply an appropriate form of the verb *be* in the first blank and an appropriate present participle in the second.

EXAMPLES: a. There <u>isn't</u> much water <u>running</u> in the rivers now.
             b. There <u>is</u> a concert <u>taking</u> place at school tonight. (*To take place* means *to occur* or *to happen*.)

1. There _____ something _____ on the stove.

2. There _____ a few birds _____ in our peach tree.

3. There _____ nobody _____ on the moon.

4. There _____ anyone _____ about me behind my back.

5. There _____ someone outside in the hall _____ for you.

6. There _____ anyone _____ on that mountain.

7. There _____ a political discussion _____ place today.

8. There _____ any roses _____ in my garden this summer.

9. There _____ a good horse _____ in the next race.

10. There _____ something very important _____ place in my life right now.

Now supply your own subjects.

11. There_____ about me behind my back.

12. There_____ at the White House today.

13. There_____ in the park today.

14. There_____ in the other room.

15. There_____ in the next game.

16. There_____ in my company.

Now complete the sentences with appropriate words.

17. There is a political rally _____.

18. There is somebody _____.

19. There is nobody _____.

20. There isn't anything/anybody _____.

21. There are a few people _____.

22. There are a lot of athletes _____.

2.11

Focus: *Yes-No* Questions and Answers with Expletive *There*

Yes-no questions in the present continuous tense with expletive *there* are formed by inserting the expletive between the auxiliary and the subject: *Is there anyone living in that house?* *Are there a lot of people waiting for the bus?* The expletive always appears in *yes-no* answers: *Yes, there are; No, there aren't.*

Supply an appropriate form of the verb *be* in the first blank and an appropriate present participle in the second.

EXAMPLES: a. Are there any people swimming in the pool?
              b. Is there anyone working in the other office?

1. _____ there anything _____ on the stove?

2. _____ there something _____ you? (Use *bothering. To bother* means *to irritate* or *to disturb*.)

3. _____ there anyone _____ you on the project?

4. _____ there someone _____ at that desk?

5. _____ there a meeting _____ place tomorrow?

6. _____ there anyone special _____ you to the party?

7. _____ there any Chinese _____ in your English class?

8. _____ there a lot of people _____ in your company?

9. _____ anything important _____ place in your life now?

Now complete the sentences with appropriate words.

10. Is there a good horse/runner_____?

11. Is there anything special _____?

12. Is there someone_____?

13. Are there any Japanese _____?

14. Is there an election_____?

15. Are there many people _____?

16. Is there a good pitcher/catcher_____?

17. Is there any water _____?

18. _____ for you at home?

19. _____ a blue dress in this room?

20. _____ place today?

21. _____ in your company?

22. _____ in the kitchen?

23. _____ at school tonight?

2.12

WHO, WHOM, AND WHOSE IN INFORMATION QUESTIONS

1. The interrogative pronoun *who* occurs as the subject of an information question: *Who is living with you? My sister is living with me; Who is doing the job? I am doing the job; Who is leading the country? The President is leading the country.*

2. *Whom* is the object form of *who* and serves two functions: (a) as the object of a verb: *Whom do you love? I love my wife; Whom do you know in Hong Kong? I don't know anyone in Hong Kong;* or (b) as the object of a preposition: *To whom are you writing? I am writing to my father; For whom are you voting? I am voting for nobody.*

3. Today, *whom* rarely appears in informal usage; for example, the sentences *With whom is the Ambassador having a meeting?* and *To whom is the government responsible?* are very formal in tone and represent the kind of language used in official documents, in business and legal English, and in academic papers.

4. In formal usage, a preposition precedes *whom* in an information question: *For whom is your lawyer working? To whom are you going to send the letter?* In informal usage, *who* replaces *whom* and the preposition appears at the end of the question: *Who is your lawyer working for? Who are you going to send the letter to?* A preposition appearing in this position is called a POSTPONED PREPOSITION.

5. When they occur, postponed prepositions are sometimes followed by an adverb of time or a prepositional phrase: *Who are you thinking about now? Who are you staying with for the time being? Who are you sitting with at the next meeting? Who is he in love with now?*

6. You may remember that *whose* is the possessive form of *who* and usually precedes a noun: *Whose jacket are you wearing?* However, when a noun object is understood, *whose* can appear alone: *Whose [jacket] do you have on? Whose [typewriter] are you using today?*

2.13

GRAMMAR EXERCISE   Name _____ Date _____

> Focus: Who, Whom, and Whose in Information Questions.

Supply *who, whom,* or *whose* in the blanks. Use *whom* only in sentences introduced by a preposition. Practice formal and informal usage of *who(m)*.

EXAMPLES: a. From whom do you usually get legal advice?
b. Who lives with you?
c. Whose parents are coming to the graduation ceremonies?
d. Who (whom) do you love the most in the world?

1. _____ wears a red and white costume, has a long white beard, and lives at the North Pole? _____ does he live with?

2. To _____ do you pay taxes? _____ prepares your income tax return?

3. _____ book is that lying on the floor under the table?

4. _____ do you usually see first in the mornings?

5. _____ cooks better in your family, your Mom or Dad?

6. _____ do you usually sit between during the class?

7. _____ coat is that hanging on the hook near the door?

2.13 (Continued)

8. From _____ are you receiving this incorrect information?

9. For _____ does the President of the United States work?

10. _____ does your father work for? To _____ does he report?

11. _____ children are going to school?

12. _____ takes care of your children during the day?

13. _____ dictionary are you using? _____ is using my desk?

14. _____ lives in Buckingham Palace in London?

15. With _____ does the Queen live? _____ do you live with?

16. _____ do you know in Paris? _____ family lives in France?

17. (at the Ambassador's office) To _____ do you want to speak? (at the store) _____ do you want to speak to?

18. _____ does this package belong to? _____ package is it?

19. _____ is appearing in that movie? _____ are you going to the movies with tonight? _____ are you taking?

20. To _____ is the President delivering the speech?

21. _____ did the store deliver the package to by mistake?

22. _____ dog is that playing in our vegetable garden?

23. _____ in this room likes to dance? _____ did you dance with last night? _____ wife is Bob dancing with now?

24. _____ do I remind you of? (*To remind* means *to make one remember*.)

25. _____ in this group drives a car?

26. _____ car is that across the street? Is it yours?

27. From _____ are you receiving that confidential information?

28. _____ has the correct time? _____ watch is this?

2.14

GRAMMAR EXERCISE   Name _____ Date _____

Focus: Information Words as Subjects

In an information question the subject of a sentence usually follows an auxiliary verb: *What do you like to eat? Where are you living now?* However, when an information word (or words) serves as the subject of an information question, the usual question form is not used. *What happens at the meeting every day? How many people live in Peking?*

Fill in the blanks with appropriate information words. Use *who, what, what kind of,* or *how many.*

EXAMPLES: a. <u>What</u> is very small, has a little tail, and likes to eat cheese?
           b. <u>Who</u> has the best pronunciation in your English class?

1. _____ is happening in the world right now?

2. _____ is coming to our house for dinner tonight?

3. _____ people live in the world/China/your native country?

4. _____ comes from South America/Europe in the class?

5. _____ has the most beautiful house in London?

6. _____ animal lives in trees, has a long tail, and likes to play all the time?

7. _____ is your ideal person?

8. _____ is the King of the jungle?

9. _____ comes from the sun?

10. _____ animal gives us milk? _____ gives us oxygen?

11. _____ speaks English with a Spanish accent in this class?

12. _____ people work in your father's factory?

13. _____ flowers grow best in your garden?

14. _____ animal has a very long neck and is the tallest of existing animals?

15. _____ is the largest animal in Africa/the world?

16. _____ insect makes something that is very delicious to eat?

17. _____ lives at the North Pole?

18. _____ is troubling you? _____ is bothering you?

19. _____ programs appear on TV in your hometown?

20. _____ drives a car in your family?

21. _____ is happening in this room right now?

22. _____ in this room comes to school on the bus?

23. _____ has the answer to the mystery of life?

24. _____ animal is always washing itself?

25. _____ people live in your house/apartment?

2.15

Focus: Postponed Prepositions

In informal usage, postponed prepositions may occur in information questions that begin with *what* and *who*. *What* refers to things and *who* refers to people.
Reminder: *Who* is used informally as a substitute for *whom*.
Pronunciation Note: (a) *Who is* sounds like *hooze*. (b) *Who are* sounds like *who-er*. (c) *What is* sounds like *whats*. (d) *What are* sounds like *what-er*.

Fill in the blanks with *about, at, in, for, from, of, to*, or *with*.

EXAMPLES: a. Who are you always thinking <u>about</u>?
             b. What are you pointing <u>at</u> with your pencil?

1. Who is your sister living _____ in Los Angeles?

2. Who are you talking _____ on the phone?

3. Who are you cooking that food _____?

4. Who does this jacket belong _____? Who do I remind you _____?

5. Who are you sitting next _____ in class tomorrow?

6. Who are you having dinner _____ tonight?

7. What are you washing your dishes _____?

8. Who do you work _____?

9. Who are you sending that letter _____? Who do you usually receive letters _____?

10. What do you eat soup _____? What pot are you cooking the chicken _____?

11. What are you always dreaming _____?

12. Who is Tom waiting _____ at the corner?

13. Who do you usually sit _____ in class?

14. Who are you sitting in back _____? . . . close _____? . . . in front _____?

15. What do you brush your teeth _____?

16. Who are you going to vote _____ in the next election?

17. Who is your sister getting married _____? (Use *to* here.)

18. What are you reading _____ in that magazine?

19. Who is she going to dance _____ at the next dance recital (concert)?

20. What is the professor talking _____ at the next lecture?

21. Who are your children playing _____ in the playground?

22. What are you thinking _____ at this very moment (right now)?

23. What are you pointing _____? Who are you staring _____?

24. What are you looking _____? (Use *at* or *for* here.)

25. What is your teacher talking _____ next?

2.16

BE GOING TO

1. *Be going to* + a base form is used for an event that is to take place in future time: *The twentieth century is going to end soon; All of us are going to be at the graduation ceremonies tomorrow night.*

2. Contractions of subject pronouns and the verb *be* occur in informal usage: *I'm going to reveal this information to the police; We're going to leave in a few minutes.*

3. Negative verb phrases are formed by inserting *not* between *be* and *going to*: *The government is not going to release the political prisoners; I'm not going to tell anyone the secret.*

4. *To go* in a verb phrase with *be going to* may be omitted: *They are going [to go] to the concert tomorrow; We're going [to go] to the festival next week.*

5. The duration of an event in future time may also be expressed with *be going to*. When this occurs, the preposition *until* often appears in a time expression: *We're going to be in Berlin until the end of the month; I'm going to practice until the end of the day.*

6. When expressing the duration of an event in the future, the preposition *for* also occurs in an expression of time: *The patient isn't going to stay in the hospital for a long time; We're going to be in London for a few days. For* is sometimes omitted: *They're going to be in Paris [for] a few weeks; My brother isn't going to stay at the party [for] a long time.*
   Pronunciation Note: When we are speaking quickly, *going to* sounds like *gonna: We're "gonna" be early; They're "gonna" go late.* **This contraction does *not* occur when we are speaking slowly.**
   Note: The future tense with *will* is discussed in Chapter 9.

2.17

GRAMMAR EXERCISE   Name _____ Date _____

   Focus: *Be Going to*

Fill in the blanks with appropriate verb phrases containing *be going to* + a base form. Use the base forms given in the parentheses.

EXAMPLES: a. (change) The nature of a male lion isn't going to change.
            b. (be) Everyone is going to be at the graduation ceremonies.

1. (enter) Our son _____ the university in September.

2. (watch) We _____ TV for a couple of hours tonight.
   Note: No preposition appears in *watch TV (but look at TV)*; also, no preposition appears in *enter the university, enter the room,* or *enter the war (but go to the university, come into the room).*

3. (last) Tomorrow's meeting _____ for about three hours.

4. (come) The world _____ to an end tomorrow.

5. (be) A few people _____ absent from class tomorrow.

2.17 (Continued)

6. (do) Unfortunately, the police _____ anything about the problem of crime in the city.

7. (introduce) Our company _____ a new product to the public. (make) We _____ a lot of money.

8. (go) We _____ anywhere special on our next vacation.

9. (rise) The sun _____ at 6:27 tomorrow morning.

10. (stay) My boss _____ in Boston until the end of the week.

11. (get) Be careful! You _____ into trouble.

12. (last) The party _____ until around midnight.

13. (do) We _____ anything special this coming weekend.

14. (get) Fortunately, his parents _____ a divorce.

15. (announce) The government _____ its decision tomorrow.

16. (help) Unfortunately, this medicine _____ the patient.

17. (water) I _____ my house plants tomorrow.

18. (last) The discussion _____ for about an hour.

19. (talk) He _____ about anything in particular at the meeting.

20. (take) No election _____ place this year.

21. (stay) We _____ here until the end of the day.

Now complete the sentences with your own words.

22. The police/fireman _____.

23. The mailman/garbage man _____.

24. The meeting/program/debate _____.

25. The President/Pope/Queen _____.

26. It (talk about weather) _____.

27. I/you/s/he _____.

2.18

GRAMMAR EXERCISE   Name _____ Date _____

Focus: *Yes-No Questions with Be Going to*

The subject of a sentence is inserted between *be* and *going to* in a *yes-no* question with *be going to*: **Are you going to** *take a vacation this coming summer?*

Supply an appropriate form of the verb *be* in the first blank and an appropriate base form in the second blank.

EXAMPLES: a. <u>Are</u> we going to <u>take</u> a break in a few minutes?
              b. <u>Are</u> you going to <u>go</u> to Europe next summer?

1. _____ your brother going to _____ the university this fall?

2. _____ your roommate going to _____ from the university soon?

3. _____ you going to _____ our secret to anyone?

4. _____ your father going to _____ here until the end of May?

5. _____ Jack going to _____ his girlfriend tomorrow night?

6. _____ you going to _____ TV for very long?

7. _____ we going to _____ lunch with anyone in particular?

8. _____ the children going to _____ to bed early tonight?

9. _____ you going to _____ a nap this afternoon after lunch?

10. _____ she going to _____ any postcards to her family?

Now supply any appropriate words.

11. _____ into trouble with your boss?

12. _____ here for very long?

13. _____ dinner with some friends?

14. _____ the train this afternoon?

15. _____ a master's degree?

16. _____ in this city forever?

17. _____ married soon?

18. _____ a car?

19. Is your father going to _____?

20. Is your boss going to _____?

21. Is the movie going to _____?

22. Are the police going to _____?

23. Is the sun going to _____?

24. Is the medicine going to_____?

25. Are you going to _____?

26. Is tomorrow going to _____?

2.19

Focus: The Duration of an Event in Future Time

Supply an appropriate form of the verb *be* in the first blank and an appropriate base form in the second.

EXAMPLES: a. We <u>are</u> going to <u>stay</u> in Chicago until the end of spring.
b. I'<u>m</u> going to <u>be</u> at the library until one o'clock.
c. She'<u>s</u> going to <u>remain</u> in school until the end of the year.

1. We _____ going to _____ in Boston for only a few days.

2. I _____ going to _____ at the dentist's for just an hour.
Note: The adverbs *only* and *just* are often used to emphasize a small amount of some <u>thing</u> or <u>time</u>.

3. My sister and I _____ going to _____ our parents for just a week.

4. Those lucky people _____ going to _____ at the beach for a month.

5. Carlos and Maria _____ going to _____ in this country for the rest of their lives.

6. I _____ going to _____ at my mother's house for just an hour.

7. We _____ going to _____ in the mountains for the whole summer.

8. The patient _____ going to _____ in a sanatorium for the rest of his life.

9. I _____ going to _____ at this desk until the end of the day.

10. I _____ going to _____ my friends in Rome for only a few days.

Now complete the following *yes-no* questions with appropriate base forms and time expressions.

11. Is the patient going to _____?

12. On your next vacation, are you going to _____?

13. Next winter, are you going to _____?

14. Tomorrow, are your parents going to _____?

15. This coming Christmas, are you going to_____?

Now supply the prepositions *for* or *until* in the blanks.

16. We're going to be in Colombia _____ at least a week. (*At least* means *the minimum of.*)

17. My office is going to be very busy _____ the end of the week.

18. I'm going to be at my cousin's _____ just a short while.

19. He's going to work for the company _____ the end of the year.

20. I'm going to be at the store _____ just a few minutes.

21. He's going to be in this school _____ the end of the semester.

22. She's going to live in this country _____ at least a year.

2.20

GRAMMAR EXERCISE   Name _____ Date _____

Focus: Information Questions with *How Long*

An information question with *be going to* that begins with the information words *how long* asks for the length of an event. The usual pattern of such a sentence is *how long* + *be* + subject + *going to* + base form. The preposition *for* may precede *how long* but its use is optional: [For] *how long are you going to remain a student?*

Pronunciation Note: (a) *How long are* sounds like *how long-er*. (b) *How long is* sounds like *how longiz* (or sometimes *longz*).

Supply an appropriate form of the verb *be* in the first blank and an appropriate base form in the second

EXAMPLES: a. For how long <u>are</u> you going to <u>live</u> in this country?
              b. How long <u>is</u> your boy going to <u>stay</u> at the beach today?

1. How long _____ you going to _____ at this school?

2. For how long _____ your father going to _____ for the company?

3. How long _____ you going to _____ in your present apartment?

4. How long _____you going to _____ in this room today?

5. How long _____ your husband going to _____ his car?

6. How long _____ that country going to _____ a military government?

7. For how long _____ your car going to _____ at the garage?

8. How long _____ your boss going to _____ angry at you?

Now supply *how long* + *be* + subject + *going to* + base form.

9. _____ on the phone?

10. _____ English?

11. _____ TV tonight?

12. _____ a socialist government?

13. _____ this bad weather?

14. _____ in the White House?

Now complete the sentences with any appropriate words.

15. How long is the patient going to_____?

16. How long is the prisoner going to _____?

17. How long are the astronauts going to_____?

18. How long is the examination going to _____?

19. How long is your mother/father going to _____?

2.21

Focus: *Be Going to* + *Be* + Present Participle

Statements with *be going to* + *be* + a present participle are used to emphasize the continuing nature (duration) of an event in future time: *The earth **is going to be revolving** around the sun for millions of years more.* *Not* is inserted between *be* and *going to* in negative verb phrases: ***I'm not going to** be doing anything special this coming weekend.*

Supply appropriate present participles in the blanks.

EXAMPLES: a.   The patient is going to be <u>walking</u> with a cane for a while.
                b.   We aren't going to be <u>using</u> our dictionaries during the test.

1.   My parents are going to be _____ me for a couple of weeks in June. They're going to be _____ in my guest room.

2.   Unfortunately, the patient isn't going to be _____ well for a long time. She's going to be _____ better, however.

3.   I'm going to be _____ my typewriter for a couple of more years.

4.   The students are going to be _____ an exam for an hour.

5.   The surgeon is going to be _____ on the patient for a couple of hours. He's going to be _____ a newly developed technique.

Now supply *be (not) going to* + *be* + a present participle in the blanks.

6.   The days _____ longer/shorter soon.

7.   He _____ any English courses next semester.

8.   The director _____ about anything special at the next meeting. I'm not going to be going.

9.   Our baby _____ with a spoon soon.

10.   The birds _____ south/north soon.

11.   We _____ in Paris for quite a while. (*Quite a while* means *a long time*.)

12.   My office is going to be busy tomorrow. My phone _____ all day long. I _____ hard.

13.   They _____ any alcohol at the party tomorrow.

14.   I _____ English for quite a while.

15.   We _____ to our lawyer about the problem soon.

16.   Please wait for me. I _____ on the phone for only a couple of more minutes.

17.   According to the radio, it _____ until the end of the week.

18.   I _____ at this desk until the end of the class.

2.22

GRAMMAR EXERCISE   Name _____ Date _____

Focus: *How Long* Questions with *Be Going to*

An information question with the following pattern frequently occurs: *How long are the stores going to be staying open during the Christmas holidays?*
Reminder: *Be going to* + base form and *be going to* + present participle are essentially interchangeable; the present participle is used only for <u>emphasis</u>.

Supply an appropriate form of the verb *be* in the first blank and an appropriate present participle in the second.

EXAMPLES: a. How long <u>is</u> the surgeon going to be <u>operating</u> on the patient?
              b. How much longer <u>is</u> our baby going to be <u>wearing</u> diapers?

1. How much longer _____ your son going to be _____ braces on his teeth?

2. How long _____ your parents going to be _____ with you?

3. For how long _____ we going to be _____ our next break?

4. How much longer _____ it going to be _____? It sure is wet!

5. How long _____ the children going to be _____ in the pool?

6. How long _____ the architect going to be _____ on the project?

7. How long _____ Dad going to be _____ in the garden?

8. How much longer _____ we going to be _____ about financial problems?

Now supply *how long* + *be* + subject + *going to be* + present participle.

9. _____ in the kitchen?

10. _____ for an answer?

11. _____ at this school?

12. _____ that book?

13. _____ that medicine?

14. _____ your friends?

Now complete the sentences with any appropriate words.

15. How much longer is your father going to _____?

16. How long are the children going to _____?

17. How long are the students going to _____?

18. How long is the mechanic going to _____?

19. How long are those tourists going to _____?

20. How long is your mother going to _____?

21. How long are we going to _____?

22. How long are the birds going to _____?

2.23

THE IMPERATIVE MOOD

1. The IMPERATIVE MOOD is used for (a) making requests, (b) expressing commands, and (c) giving instructions.
   Note: The polite word *please* is frequently (and best) used in a command or request, at the beginning of a sentence and sometimes at the end if the sentence is short.

2. In a command the subject of a sentence (always the second person) does not appear but is understood: [*You*] *please close your books;* [*You*] *sit down, please.*

3. A verb in the second person singular (or plural) is always the complete verb in an imperative sentence: *Please **give** my love to your family;* ***Stop** that noise;* ***Close** the door, please.*

4. *Don't,* the contraction of *do not,* is used at the beginning of an imperative sentence, but it is more polite to precede the word with *please;* (*Please*) *don't touch that painting;* (*Please*) *don't be late.*

5. A few adverbs of frequency may precede the verb in a command: ***Always** take this medicine after meals; Don't **ever** tell our secret;* ***Never** waste your time at school.*

6. The understood subject of a command is usually second person, singular or plural, but *let's* (*let* + *us*) + a base form may also occur: ***Let's go** to the movies;* ***Let's take** a break. Not* appears in the negative form: ***Let's not have** dinner too early;* ***Let's not eat** at home tonight.*

7. A person's name or title usually occurs at the beginning of a command: *Jack, please give me that magazine; Doctor, please make me well;* but if the command is short, the name or title may appear at the end: *Give me that, Jack; Help me, Doctor.*
   Note: In writing, a comma appears before or after the name; in speaking, a pause occurs.

8. *Would you* (*please*) + a base form is very often used in a polite request: ***Would you please pass** the sugar; Timmy, **would you please stop** teasing the cat.*
   Note: It is customary not to use a question mark in this pattern.

2.24

GRAMMAR EXERCISE   Name _____ Date _____

Focus: The Imperative Mood

Supply appropriate verbs in the blanks:

be	enjoy	help	look	put	spend	tell
cook	get	keep	mail	repeat	stand	turn
do	go	lend	obey	ride	stay	
eat	have	listen	pass	sit	take	

EXAMPLES: a. Would you please <u>repeat</u> that question more slowly.
               b. Please don't <u>be</u> selfish with your toys, Buddy.

1. Children, Please don't _____ your hands on the wall.

2. Would you please _____ the salt, Anna.

3. Please _____ this information a secret between us.

4. Darling, _____ sure to take your medicine after breakfast.

5. Never _____ between the cars of the train.

6. Let's _____ in a restaurant tonight. Let's _____ to a movie afterwards.

7. Would you please _____ your name at the top of the page.

8. Let's _____ married. Let's _____ to Hawaii on our honeymoon.

9. _____ your parents, Billy. Betty, _____ to your mother.

10. Dear, please don't ever _____ our secret.

11. _____ your dinner, everyone.

12. _____ a nice day. _____ a wonderful evening.

13. Dad, would you please _____ me your car.

14. Would everyone in the room please _____ down.

15. Richard, let's _____ a drive up to the mountains today.

16. Class, would you please _____ at the examples on the next page.

17. Children, don't ever _____ cruel to animals.

18. Let's _____ out to dinner tonight. Let's not _____ at home.

19. Linda, would you please _____ me with this job.

20. Don't _____ home late, children.

21. Dear, would you please _____ this letter for me on your way to work.

22. Danny, would you please _____ the radio off.

23. Please _____ off the grass.

24. Class, would you please _____ your homework in ink.

25. Honey, let's _____ to the beach on our vacation this year.

26. Mom, would you please _____ steak for dinner tonight.

27. Let's not _____ a lot of money on Christmas presents this year.

28. Let's _____ another cocktail.

29. Let's _____ a walk in the park. Let's not _____ to work.

30. Darling, please _____ me about your problem at school.

31. Always _____ fish in the refrigerator.

32. Let's _____ a little break.

2.25

REFLEXIVE PRONOUNS

	Singular	Plural
First person	myself	ourselves
Second person	yourself	yourselves
Third person	herself	themselves
	himself	
	itself	

1. A mirror reflects an image of ourselves. Like a mirror, a REFLEXIVE PRONOUN refers back to the subject of a sentence: For example, in *Vain people are always looking at themselves in a mirror,* the reflexive pronoun *themselves* refers back to the subject of the sentence, *vain people.*

2. A reflexive pronoun always appears as an object and frequently the object of a preposition: *I am angry **at myself;** She doesn't believe **in herself;** He is always talking **to himself.***

3. We sometimes use a reflexive pronoun to intensify (make stronger) a pronoun or noun subject: *I **myself** am going to complain to the government; **We ourselves** are responsible for our actions; **The thief himself** says he stole the money.*

4. Reflexive pronouns may function as the direct object of a verb: *Our cat is always **washing itself;** Many people don't **understand themselves;** We enjoy **ourselves** a lot.*

5. Reflexive pronouns may also function as the indirect object of a verb: *I am going to buy a watch for **myself** (= I am going to buy **myself** a watch); She is giving a present to **herself** (= She is giving **herself** a present).*
   Note: The difference between direct and indirect objects is discussed in Chapter 3.

6. Idiomatically, a reflexive pronoun preceded by the preposition *by* means *alone; I want to go to the party **by myself** (alone); That poor old woman lives all **by herself** (alone); Artists and writers usually work **by themselves** (alone).*

2.26

GRAMMAR EXERCISE   Name _____ Date _____

Focus: Reflexive Pronouns

Fill in the blanks with appropriate reflexive pronouns (*myself, yourself, herself, himself, itself, ourselves, yourselves, themselves*).

EXAMPLES: a. You yourself are responsible for your actions.
              b. A computer doesn't compute by itself.

1. Egotistical people are always talking about _____.

2. The Queen _____ is going to present the awards at the ceremonies.

3. I'm giving _____ a new car on my birthday.

4. Please make _____ another cocktail, Clarice.

5. Most people don't like to live by _____.

6. Grandma (informal for *grandmother*) fell down and hurt _____.

7. Grandpa (informal for *grandfather*) bought _____ a new pipe.

8. What a stupid mistake I made! I really don't understand _____.

9. In the homework the students test _____.

10. It's a good idea for you to do your homework by _____.

11. The President _____ is coming to our house for dinner tonight.

12. My wife's cat is always washing _____. I _____ don't like cats. My little canary is always looking at _____ in his mirror. Dogs don't like to be by _____.

13. The patient is always taking _____ into a world of fantasy.

14. Bill and Cora are very much in love and prefer to be by _____.

15. They're enjoying _____ a lot.

16. Our little boy cannot dress _____. He cannot cross the street by _____.

17. Do you ever laugh at _____? Do you live by _____?

18. Let's make a toast to _____. Let's make _____ another drink.

19. Their little girl is always getting _____ into trouble.

20. Some people care little for _____.

21. There is a hermit living by _____ on the top of the mountain.

22. We always enjoy _____ on our European vacations.

23. Well, Mr. Smith, would you please tell me about _____.

24. We always enjoy _____ in class.

25. Don't cut _____ with that knife, Jack.

26. Does your mother do her hair _____?

27. Be careful! Don't hurt _____ on that machine.

28. How well do you know _____?

29. Does your father work for _____?

30. Selfish people are always thinking about _____.

31. Do you usually enjoy _____ at school/work?

2.27

GRAMMAR EXERCISE   Name _____ Date _____

> **Focus: Adjective Phrases with Prepositions**

> ADJECTIVE PHRASES are used to modify (describe) nouns. Unlike adjectives, they follow the noun that they modify: *The children **in the playground** are having a good time; The flowers **in that vase** are dying.* Adjective phrases consist of a preposition and a noun with or without modifiers.

Supply appropriate prepositions (*at, for, in, of, on, up, with*) in the blanks in order to complete the adjective phrases.

EXAMPLES: a. All the sentences <u>in</u> this exercise contain adjective phrases.
           b. The director <u>of</u> my school is from Brazil.

1. The desk _____ the front _____ the room is the teacher's.

2. The plane _____ _____ the sky is a jet.

3. He is in love with a girl _____ his math (mathematics) class.

4. The sentences _____ the blackboard are good examples.

5. The explanations _____ this book are about English grammar.

6. The book _____ my biology class costs a lot.

7. The music _____ the radio is too loud.

8. The lamp _____ my bedroom desk is broken.

9. The ring _____ her index finger is gold.

10. The money _____ the drawer is for the delivery boy.

11. Her husband is _____ his forties (between the ages of forty and fifty).

12. The movie _____ that theater is for adults only.

13. A person _____ the front office is asking for you.

14. There is a boy _____ red hair in my algebra class.

15. The house _____ the corner belongs to my teacher.

16. The information _____ this report isn't correct.

17. The fish _____ the refrigerator is spoiled.

18. The books _____ the top shelf are mine.

19. The woman _____ this photograph is my grandmother.

20. The car _____ the garage belongs to me.

21. The house _____ the corner _____ Park Avenue and Fifth Street is for sale.

22. The movie _____ TV now is about a boy _____ green hair.

23. The actor _____ that movie was terrible.

24. The pollution _____ the air is getting worse.

25. The life _____ a mosquito is short.

26. The author _____ this book is originally from California.

2.28

Focus: Linking Verbs

1. A LINKING VERB links (connects) a subject to the rest of the sentence. The linking verbs are *be, appear, look, seem, feel, taste, smell,* and *sound.*

2. Adverbs of manner (e.g., *quickly, badly, carefully,* and *slowly*) do not follow linking verbs; such verbs are followed by adjectives: *I am happy; She looks sick; That smells bad; I feel sad; That sounds beautiful.*

3. *Appear* and *look* are sometimes not linking verbs: *She appears sick* (but *That actress appears frequently on TV*); *The dog looks hungry* (but *The dog looked hungrily at the food on the table*).

4. When *well* refers to a state of good health, it is an adjective and may follow a linking verb: *She sings well* (adverb); *She feels well* (adjective); *She dances well* (adverb); *She looks well* (adjective).

Fill in the blanks with adjectives or adverbs.

EXAMPLES: a. (good) This ice cream tastes <u>good</u>.
              b. (good *or* well) Doctor, one of the patients doesn't feel <u>well</u>.

1. (sad) I feel _____ about the poor children in our town.

2. (happy) Bill and Grace Johnson look _____.

3. (angry) John looked _____ at me.

4. (good *or* well) Unfortunately, she doesn't feel _____. She's entering the hospital soon.

5. (correct) This report looks _____.

6. (correct) She speaks French _____.

7. (fast) That horse looks _____. He drives his car _____.

8. (beautiful) Her voice sounds _____.

9. (good) This spaghetti looks, smells, and tastes _____.

10. (unhappy) He seems _____. He's living _____ with his wife.

11. (crazy) That dog appears a little _____.

12. (frequent) She appears _____ on the stage in London.

13. (clever) She looks very _____. She does everything _____.

14. (beautiful) She looks _____. She sings _____.

15. (good) Their little boy is _____ at baseball.

16. (delicious/terrible) This food smells _____. but it tastes _____.

17. (good *or* well) My girlfriend looks _____ in her new dress.

18. (hard) That exercise looks _____. He works _____.

19. (good *or* well) Bill's taking medicine; he doesn't feel _____.

20. (bad) He feels _____ about his situation at school.

Note: Following feel, *bad* means *sad* or *unhappy.*

2.29

GRAMMAR EXERCISE   Name _____ Date _____

Focus: Reviewing Prepositions

Supply appropriate prepositions in the blanks. Do this exercise as a quiz.

at	by	during	from	into	on	to	up
between	down	for	in	of	out	until	

1. What time do you usually get _____ school?

2. He's going back _____ China _____ September.

3. A good friend _____ mine lives _____ 400 West Main Street.

4. They're going to stay here _____ the end of the week.

5. Please look _____ the list _____ irregular verbs _____ the back _____ your book. It is _____ the Appendix.

6. Her birthday is _____ July 25.

7. I don't like to eat _____ myself. Look _____ yourself, Billy.

8. Do you usually watch TV _____ the evening?

9. The world atlas is _____ the top shelf _____ the bookcase.

10. Is your son studying _____ the university now?

11. What time is the King going to arrive _____ the reception?

12. When is our plane going to land _____ Singapore?

13. Our son wants to get _____ the University of Wisconsin.

14. What time do you usually get _____ of class?

15. My school is _____ the corner _____ Fifth Avenue and Park Street.

16. His store is _____ Main Street _____ Broadway and Hill Street. It is next _____ a large bank.

17. Would you please deliver this package _____ a friend _____ mine.

18. I'm always very busy _____ the beginning _____ the end _____ a working day.

19. I always walk _____ the stairs in my apartment house, but I always take the elevator _____.

20. We are far _____ the beginning _____ this exercise.

21. Fortunately, we're going to be using our dictionaries _____ the next examination. The exam is going to be _____ Friday.

22. Whose car is that _____ front _____ ours?

23. His sister is getting married _____ a man from South America.

24. What programs are good _____ TV tonight?

25. Our apartment is _____ the sixth floor.

THE SIMPLE PAST TENSE

3

3.1

EVENTS AT A DEFINITE TIME IN THE PAST

1. *Was* and *were* are the two forms that appear in the conjugation of the verb *be* in the simple past tense.
   Note: No contractions of *was* and *were* occur with subject pronouns.

	Singular	Plural
First person	I was	we ⎫
Second person	you were	you ⎬ were
Third person	he ⎫	they ⎭
	she ⎬ was	
	it ⎭	

2. In the negative form of the verb *be* in the simple past tense, the adverb *not* follows the verb. *Wasn't* and *weren't* are the contracted forms of *was not* and *were not*.

I wasn't	we ⎫
you weren't	you ⎬ weren't
he ⎫	they ⎭
she ⎬ wasn't	
it ⎭	

3. In *yes-no* questions, *was* or *were* is placed before the subject of the sentence: ***Was Columbus** a Spaniard? **Were the people** responsible for the war?*
   Yes-no questions with the expletive *there* are formed by inserting the expletive between the verb and the subject: ***Were there many people** in England at the time of Shakespeare? **Was there much happiness** in his life?*

YES-NO ANSWERS WITH THE VERB *BE*

Yes, ⎰	I was. you were. he (she, it) was. we (you, they) were.	No, ⎰	I wasn't. you weren't. he (she, it) wasn't. we (you, they) weren't.

Note: Noncontracted forms are used for emphasis: *Was Columbus a Spaniard? No, he was not.*

Suggestion: When the group reaches the end of this chapter, that may be a good time for covering the material on numbers, dates, and arithmetic in the Appendix.

3.2

GRAMMAR EXERCISE   Name _____ Date _____

Focus: Affirmative Statements with the Verb *Be*

Fill in the blanks with *was* or *were*.

EXAMPLES: a. Once upon a time (a long time ago), there <u>was</u> a young girl named Snow White.
                    b. Romeo and Juliet <u>were</u> young lovers in the city of Verona.

1. According to the Bible, Adam and Eve _____ the first man and woman.

2. At one time London _____ the most important city in the world.

3. Rome _____ one of the most important cities in the ancient world. It _____ the capital of a great empire.

4. Alexander Graham Bell _____ the inventor of the telephone.

5. Neil Armstrong _____ the first man on the moon.

6. In the Bible, Cain and Abel _____ the sons of Adam and Eve. As the story goes, Abel _____ good and Cain _____ bad.

7. The Wright brothers _____ the inventors of the airplane.

8. Marie Curie _____ the discoverer of polonium and radium.

9. The assassination of John F. Kennedy _____ a great tragedy for the people of the world.

10. The Russian Revolution _____ an event of great historical importance. It _____ the beginning of a new era.

11. Two important men in Cleopatra's life _____ Julius Caesar and Mark Antony. She _____ the Queen of Egypt around two thousand years ago.

12. The Spanish Empire _____ at its height during the eighteenth century. Its most important colonies _____ in Latin America.

13. Christopher Columbus _____ the discoverer of the New World.

14. Paul VI _____ the first Pope of the Roman Catholic Church to visit the Americas.

15. The Chinese _____ the first people to use explosives.

16. Charles Lindbergh _____ the first person to fly across the Atlantic Ocean. He was called the "lone eagle."

17. Elizabeth I _____ the Queen of England and Ireland from 1558 to 1603. She _____ the daughter of Henry VIII.

18. Greece _____ a center of culture in the ancient world.

19. Once upon a time, there _____ a young girl named Cinderella.

20. Latin _____ the language of the Roman Empire.

21. The Egyptians _____ the first people to use paper.

22. Many scientists _____ responsible for the development of the atomic bomb. Albert Einstein _____ one of them.

3.3

GRAMMAR EXERCISE   Name _____ Date _____

Focus: Affirmative and Negative Statements with the Verb *Be*

Fill in the blanks with affirmative or negative forms of the verb *be* in the simple past tense.

EXAMPLES: a. The atomic bomb <u>was not</u> the invention of one scientist.
               b. According to some people, the Vikings <u>were</u> the first Europeans to come to the New World.

1. Some people say Columbus _____ the first European to land in the New World.

2. The life of a man two thousand years ago _____ short.

3. The astronaut's journey to the moon _____ an easy trip.

4. We _____ in this room last Sunday.

5. In pre-revolutionary China, life _____ wonderful for a few.

6. My parents _____ in Russia last year.

7. The war in Vietnam _____ a tragedy.

8. It _____ easy for the people of the world to understand the assassination of President Kennedy.

9. According to many scientists, the beginning of the world _____ a meeting of natural forces.

10. Life _____ easy for the slaves in the South before the American Civil War.

11. The First World War _____ a terrible event.

12. The economy of the world _____ good during the 1930's.

Now complete the following sentences.

EXAMPLES: c. Yesterday <u>wasn't a very nice day.</u>
               d. George Washington <u>was the first</u> President of the United States.

13. Adam and Eve/Cain and Abel _____.

14. The party/meeting/class _____.

15. The President/Ambassador _____.

16. The Watergate scandal _____.

17. Before the revolution, the people _____.

18. During the war, the economy _____.

19. During our argument, I/s/he _____.

20. Before his/her marriage, s/he _____.

21. After the examination, I _____.

22. On the first day of this class, I _____.

23. My sister/brother _____.

24. [supply name] _____.

3.4

GRAMMAR EXERCISE   Name _____ Date _____

Focus: The Verb *Be* with Expletive *There*

Fill in the blanks with *was* or *were*.

EXAMPLES: a. There <u>were</u> many reasons for the fall of the Roman Empire.
                    b. There <u>was</u> a terrible earthquake in Guatemala in 1976.

1. There _____ hundreds of people watching the parade.

2. There _____ thousands of people at the public execution of Marie Antoinette. There _____ no good reason for her death.

3. There _____ approximately four million people in England during Shakespeare's time.

4. There _____ a woman on the English throne at that time.

5. There _____ many students who took the course last year.

6. There _____ almost a million casualties in the American Civil War.

7. There _____ a lot of lightning during the storm last night.

8. There _____ a lot of corruption in the government before the revolution. There _____ many reasons for the people's revolt.

9. There _____ two important men in Cleopatra's life.

10. There _____ no good reason for the First World War.

3.5

GRAMMAR EXERCISE

Focus: *Yes-No* Questions and Answers

Supply *was* or *were* in the first blank and complete the following *yes-no* answers.

EXAMPLES: a. <u>Was</u> the General's decision to attack wrong? Yes, <u>it was.</u>
                    b. <u>Were</u> there any good reasons for the war? No, <u>there weren't.</u>

1. _____ I correct in my calculations? Yes, you _____.

2. _____ Helen of Troy a beautiful woman? Yes, _____.

3. _____ Christopher Columbus from Spain? No, _____.

4. _____ it cold at the football game? Yes, _____.

5. _____ there a few people at the park? Yes, _____.

6. _____ I wrong to complain to the police? No, you _____.

7. _____ you by yourself at the concert? No, I _____.

8. _____ there a good reason for your mistake? Yes, _____.

9. _____ the wine at the dinner party good? Yes, _____.

10. _____ that decision easy to make? Yes, _____.

3.6

Focus: Information Questions with the Verb *Be*

In an information question with the verb *be* in the simple past tense, the verb always follows the information word(s): ***Who was Albert Einstein? Where was the Garden of Eden? Who was it on the phone?***

Fill in the blanks with *who(m)*, *what*, or *where*, and *was* or *were*.

EXAMPLES: a. <u>Who was</u> Thomas Alva Edison?

           b. <u>Where were</u> you last Christmas?

1. _____ Adam and Eve, according to the Bible?

2. _____ their sons?

3. _____ the language of the Roman Empire?

4. _____ Mohammed's first wife/the last Queen of France/Helen of Troy/Cleopatra/ Marie Curie/Eva Peron/Helen Keller/Florence Nightingale/Queen Victoria?

5. _____ Shakespeare's wife/George Washington's wife?

6. _____ you in the summer of 1976/the winter of '76/77?

7. _____ you/your mother/your father born?

8. _____ you last night/last week/last month/last year?

9. _____ the President on Sunday afternoon?

10. _____ the Garden of Eden/Atlantis/the capital of the Roman Empire?

11. _____ you an hour ago/four hours ago/two days ago/a year ago?

12. _____ I on this day a year ago?

13. _____ Dwight D. Eisenhower/Franklin D. Roosevelt/Winston Churchill/Charles de Gaulle/Joseph Stalin/Lenin/Karl Marx/Che Guevara/Confucius/Sigmund Freud/Mao Tse-tung/Charles Lindbergh/Alexander Graham Bell/George Washington/Simon Bolivar/ Hernand Cortes?

14. _____ an important general in the Second World War (in the United States, Germany, Italy, Japan, France, Russia)?

15. _____ you with on Thursday evening?

16. _____ the Wright brothers?

17. _____ your girlfriend/boyfriend the night before last?

18. _____ you yesterday morning/afternoon?

19. _____ you with on your last birthday?

20. _____ Hitler/Napoleon/Ivan the Terrible/Ghengis Khan?

21. _____ they with on their last vacation?

22. _____ the first Europeans in the New World?

3.7

REGULAR VERBS

1. In the simple past tense, regular verbs end in -ed in all persons.

	Singular		Plural	
First person	I		we	
Second person	you	worked	you	worked
Third person	he		they	
	she			
	it			

Rules for Spelling Past Forms

2. (a) Usually, we can make the past tense form of a verb by simply adding -ed: (open) Marco Polo **opened** the door to China; (sail) Columbus and his crew **sailed** for two months on their voyage to the New World; (fail) Hitler **failed** to conquer Europe.

(b) When a regular verb ends in -y preceded by a consonant, we change the -y to an -i and add -ed: (carry) The rocket **carried** the astronauts into space; (hurry) They **hurried** to finish the project on time; (try) Alexander the Great **tried** to conquer the ancient world.

(c) When a regular verb ends in -y preceded by a vowel, we do not make a change, but only add -ed: (stay) We **stayed** in Madrid for seventeen days; (play) We **played** cards last night; (pray) We all **prayed** for peace.

(d) When a regular verb ends with a single consonant preceded by a single stressed vowel, we double the consonant before adding the -ed: (stop) The people finally **stopped** the war; (step) The bride and groom **stepped** toward the altar; (permit) The police **permitted** us to pass through the barricades.

(e) When a regular verb ends in -e, only -d is added: (change) They suddenly **changed** my schedule; (place) Napoleon **placed** his crown on himself; (encourage) They **encouraged** their children to enter the university.

3.8

PRONUNCIATION EXERCISE

Focus: Verbs Ending with a t or d Sound

When a base form ends in a t or d sound, the final syllable in the past form of regular verbs is pronounced.

Practice pronouncing the past forms in the following lists.

-ted			-ded	
benefited	expected	reported	attended	landed
collected	invited	started	decided	needed
corrected	omitted	tasted	ended	recorded
elected	permitted	waited	graded	reminded

3.8 (Continued)

Name _____ Date _____

In the blanks, supply appropriate past forms from the lists on page 111.

EXAMPLES: a. Unfortunately, they <u>omitted</u> my name from the winners' list.
          b. All the newspapers <u>reported</u> the story about the kidnapping.

1. They _____ me the president of the club.

2. We _____ a wedding on Saturday afternoon.

3. The sanitation department _____ the garbage early today.

4. We _____ a long rest after our tiring business trip.

5. Our plane _____ at Orly Airport exactly on time.

6. S/he _____ the students' homework very carefully.

7. We _____ to get to Chicago quickly.

8. The meeting _____ early and _____ late.

9. Enrico Caruso _____ many records in the earlier part of this century.

10. The singer at the concert _____ me of an old friend of mine.

11. The dinner _____ delicious.

12. They finally _____ to get married.

13. We _____ for you for three hours at the station.

14. Fortunately, the patient _____ from the medicine.

15. They _____ us to their graduation ceremony.

16. The victim _____ the details of the crime to the police.

17. The office manager _____ everyone to go home early.

18. Napoleon's life _____ on the island of Saint Helena.

19. My teacher carefully _____ the final examinations.

20. The patient _____ to take a lot of medicine.

21. The fish at dinner last night _____ bad.

3.9

PRONUNCIATION EXERCISE

Focus: Past Forms Ending with a *t* Sound

1. When base forms that end in -*k*, -*p*, -*f*, -*gh*, -*s*, -*ce*, -*sh*, -*ch*, and -*x* become -*ed* past forms, they end with a *t* sound.

Practice pronouncing the past forms in the following lists.

-sh	-k	-x	-ce(-s sound)	-ch	-p
finished	asked	fixed	noticed	watched	stopped
washed	looked	boxed	practiced	patched	helped
pushed	liked	taxed	danced	hatched	wrapped
crashed	locked	waxed	introduced	latched	dropped
mashed	walked	mixed	produced	touched	clapped

2. When a past form that ends with a *t* sound precedes a word that begins with *a*, *e*, *i*, *o*, *u*, *w*, *h*, or *y*, the two words combine in pronunciation into one word.

Practice pronouncing the combined words in italics in the following sentences. Read the sentences aloud.

1. The children *laughed at* the clown. He *laughed with* them.
2. The scientist *worked on* the project for many years.
3. The present was beautiful. I *wrapped it* in special paper.
4. I *helped a* blind man to cross the street yesterday.
5. I *typed a* few letters last night.
6. My company *introduced a* new product last year.
7. I *watched a* good program on TV this evening.
8. The dancers *danced a* tango. Then they *danced a* rhumba.
9. The clown *walked on* his hands.
10. The soprano *practiced a* new song.
11. I *introduced a* new student to the class today.
12. Mom *fixed a* wonderful Thanksgiving dinner. I *baked a* pie.
13. I *washed all* the dishes after dinner.
14. We *stopped at* the store for some groceries.
15. She *locked her* door. I *asked her* a question.
16. The tennis player *dropped his* ball.
17. I *noticed a* good bargain at the store.
18. The flag *flapped in* the wind. The baby *clapped her* hands.
19. I *stopped at* the red light. I *stopped at* a friend's house.
20. He *kissed her*. She *kissed him*. The mother *kissed her* baby.
21. I *cooked a* big dinner for myself. We *cooked a* goose.
22. I *worked on* my homework for several hours.
23. I *smoked a* cigarette after dinner. He *smoked a* pipe.

3.10

PRONUNCIATION EXERCISE

Focus: Past Forms Ending with a *d* Sound

All past forms except for those described in exercises 3.7 and 3.8 end with a *d* sound. Like a past form ending with a *t* sound, when a past form that ends with a *d* sound precedes a word that begins with *a, e, i, o, u, w, h,* or *y,* the two words combine in pronunciation into one word.

Practice pronouncing the combined words in italics in the following sentences. Read the sentences aloud.

1. His father *died a* long time ago.
2. Unfortunately, he *owed a* lot of money to the bank.
3. Mary *married Anthony* in a church.
4. The manager *explained office* procedures to the new secretary.
5. They *lived in* Hong Kong for a long time.
6. The orchestra *played a* symphony by Beethoven.
7. He *received a* very good grade in the course.
8. We *arrived at* the party late.
9. The children *played in* the playground all afternoon.
10. A terrible accident *occurred on* the highway last night.
11. They *showed a* good movie on TV last night.
12. The doctor *called on* some patients at the hospital.
13. Cleopatra *killed herself.* She *lived in* Egypt a long time ago.
14. I *cleaned up* the apartment all day yesterday.
15. The patient *died in* his sleep.
16. The store *closed at* five. It *opened again* at nine.
17. We *stayed at* the movies for three hours.
18. They *opened a* new store on Broadway.
19. I *borrowed a* thousand dollars from the bank.
20. We *figured out* the problem yesterday. (*To figure out* means *to solve.*)
21. John *called at* night. He *called up* everybody.
22. I *mailed a* letter to the President.
23. We *enjoyed ourselves* at the party.
24. Greta Garbo *appeared in* many wonderful movies.
25. She *prepared her* speech well.
26. They *transferred a* new student to my class.
27. He *prepared a* wonderful dinner for us.
28. They *offered us* a lot of money for our house.
29. He *shaved off* his beard a couple of weeks ago.
30. They *turned off* the electricity a couple of minutes ago.

3.11

Focus: Past Forms of Irregular Verbs

Note: In the Appendix there is a list of commonly used verbs that are irregular in the past tense.

Make past forms out of the base forms given in the parentheses and supply them in the blanks.

EXAMPLES: a. (hide) I <u>hid</u> some money in my dictionary.
   b. (put) The firemen <u>put</u> out the fire in only a few minutes.

1. (have) We _____ a wonderful time at the party last night.

2. (ring) The bell _____ just a few minutes ago.

3. (drink) I _____ three cups of coffee for breakfast.

4. (do) The children _____ something naughty this morning.

5. (wake) The baby _____ up only a few minutes ago.

6. (catch) He _____ a very bad cold on the camping trip.

7. (blow) The wind _____ down a tree in front of our house.

8. (feed) I _____ the cat its breakfast a short while ago.

9. (find) Jackie _____ some money on the street a couple of days ago.

10. (get) We all _____ wet during the rainstorm yesterday.

11. (come/stand) The Queen _____ into the room and everyone _____ up.

12. (hold) Our teacher _____ the class in the park last Tuesday.

13. (see) I _____ a fantastic movie on TV last night.

14. (take) We _____ a drive to the country last weekend in our car.

15. (read) I _____ a lot of books for the course on Shakespeare.

16. (spend) We _____ a lot of money on our last vacation.

17. (wear) My mother _____ a marvelous dress to the party last night.

18. (go) We _____ to bed very early last night.

19. (bite) Our dog _____ a little girl on her arm yesterday morning.

20. (break) His girlfriend _____ her promise to him.

21. (leave) My boss _____ his office for a business appointment an hour ago.

22. (hear) I _____ some terrible news on the radio a few minutes ago.

23. (take) He _____ three courses in mathematics last semester.

24. (forget) I _____ to take those books back to the library.

25. (cost) Grandpa's operation last summer _____ a lot of money.

26. (lend) My roommate _____ a couple of dollars to me.

27. (eat) I _____ some very good Chinese food last night.

3.11 (Continued)

28. (feel) The patient _____ very well yesterday, fortunately.

29. (meet) Romeo _____ Juliet at a party a long time ago.

30. (begin) The movie _____ with a fantastic automobile chase.

31. (fly) We _____ to Japan on Japan Airlines last summer.

32. (tear) I _____ one of my best shirts on a nail the other day.

33. (write) He _____ several letters to his family last week.

34. (rise) The sun _____ at 7:37 yesterday morning.

35. (run) A very good horse _____ in the last race.

36. (buy) I _____ a very fast motorcycle for myself yesterday.

37. (win) All of us _____ a lot of money in the last race.

38. (withdraw) I _____ $75.00 from my bank account yesterday.

39. (understand) I _____ almost everything during the last class.

40. (sleep) The baby _____ for almost three hours yesterday afternoon.

41. (cost) Their furniture _____ several thousand dollars.

42. (drive) We _____ our car out to the Far West last summer.

43. (hit) My favorite player _____ three home runs in the last game. (bet) I _____ ten dollars on the game.

44. (bring) Our teacher _____ his little boy to the last class.

45. (choose) Unfortunately, I _____ the wrong horse in the last race. (lose) I _____ ten dollars.

46. (pay) We _____ $55,000 for our new house.

47. (teach) My teacher _____ in Africa for several years.

48. (shrink) My favorite shirt _____ in the last wash.

49. (speak) We _____ to a lot of people at the reception.

50. (grow) We _____ lettuce in our garden last summer.

51. (sell) Russia _____ Alaska to the United States.

52. (set) The sun _____ yesterday afternoon in a blaze of glory. (be) The colors _____ glorious.

53. (sing) The soprano _____ some of my favorite songs.

54. (hurt) Jim _____ himself in a skiing accident last winter.

55. (lay) I _____ my school material on my desk.

56. (fall) Our son _____ in love with the girl next door.

57. (freeze) The water in the lake _____ yesterday afternoon.

58. (cast) I _____ my vote for the winner in the last election.

3.11 *(Continued)*

Name _____ Date _____

59. (fight) My favorite boxer _____ with the champion at Madison Square Garden last night. (beat) Unfortunately, the champion _____ him in the third round.

60. (swim) Our children _____ a lot last summer on their vacation.

61. (ride) Jimmy _____ to school on his bike yesterday morning.

62. (hang) I _____ the new painting in the dining room.

63. (keep) We _____ our last car for seven years.

64. (shake) I _____ the Ambassador's hand at the party.

65. (sit) I _____ between John and Frank at the last meeting.

66. (steal) Somebody in her office _____ her purse last week.

67. (dig) The phone company _____ a big hole in the street yesterday.

3.12

THE NEGATIVE FORM AND YES-NO QUESTIONS

1. Except for the verb *be,* regular and irregular verbs have the same negative form in the simple past tense. *Did,* the past form of *do,* is used as an auxiliary in a negative verb phrase. *Not* is inserted between *did* and a base form to complete the phrase: *At the end of his political career, Richard Nixon **did not have** the support of the American people; Jesus **did not live** a long life.*

		Singular		Plural	
First person	I	⎫		we	⎫
Second person	you	⎬ did not do		you	⎬ did not do
Third person	he, she, it	⎭		they	⎭

2. In informal usage, *didn't,* the contraction of *did not,* occurs: *We **didn't win** the last game; I **didn't see** anybody in particular at the store.*

3. *Did* is also used to form a *yes-no* question; it is put at the beginning of a question, followed by the subject and a base form: ***Did the Vikings get** to America before Columbus? **Did Magellan go** around the world?*

	I	⎫		we	⎫
Did you	⎬ do it?	Did you	⎬ do it?
	he, she, it	⎭		they	⎭

4. *Did* also appears in *yes-no* answers: *Did he make a mistake? Yes, he **did**; No, he **didn't**.*

Yes-No Answers with *Did*

	I	⎫		we	⎫
Yes, you	⎬ did.	No, you	⎬ didn't.
	he, she, it	⎭		they	⎭

Note: The noncontracted form of a *no* answer is used for emphasis: *Did you take my money? No, I did not.*

3.13

Name _____ Date _____

        Focus: Negative Verb Phrases

Fill in the blanks with negative verb phrases (*did* + *not* + base form), using the base forms in the following list.

anticipate	cost	expect	listen	see	want
arrive	discover	get	meet	send	watch
believe	eat	go	pay	take	win
build	enjoy	like	read	understand	

EXAMPLES: a. Winston Churchill <u>did not anticipate</u> the fall of the British Empire. He <u>didn't expect</u> it.
             b. They <u>didn't build</u> Rome in a day. (old saying)

1. The American people _____ Richard Nixon's story.

2. The Communists _____ the war in Vietnam easily.

3. I _____ the teacher's explanation of the formula.

4. Marie Curie _____ radium and polonium by herself. She had a lot of help from her husband.

5. I _____ to the doctor's office on time. (*On time* means at a specific time; *in time* means before a specific time.)

6. We _____ to the station in time to catch the bus.

7. I _____ at the meeting in time to hear the speech.

8. I _____ any French courses last semester.

9. The United States _____ the Russians much for Alaska.

10. We _____ the movie *King Kong*.

11. My sister _____ out with her boyfriend last Saturday night.

12. Many young men _____ to fight in the last war.

13. Before the revolution, the rich _____ to the voice of the poor. They _____ attention to their needs.

14. Adam and Eve _____ to God's command.

15. I _____ any interesting people on my last vacation.

16. We _____ any Christmas cards last year.

17. Our plane _____ in London on time; we were an hour late. Consequently, we _____ to our hotel in London in time for our business meeting.

18. We _____ anything special on TV last night.

19. We _____ *Hamlet* in the course on Shakespeare last semester. I _____ the course.

20. Fortunately, our vacation _____ much last summer.

21. I _____ a very good grade on the final examination.

3.14

GRAMMAR EXERCISE   Name _____ Date _____

Focus: *Yes-No* Questions and Answers

Supply appropriate base forms in the blanks, using the base forms in the following list. Practice asking and answering the questions. **Pronunciation Note**: *Did you* sounds like *did-jew*.

arrive	eat	forget	invent	send	understand
discover	enter	get	make	study	work
do	feel	go	marry	take	wax
drink	find	have	meet	tell	

EXAMPLES: a. Did you <u>wax</u> the floors in your apartment yesterday?

b. Did you <u>have</u> a nice time at the cocktail party last night?

1. Did your father _____ your mother in your hometown?

2. Did the doctor _____ at the hospital in time to save the patient?

3. Did you _____ out with your friends last night?

4. Did you _____ lunch with your parents yesterday?

5. Did Alexander Graham Bell _____ the telephone?

6. Did you _____ out your girlfriend/boyfriend last night?

7. Did you _____ your homework at the library yesterday afternoon?

8. Did your parents _____ you a letter last week?

9. Did anybody _____ this room through the window today?

10. Did you _____ to school early or late today?

Now supply *did* + subject + base form in the blanks.

11. _____ a good time on their last vacation?

12. _____ our secret to anybody in this class?

13. _____ the train or bus this morning?

14. _____ up late or early yesterday morning?

15. _____ to church the Sunday before last?

16. _____ any mistakes in the last examination?

Now complete the following sentences, using a variety of base forms.

17. Did your teacher_____?

18. Did your lawyer _____?

19. Did the police _____?

20. Did your doctor _____?

21. Did your boss/secretary/co-worker _____?

22. Did everyone in this class _____?

3.15

INFORMATION QUESTIONS

1. The auxiliary *did* is also used in an information question in the simple past tense. The usual pattern is information word(s) + *did* + subject + base form: ***When did the S.S. Titanic sink? When did Neil Armstrong land*** *on the moon?* ***How did you feel*** *yesterday?*

	Singular			Plural		
First person		I			we	
Second person	How did you	you	} go?	How did you		} go?
Third person		he			they	
		she				
		it				

2. A common response to an information questions is just a prepositional phrase: *Who(m) did you give the package to? . . . (to) Mary; Where did you put my dictionary? . . . (on) the table; Who(m) did you have dinner with last night? . . . (with) my parents; How did you get to school? . . . (on) the bus; How did you get to the island? . . . (on) my boat.* Or we may respond with just a subject and a past form: *How did you get to the island? . . . I swam; How did you get to Rome? . . . I flew; What did you do last night? . . . I studied.*

3. Postponed prepositions may occur in information questions: *Who(m) did you give the package* **to?** *What shelf did you put the atlas* **on?** *What school did you go* **to?** *What institute did you study* **at?**
   Reminder: Postponed prepositions sometimes precede prepositional phrases and time expressions: *Who(m) did you dance with* **at the party?** *What university did you study at* **in the Soviet Union?** *Who(m) did you speak to* **at the conference?**

4. Information questions in the simple past tense may also occur without the help of the auxiliary *did*. This takes place when the information word(s) is the subject of a sentence: ***How many people*** *died in the earthquake in Guatemala in 1976?* ***Who*** *gave you your name?* ***What*** *happened to Richard Nixon?*

5. The usual response to these *who* questions is a short answer with a subject + *did* or *didn't*: *Who came to school early?* ***I did;*** *Who went home late?* ***I didn't;*** *Who flew across the Atlantic first?* ***Lindbergh did;*** *Who left this book on the table?* ***I didn't.***

3.16

GRAMMAR EXERCISE

Focus: Information Questions with *Did*

Supply appropriate base forms in the blanks. The words in the following list are only some of the base forms that may be used in this exercise. **Pronunciation Reminder**: *Did you* sounds like *did-jew.*

buy	cook	dream	go	leave	purchase	speak	vote
come	dance	get	have	pay	send	travel	

EXAMPLES: a. What did you <u>do</u> last night after dinner?
           b. Who did you <u>go</u> with to the graduation ball (a formal dance)?

3.16 (Continued

1. What time did your roommate _____ up yesterday morning?

2. Where did you _____ your folder/briefcase/dictionary?

3. What did you _____ for dinner last night/the night before last?

4. What time did you _____ home last night?

5. Who did you _____ with at the graduation ball?

6. Who did the people _____ for in the last election?

7. What color curtains did your mother _____ for the dining room?

8. What time did you _____ school yesterday afternoon?

9. Who did you _____ to on the phone last night?

10. What did you _____ for lunch/breakfast yesterday?

Now supply information word(s) + *did* + subject + base form.

11. _____ for in the last election?

12. _____ for this book?

13. _____ a letter to last night?

14. _____ English before this course?

15. _____ dinner with last night?

16. _____ after the last class?

17. _____ about last night?

18. _____ to at the police station?

Now complete the sentences. Use a variety of base forms.

19. How much money did you _____?

20. What kind of TV _____?

21. What countries _____?

22. Who did you _____?

23. How did you _____?

24. Where did _____?

25. What did_____?

26. How much _____?

27. What kind of _____?

28. How_____?

3.17

GRAMMAR EXERCISE   Name _____ Date _____

Focus: Information Questions without *Did*

Supply appropriate past forms in the blanks, making past forms out of the base forms in the following list.

assassinate	come	fight	go	lead	steal	write
be	discover	find	invent	live	take	
bring	do	fly	kill	lose	teach	
build	eat	give	know	see	win	

EXAMPLES: a. Who <u>taught</u> this class yesterday?
            b. Who <u>was</u> the first man on the moon?

1. Who _____ into this room first/last today?

2. Who _____ in the Garden of Eden?

3. Who _____ the forbidden fruit first, Adam or Eve?

4. Who _____ polonium and radium/penicillin?

5. Who _____ Julius Caesar/John F. Kennedy/Abraham Lincoln/Martin Luther King/ Che Guevara?

6. Who _____ the telephone/the wireless/dynamite/the atomic bomb/television/the electric light bulb/the phonograph/the printing press?

7. Who _____ the Bible/*Romeo and Juliet*/*Gone with the Wind?*

8. Who _____ in the war in Vietnam/Korea?

9. Who _____ money on the street yesterday?

10. Who _____ an umbrella to school today?

11. Who _____ to the movies last night?

12. Who _____ my money out of my coat pocket?

13. Who _____ my dictionary off my desk?

14. Who _____ the sweater that I lost?

15. Who _____ Germany/the United States/Italy/the Soviet Union during the Second World War?

16. Who _____ the American Civil War/the Spanish Civil War?

17. Who _____ the pyramids/the Great Wall of China?

18. Who _____ around the world first/across the Atlantic first?

19. Who _____ you your watch/your necklace/your ring/your name?

20. Who _____ the movie *Gone with the Wind*/*The Exorcist?*

21. Who _____ the answer to the riddle? (A *riddle* is a question requiring some thought to answer. Riddles often take the form of a joke; for example, "What is black and white and read (red) all over?" . . . a newspaper, of course.)

3.18

DIRECT AND INDIRECT OBJECTS

1. A noun (or pronoun) that is the DIRECT OBJECT of a verb usually answers the questions *What?* or *Whom?* and follows the verb directly: *Yesterday, he bought a **Rolls-Royce*** (<u>What</u> did he buy yesterday?); *His wife saw **him** at the car dealer's* (<u>Whom</u> did his wife see at the car dealer's?).

2. A noun (or pronoun) that is the INDIRECT OBJECT of a verb answers the questions *To Whom?* or *what?* or *For whom?* or *what?* and follows the verb indirectly, after a direct object, in a prepositional phrase: *Yesterday, he bought a Rolls-Royce **for his wife*** (<u>For whom</u> did he buy a Rolls-Royce yesterday?).
   Reminder: Reflexive pronouns may be used as indirect objects: *I bought **myself** a new watch; She gave **herself** a quick look in the mirror.*

3. Alternatively, an indirect object may precede a direct object, omitting the "to" or "for" of the prepositional phrase: *He bought a Rolls-Royce **for his wife** = He bought **his wife** a Rolls-Royce.*

4. When an indirect object precedes a direct object, do not use the prepositions *to* or *for*. These two prepositions are used in prepositional phrases that follow direct objects. Compare:

Indirect Object Preceding Direct Object	Prepositional Phrase Following Direct Object
*He built **himself** a house.*	*He built a house **for himself**.*
*She owes **the bank** money.*	*She owes money **to the bank**.*

5. A common mistake that students make is to put *to* or *for* in front of an indirect object that is preceding a direct object in a simple sentence. Compare:

Correct	Wrong
I gave John the book.	*I gave to John the book.*
We bought ourselves a car.	*We bought for ourselves a car.*

6. Some verbs followed by direct object + prepositional phrase with *to*:

bring	hand	offer	pay	send	take	tell
give	lend	owe	sell	show	teach	write

7. Some verbs followed by direct object + prepositional phrase with *for*:

bake	build	buy	draw	find	get	knit	make	reserve

3.19

GRAMMAR EXERCISE

Focus: Direct and Indirect Objects

On a separate piece of paper, change the following sentences so that indirect objects precede direct objects. Omit *to* or *for*.

EXAMPLES:
  a. He gave a bouquet to Mary. *He gave Mary a bouquet.*
  b. Mary made a blouse for herself. *Mary made herself a blouse.*

1. I lent a thousand dollars to a friend.
2. The policeman drew a map for me.
3. I showed the message to John.
4. Mom baked a birthday cake for Timmy.
5. My mother taught French to me.
6. I reserved a rented car for myself.
7. I handed the check to the waiter.
8. She sent a telegram to her father.
9. He wrote a letter to the president of the company.
10. They bought a car for their son.
11. My neighbor sold his car to me.
12. I found a nice present for my mother.
13. I got some new toys for our baby.
14. I made another cocktail for myself.

Now change the following sentences so that prepositional phrases follow direct objects. Add *to* or *for*.

EXAMPLES:
  c. He taught me the tango. *He taught the tango to me.*
  d. Billy built himself a tree house. *Billy built a tree house for himself.*

15. I lent him my typewriter.
16. I bought myself a new bike.
17. He gave his grandfather a box of cigars.
18. Dad baked Mom a beautiful birthday cake.
19. The architect showed us the plans.
20. My doctor gave me this prescription.
21. She knit herself a beautiful sweater.
22. Bob found himself a girlfriend.
23. Dick sold Ellen his car.
24. We bought ourselves the best tickets.
25. Santa Claus gave Nancy a doll house.
26. Monica made herself another evening dress.
27. He handed his wife the check.
28. They showed me the secret report.

3.20

GRAMMAR EXERCISE   Name _____ Date _____

Fill in the blanks with *to* or *for*.

EXAMPLES: a. I'm going to lend my car to Bill.
             b. I wanted to get a new doll for my daughter.

1. We're sending this letter _____ the President tomorrow morning.

2. I'm cooking these cookies _____ my neighbors' children.

3. I need to send a letter _____ my parents.

4. Mary is knitting a sweater _____ her brother.

5. My grandfather is giving all his money _____ the Red Cross.

6. She told the story of Cinderella _____ the children.

7. He wants to buy a new stereo _____ himself.

Now supply *to* or *for* or zero preposition (0) in the blanks. **Reminder**: Zero (no) preposition occurs before indirect objects that precede direct objects.

EXAMPLES: c. The professor gave 0 that student a bad grade.
             d. She gave a bad grade to the student.

8. Please make things easy _____ yourself.

9. Please make _____ yourself another drink.

10. He got a dozen roses _____ his wife on her birthday.

11. She got _____ him a new set of golf clubs last Christmas.

12. My company owes a lot of money _____ the bank.

13. We're going to give _____ ourselves a vacation in Spain.

14. My girlfriend is going to knit some socks _____ me.

15. The company offered _____ John a fantastic job in Saudi Arabia.

Now supply *to* or *for* + prepositional phrase in the blanks.

16. My Mom baked a wonderful cake _____.

17. They reserved a hotel room _____.

18. Jack told a funny story _____.

Now supply an appropriate indirect object in the blanks.

19. He got _____ a beautiful new car.

20. We owe _____ a vacation.

21. I gave _____ a very large tip (money for service rendered).

3.21

TWO-WORD VERBS

1. A verb and a preposition may be combined to form a TWO-WORD VERB. The preposition in such a verb is referred to as a PARTICLE: *Grandma **fell down** and hurt herself; Please **turn off** the lights; Did you **call up** your boss?*

2. There are two kinds of two-word verbs, SEPARABLE and INSEPARABLE. In separable verb-preposition combinations, the particle may occur before or after the noun object: *John turned off **the lights** this morning* or *John turned **the lights** off this morning; Did you call up **your boss?*** or *Did you call **your boss up?***
   Note: When a noun object is moved, time expressions and prepositional phrases still remain in final position: *They called off the game yesterday morning = They called the game off yesterday morning; I hung up my coat in the closet = I hung my coat up in the closet.*

3. If the object is a pronoun, it is always inserted between the verb and the particle in a two-word verb: *I turned **it** off* (never: *I turned off **it***); *We called **it** off* (never: *We called off **it***).

4. In inseparable verb-preposition combinations, a (pro)noun object always follows the particle; an inseparable two-word verb is never separated; *We **called on** some old friends* (never: *We **called** some old friends **on***); *I'm **looking for** a cheap apartment* (never: *I'm **looking** a cheap apartment **for***).

5. Some separable two-word verbs:

   blow out (a candle): extinguish
   call off (a game, a meeting): cancel
   call up (a person): telephone
   do over (a letter, homework): do again with corrections
   figure out (a problem): solve

6. Some inseparable two-word verbs:

   get on (a bus): board
   get over (a disappointment, an illness): recover from
   look after (children): take care of
   wait on (a person): serve

   Note: A two-word verb frequently has more than one meaning. Any good dictionary will have most of the definitions of two-word verbs.

3.22

GRAMMAR EXERCISE

Focus: Separable Two-Word Verbs

On a separate piece of paper, rewrite the following sentences so that the object nouns precede the particles.

EXAMPLES: a. Please *take off* (remove) your coat in the hall. *Please take your coat off in the hall.*
b. *Call up* (telephone) the police. *Call the police up.*

1. I *turned off* (extinguished) the lights.
2. Please *clean up* (clean thoroughly) your room, Nancy.
3. Waiter, would you please *clean off* (clean thoroughly) this table.
4. I'm going to *clean out* (clean thoroughly) the closet.
5. Did he *turn down* (reject) the job offer?
6. Please *turn down* (lower the volume of) the radio.
7. Please *turn up* (raise the volume of) the stereo.
8. Did you *hand in* (submit) your homework yesterday?
9. Is the teacher going to *hand out* (distribute) new material today?
10. Please *try on* (test) this jacket.
11. Did you *try out* (test) that typewriter? (*try on* for clothing, *try out* for machinery or equipment)
12. Don't forget to *write down* (record) her phone number.
13. I want to *take off* (remove) my coat.
14. Did Billy *put on* (don) his baseball uniform?
15. I'm going to *take back* (return) this dress to the store.
16. Did you forget to *hang up* (replace) the receiver?
17. Please *hang up* (place on a hanger) your coat in the closet.
18. Did you *cross out* (draw a line or cross through) all the mistakes in the letter?
19. Would you please *blow out* (extinguish) the candles.
20. They want to *call off* (cancel) the game.
21. They're going to *put off* (postpone) the meeting until tomorrow.
22. Please *do over* (do again) this letter.
23. Do you want me to *figure out* (solve) this problem for you?
24. Children often like to *make up* (invent) stories. (*To make up stories* is sometimes used to mean *to lie.*)
25. My company *laid off* (fired) ten men.
26. His company *took on* (hired) a lot of new workers.
27. Please *look over* (examine, review) the report carefully.
28. Please *point out* (indicate) the mistakes in this letter.
29. My dentist is going to *pull out* (remove) two of my teeth.

3.23

GRAMMAR EXERCISE

Name _____ Date _____

Focus: Inseparable Two-Word Verbs

In each blank, supply an appropriate inseparable two-word verb from the following list.

break down: go out of order
call on: visit (formal)
come out: be published
get on: board
get up: arise

go over: review
go with: harmonize with
look after: take care of
pick on: annoy, tease
take after: resemble

take off: leave the ground
    (for planes)
wait on: serve
wake up: stop sleeping

EXAMPLES: a.   What time do you usually wake up?

           b.   Who do you take after, your mother or father?

1. When is your new book finally going to _____?

2. Why did your car _____ so suddenly?

3. The French Ambassador is going to _____ the President today.

4. Class, please _____ the past material before the examination.

5. Is our plane going to _____ in a few minutes?

6. Dickie, please don't _____ your little brother.

7. Does their new baby _____ him or her?

8. We need a waiter to _____ us.

9. Sh! We don't want the baby to _____.

10. This shirt doesn't _____ these pants; it's the wrong color.

11. I _____ my neighbor's children two afternoons a week.

12. What time are you going to _____ tomorrow morning?

13. The old lady will be able to _____ the plane before the other passengers.

Now supply past forms of two-word verbs.

14. I _____ at 7:30 yesterday morning.

15. That author's new book _____ two months ago.

16. The plane _____ for Moscow at midnight.

17. Unfortunately, our car _____ during our last vacation.

18. He _____ quickly and left the room.

19. I _____ the wrong bus yesterday morning. I was late to work.

20. At my lawyer's office yesterday, I _____ the contract carefully.

21. Carl _____ all the past material before the final exam.

22. I _____ some very important customers yesterday.

23. A very good waiter _____ us at the restaurant last night.

3.24

ELSE AND *BESIDES*

1. The adjective *else* frequently follows information words in questions. The word has the meaning of *other* or *in addition to*: **Who else** (in addition to us) *is going to be at the meeting?* **What else** (in addition to money) *do you want in your life?*

2. Like *else*, the adverb *besides* means *in addition to,* and the two words may occur together in the same sentence: *How else do you get to California* **besides** (in addition to) *a plane? What else do you need for a successful Thanksgiving dinner* **besides** (in addition to) *a turkey?* **Besides** (in addition to) *you, who else was absent?*

3. Besides information words, *else* appears with compound pronouns and adverbs: *Is there* **anyone else** *coming to the party besides those few? There is* **something else** *bothering him besides his problems at work; Let's go* **somewhere else** *besides the beach this year; Is there* **anything else***?*
   Note: It is easy to confuse the preposition *beside* with the adverb *besides. Beside* means *next to* while *besides* means *in addition to*: *That little boy is always* **beside** (next to) *his father.*

Name _____ Date _____

Supply *beside* or *besides* in the blanks.

EXAMPLES: a. That's our car <u>beside</u> the house.
            b. <u>Besides</u> Mary and her husband, Frank and his wife were there.

1. There are a couple of small houses _____ the lake.

2. She is always _____ her husband in time of trouble.

3. _____ school, he has a full-time job.

4. At official receptions, the First Lady stands _____ the President. (The wife of the President of the United States is called *the first lady of the land.*)

5. What else _____ the fish did they serve at the dinner party?

6. There's a large apartment building _____ our house.

7. Their house is _____ a lovely park.

8. _____ champagne, they served red wine at the dinner party last Saturday night.

9. I prefer to have my phone _____ my bed.

10. _____ the rainy weather, a bad cold spoiled my vacation.

11. Children don't usually like to sit _____ the teacher's desk.

12. _____ my phone bill, my rent and gas bills are very high.

3.25

          Focus: *Else*

Supply *else* with an appropriate information word or compound pronoun in the blanks.

EXAMPLES: a. Do you want anything else besides a ham sandwich?

              b. What else do you want besides money?

1. Besides John, Mary, and Bill, _____ is going to be at the meeting?

2. Besides your financial problems, is there _____ bothering you?

3. _____ do you need for your English class besides a dictionary?

4. Besides that terrible event, _____ happened on your vacation last summer?

5. _____ besides the teacher and the other students is going to be in your class tomorrow?

6. Is _____ besides yourself going to be at home tonight?

7. _____ besides the train do I get to the country?

8. Besides cigarettes, _____ is bad for our health?

9. Besides your family, _____ is important in your life?

10. _____ do you want besides a cola?

11. Is there _____ you want besides a good job?

12. _____ gave you a birthday present besides your mother and father?

13. _____ besides Florida is nice in the winter in the United States?

14. _____ is on your mind besides your problems at work?

15. _____ did you do last weekend besides eat and sleep?

16. _____ do you want besides a good grade in the course?

17. Besides John, _____ do you know in Chicago?

18. _____ besides Shakespeare wrote plays in the sixteenth century?

19. _____ are they going to serve at Christmas dinner besides the goose?

20. Is there _____ in your safe deposit box besides money?

21. Besides that, _____ do you want?

22. _____ did you go last summer besides the beach?

23. _____ besides water do you need on a trip through the Sahara Desert?

24. _____ do you want besides money, success, and fame?

3.26

SUBSTITUTION WITH PRONOUNS

1. We use pronoun substitutes in a statement or question in response to another statement or question in order to avoid repetition: *I have on a new **shirt** (Do you like **it**?*); *Do you like Chinese **food?** (I love **it**)*; ***Patricia** is a nice woman (Do you know **her**?*); ***Mr. and Mrs. Williams** are my neighbors (Do you know **them?***).

2. *One(s)* occur as a substitute for countable nouns. *These are wonderful **oranges** (Do you want **one?***); *We have three sizes of eggs for sale (I'll take a dozen small **ones***). *Some* (any) is used as a substitute for uncountable nouns: *This is delicious **ice cream** (Do you want **some** [**any**]?*).

3. The interrogative pronoun *which* is used in questions with *one(s)*. When there is a small choice to make, *one* occurs: *Here is a Japanese **camera** and that is a German **camera** (Which **one** do you like?*).
   When we have a larger choice, *ones* follows *which*: *Look at all those lovely **paintings!** (Which **ones** do you like the best?*).

4. At many times, *which* and *what* are confusing to students. *Which* refers to persons or things: ***Which person** do you wish to speak to? **Which dictionary** is yours?* What is used for things: ***What time** do you have? **What** is your **address?***

5. *Which* is used when there is a choice of only a few things or persons (usually two): ***Which book** do you want to buy, the new one or the old one? **Which man** do you want to marry, Bill or John?* What is generally used when there is a choice of many things: ***What** is your name?* (there are many names); ***What country** has good weather in the winter?* (many countries have good weather in the winter).

6. Sometimes, *which* and *what* are interchangeable: *Which (what) airline are you going to take to Europe?* In this example, *which* suggests a choice of a few airlines, but *what* suggests many. However, only *what* is appropriate in the sentence *What airline is the best in the world?* (there are thousands of airlines).

3.27

Name _____ Date _____

Focus: Substitution with Pronouns

Supply appropriate pronouns in the blanks.

EXAMPLES: a. I need money to pay the waiter. Do you have <u>some</u>?
b. That's a good car, but I don't like <u>it</u>.

1. Where is my dictionary? Is _____ on my desk?

2. Look at all those bathing suits. Which _____ do you like?

3. This is delicious soup. Do you want _____?

4. I have a couple of extra dictionaries. Do you want _____?

5. That painting is a good example of French art. Do you like _____?

6. I have some chocolates in my pocket. Do you want _____?

7. Yesterday, I bought a blue jacket and a black _____.

8. Mr. and Mrs. Jackson are coming to the meeting. Do you know _____?

9. I have two friends in San Francisco. Which _____ do you know? I know many people at this school. Which _____ do you know?

10. I need soap to wash the dishes. Do you have _____?

11. I have only two cameras. Which _____ do you want to use?

12. You have a lot of friends in Texas. Which _____ are you going to see on your next vacation there?

13. Here are a lot of photographs of our class party. Which _____ do you want for yourself?

14. Isn't this a beautiful ring? Do you like _____?

15. I don't have a dictionary today. Do you have _____ for me to use for a while.

16. Here are two very good paintings. Which _____ do you like best?

17. This orange juice is very fresh. Do you want _____?

18. I need a pen with red ink to correct this homework. Do you have _____?

19. The homework last night was easy, but I didn't do _____.

20. I don't want a white shirt, I want a blue _____.

21. They have Japanese and Swiss watches. Do you prefer to buy a Japanese or a Swiss _____?

22. Which pen do you want to buy, this _____ or that _____?

23. Which man in this photograph is your father, this _____ or that _____?

3.28

GRAMMAR EXERCISE   Name _____ Date _____

Focus: *Which and What*

Supply *which* or *what* in the blanks.

EXAMPLES: a. <u>Which</u> countries border on the United States/your native country?
            b. <u>What</u> countries in the world have socialist governments?

1. _____ book is yours, this one or that one?

2. _____ is a good name for a new baby girl/boy?

3. _____ is the formula for success?

4. _____ is the best car in the world?

5. _____ is more important, money or love?

6. _____ time is best for your appointment, three or four o'clock?

7. _____ time of the year is best for a vacation in Greece?

8. _____ lion is lazy, the male or the female?

9. _____ kinds of animals live in the area around your hometown?

10. _____ do you want to do with your life?

11. _____ do you usually read on your vacations?

12. _____ dictionary is better, *Webster's* or *American Heritage*?

13. _____ airlines fly from the United States to Europe/the Orient?

14. _____ is your umbrella, the black one or the brown one?

15. _____ do you prefer in the morning, coffee or tea?

16. _____ movie do you want to see again, *Cinderella* or *Bambi*?

17. _____ part of the Bible is most interesting, the Old Testament or the New Testament?

18. _____ kind of career do you want?

19. _____ job pays more, an office job or a factory job?

20. _____ one do you want, the blue pen or the yellow one?

21. _____ person in your group is the leader?

22. _____ day of the week is best for a party?

23. _____ day do you want to go to the beach, Saturday or Sunday?

24. _____ hour is best for you to have lunch, twelve or one o'clock?

25. _____ hour in the evening is best for dinner?

26. _____ car do you want to buy, the Ford or the Toyota?

27. _____ person is your boss, Mr. Smith or Mrs. Jones?

28. _____ person in your group is from South America?

29. _____ day is Easter this year?

3.29

EXCLAMATORY PHRASES AND SENTENCES (EXCLAMATIONS)

1. An EXCLAMATORY PHRASE does not contain a subject or verb; it ends with an exclamation mark (!). The phrase begins with *what a* when a singular noun follows: ***What a** fantastic* ***record!** **What a** wonderful **day!** **What a** glorious **night!*** The phrase begins with *what* when a plural or uncountable noun follows: ***What** beautiful **flowers!** **What** delicious **food!** **What*** *strange **people!***

2. An exclamatory phrase begins with *how* when the phrase ends with an adjective: *How strange! How funny! How foolish! How wonderful!*

3. An EXCLAMATORY SENTENCE begins with an exclamatory phrase followed by the subject and balance of the sentence and, like exclamatory phrases, ends with an exclamation mark. *What a* begins the exclamation when a singular noun follows: ***What a** good **neighbor** you are! **What a** fast **horse** that is! **What a** cold and wet **day** it is!* What begins the exclamation when a plural or uncountable noun follows: ***What** wonderful **people** they are! **What** clever **students** that teacher has! **What** difficult **days** these are! **What** strength he has!*

4. An exclamatory sentence begins with *how* when the exclamatory phrase ends with an adjective or an adverb: ***How smooth** the surface of this table is! **How smoothly** they dance together! **How good** you are! **How well** you do everything! **How beautiful** she is! **How beautifully** that soprano sings!*

   Important Note: Adverbs cannot stand alone in an exclamatory phrase; they appear only in exclamatory sentences: *How well he dances!* (never *How well!*); *How quickly he runs!* (never *How quickly!*).

5. Postponed prepositions can appear at the end of an exclamatory sentence: *What a wonderful party I went **to**! What a handsome person I danced **with**! What interesting people I was introduced **to**!*

6. *Such* or *such a* may replace *what (a)* in an exclamatory sentence. When this occurs, *such (a)* follows the subject and the verb of the sentence: *She is **such a** nice person! They are **such** friendly people! This is **such a** difficult problem! These are **such** delicious oysters!*

3.30

GRAMMAR EXERCISE   Name _____ Date _____

Focus: Exclamatory Phrases and Sentences

Fill in the blanks with appropriate words, such as a (an), adjectives, or adverbs.

EXAMPLES: a. What <u>a wonderful</u> person your best friend is!
   b. How <u>well</u> your mother cooks! What a <u>good</u> cook she is!
   c. What <u>an exciting</u> movie it was!

1. What _____ night! How _____ I feel!

2. What _____ day it is! How _____ it is!

3. How _____ that foolish fellow drives his car!

4. I have such _____ headache! How _____ I feel!

5. They are such _____ people! How _____ they are!

6. What _____ woman your mother is!

7. How _____ she speaks English!

8. My upstairs neighbor is such _____ person!

9. His girlfriend has such _____ hair! She is such _____ young woman!

10. How _____ this exercise is! How _____ the students are doing! How
    _____ we are going!

11. How _____ that horse is running!

12. How _____ that little boy is!

13. *Romeo and Juliet* is such _____ play!

14. Hitler was such _____ man!

15. What _____ perfume this is! How _____ it smells!

16. How _____ that clown is!

17. What _____ dancer she is! How _____ she dances!

18. What _____ party I went to the other night!

19. What _____ people I met!

20. What _____ drink this is! How _____ it tastes!

21. What _____ food this is! How _____ it smells!

22. What _____ woman she is! How _____ she looks!

23. What _____ clothes she is wearing!

24. What _____ smile your girlfriend has!

25. What _____ class I have!

26. A cat is such _____ animal! How _____ an elephant is! How _____
    _____ a giraffe is! How _____ butterflies are!

3.31

GRAMMAR EXERCISE   Name _____ Date _____

             Focus: Reviewing Postponed Prepositions

Supply appropriate prepositions in the blanks from the following: about, at, for, in, of, on, to, with.
Reminder: *Who* often replaces *whom* in informal usage.

EXAMPLES: a.   Who did you talk <u>to</u>?
              b.   What store did you buy your coat <u>at</u>?

     1.   What are you worrying _____?

     2.   Who are you living _____?

     3.   Which table did you put my package _____?

     4.   What did you fix that broken chair _____?

     5.   Who is your cousin getting married _____?

     6.   Who does this necklace belong _____?

     7.   What are you pointing _____?

     8.   Who do I remind you _____?

     9.   Who are you voting _____?

   10.   What are you reading _____?

   11.   Which closet did you put my jacket _____?

   12.   What shelf is the French dictionary _____?

   13.   What corner do you want me to wait _____?

   14.   Who are you sending that valentine card _____?

   15.   What war did your father fight _____?

   16.   Who is your sister standing next _____?

   17.   What university is your brother studying _____?

   18.   What dentist in town are you going _____?

   19.   What do you often dream _____?

   20.   What are you thinking _____?

   21.   What kind of paint did you paint your bathroom _____?

   22.   What kind of mattress are you sleeping _____?

   23.   What company are you working _____?

   24.   What radio station do you usually listen _____?

   25.   What knife did you use to cut this meat _____?

   26.   What are you looking _____?

   27.   What kind of soap do you usually wash your dishes _____?

   28.   Which drawer did you put the telegram _____?

   29.   Which room at the library do you usually study _____?

CONJUNCTIONS AND COMPOUNDS 4

4.1

COORDINATE CONJUNCTIONS

1. The coordinate conjunctions *and, or, but,* and *so* are called CONNECTIVES because they connect a word with another word, a phrase with another phrase, or a clause with another clause.

2. Grammatical units (parts) joined by a coordinate conjunction are called COMPOUND. Two compounds that frequently appear are (a) a COMPOUND VERB: *We **danced and sang** at the party;* (b) a COMPOUND ADVERB: *The patient died **peacefully and happily;*** and (c) a COMPOUND ADJECTIVE: *She is a **beautiful and talented** actress.*

3. COMPOUND SUBJECTS are often used in a sentence. A compound subject may be (a) two pronouns joined by a coordinate conjunction: ***She and I** are going to get married;* (b) two nouns: ***Cats and dogs** don't like each other;* or (c) a noun and a pronoun: *Bill and I live together.*

4. COMPOUND OBJECTS appear as the object of a verb or preposition: *I saw **Barbara and her husband** at the football game; My father bought a new car for **my sister and me**.*

5. When two items appear in a compound, no comma is used: *Lions and elephants are afraid of each other.* When three or more items are coordinated, commas are used to separate the items; however, a comma before the conjunction preceding the last item is optional: *Mary, John(,) and Bill arrived at the meeting late; My father took my mother, my sister(,) and me to the beach.*

4.2

GRAMMAR EXERCISE

Focus: Compound Subjects

On a separate piece of paper, finish the following sentences with appropriate compound subjects. Use nouns, pronouns, and any necessary determiners (e.g., articles and possessive adjectives).

EXAMPLES: a. *Martha, Jack, and I* are coming to the meeting tomorrow.
b. *My sister and I* often argue over silly matters.
c. *Mr. Smith, his wife, and their children* were at church yesterday.

1. . . . are interesting subjects.
2. . . . were the first man and woman, according to the Bible.
3. . . . were all excellent at the dinner party last night.
4. . . . are not working.
5. . . . had a terrible fight yesterday afternoon.
6. . . . are very small countries.
7. . . . caught bad colds on their camping trip in the mountains.
8. . . . got lost on their trip in the desert.
9. . . . paid a lot of money for their children's education.
10. . . . were hurt in that terrible fire last night.
11. . . . surprised everyone and ran off and got married.
12. . . . are going to take an English course next semester.

4.2 (Continued)

      13. . . . are very expensive now.

      14. . . . are very beautiful women.

      15. . . . weren't at the last meeting.

4.3

GRAMMAR EXERCISE   Name _____ Date _____

      Focus: Compound Objects

      Note: A common mistake is to use a subject pronoun in a compound object: *She sent a present to my father and (I)*. This usage is nonstandard and does not occur in educated speech and writing.

Complete the following sentences with appropriate compound objects.

EXAMPLES: a. Yesterday, I went to <u>the store, the bank, and the drugstore.</u>

          b. My father took <u>my mother, my sister, and me</u> to the circus.

    1. I wrote letters to _____.

    2. My company fired _____.

    3. I saw _____ at the party last night.

    4. I talked to_____ on the phone last night.

    5. Nicole usually sits with _____.

    6. I went to the mountains with_____ a couple of weeks ago.

    7. Last Christmas, I gave presents to_____.

    8. I bought _____ at the store yesterday afternoon on my shopping trip.

    9. I ate _____ for lunch/dinner/breakfast.

  10. They served _____ at the dinner party last night.

  11. I forgot to put _____ in my suitcase.

  12. I sold_____ to my neighbor next door.

  13. We went to_____ on our vacation in Europe last summer.

  14. We discussed _____ during our last class.

  15. I took courses in _____ last semester at the University of Ohio.

  16. I dreamed about _____ last night.

  17. I went to _____ last Saturday.

  18. This information is a secret between_____.

4.4

Name _____ Date _____

Focus: Compound Verbs

Objects, adverbs, and prepositional phrases are often present in compound verbs: *The S.S. Titanic hit an iceberg and sank within a short time; I sent a letter to the President and got an immediate reply.*

Transform the base forms given in the parentheses into past forms.

EXAMPLES: a. He (study) <u>studied</u> hard and (get) <u>got</u> a good grade.
             b. I (get) <u>got</u> home late and (go) <u>went</u> directly to bed.

1. They (eat) _____ some bad shrimp and (get) _____ very sick.

2. They (buy) _____ a new car and (drive) _____ it down to Mexico.

3. The thief (steal) _____ the money and (hide) _____ it in a book.

4. The police (catch) _____ the thief and (put) _____ her in jail.

5. Snow White (marry) _____ the Prince and (live) _____ happily ever after (until the end of her life).

6. The patient (take) _____ the medicine and (feel) _____ much better.

7. I (park) _____ my car in the wrong place and (get) _____ a ticket.

8. Bill (see) _____ Helen and (fall) _____ in love with her at first sight (fell in love with her immediately).

9. I (get) _____ into bed and (fall) _____ asleep immediately.

10. They (invent) _____ a new mouse trap and (make) _____ a lot of money.

11. The author (write) _____ the book and (publish) _____ it himself.

12. He (drink) _____ five cocktails and (get) _____ a little drunk.

13. She (fall) _____ down and (break) _____ a leg.

14. He (bet) _____ all his money on one horse and (lose) _____ it all.

15. I (go) _____ to the bank and (deposit) _____ some money.

16. Grandpa (slip) _____ on the wet pavement and (hurt) _____ himself.

17. His father (make) _____ and (lose) _____ a lot of money.

18. We (see) _____ and (do) _____ many things on our vacation.

19. I (tear) _____ up the letter and (throw) _____ it away.

20. The movie (begin) _____ and (end) _____ with violence.

21. I (feed) _____ the baby her dinner and (eat) _____ a little bit myself.

22. They (fight) _____ and (win) _____ the battle.

23. We (fly) _____ to Puerto Rico and (have) _____ a wonderful time.

24. Picasso (draw) _____ and (paint) _____ many fine pictures.

25. I (be) _____ tired and (lie) _____ down for a little nap.

26. She (put) _____ on her coat and (leave) _____ in a hurry.

4.5

COMPOUND SENTENCES

1. A simple sentence always contains a subject and a verb: ***They live*** *in Paris.* When two simple sentences are closely related to each other, they may be combined to form a COMPOUND SENTENCE; for example, the two sentences *I went to Paris* and *I stayed for three weeks* may be joined together with the coordinate conjunction *and: I went to Paris,* **and** *I stayed for three weeks.* When two sentences appear together in a compound sentence, each sentence is called a MAIN CLAUSE (independent clause).

2. The coordinate conjunction *but* may also connect two main clauses: *It was a beautiful day,* **but** *I didn't go out.* A compound sentence with *but* shows a positive-negative contrast.

3. Main clauses can also be joined by punctuation alone. When this occurs, a SEMICOLON (;) appears between the two clauses: *I was tired; I didn't go to the movies. The party was boring; we didn't have a good time.*

4. A comma usually appears in a compound sentence with *and, or, but,* and *so;* however, when one or both main clauses are short, the comma may be omitted: *The day was hot and the night was cold; She arrived and he left.*

5. *But* main clauses are usually longer than those in the above examples; therefore, a comma is usually put between two main clauses: *Napoleon wanted to conquer Europe, but Hitler wanted to conquer the world.*

4.6

GRAMMAR EXERCISE

Focus: Compound Sentences with *And*

On a separate piece of paper, join the following sentences together with the coordinate conjunction *and.*

EXAMPLES: a. I went to the store with a friend. We bought a lot of things.
             I went to the store with a friend, and we bought a lot of things.
         b. I went to bed late. I got up late.
             I went to bed late and I got up late.

1. The teacher arrived. The class began.
2. The best apples are from the North. The best oranges are from the South.
3. We were at the beach all day. We danced all night.
4. We're leaving on our vacation tomorrow. We're going to be away for three weeks.
5. My radio isn't working. My TV isn't working.
6. This steak is excellent. The wine is superb.
7. We went to Morocco on our vacation. We had a fabulous time.

Now make up five examples of your own.

4.7

GRAMMAR EXERCISE

Focus: Compound Sentences with *But*

On a separate piece of paper, finish the following sentences with clauses introduced by *but*. **Reminder:** A *but* clause provides a contrast to the first clause.

EXAMPLES: a.   It was a beautiful day, *but I stayed in the house all day*.
              b.   He loves her very much, *but he isn't going to marry her*.

1. It's raining very hard,
2. They have a small house,
3. S/he's a very nice person,
4. I don't have much money,
5. His pronunciation is poor,
6. Mary doesn't love John,
7. S/he always studies very hard,
8. English is very difficult,
9. I didn't like the actor,
10. S/he has a good job,
11. Children are usually good,
12. I liked the food at the party,
13. We loved our hotel,
14. Paris is a beautiful city,
15. S/he doesn't like New York,
16. My vacation in Europe was expensive,
17. She's a beautiful woman,
18. The summer was hot and humid,

4.8

GRAMMAR EXERCISE

Focus: Compound Sentences with *So*

A clause introduced by *so* is called a RESULT CLAUSE because it shows the result of the first clause in a compound sentence.

On a separate piece of paper, finish the following incomplete sentences with clauses introduced by *so*.

EXAMPLES: a.   I was very tired, *so I went to bed early*.
              b.   The patient is feeling much better, *so she's going to leave the hospital today*.

1. It was a beautiful day,
2. I feel a little sleepy,
3. I didn't have an appetite,
4. It wasn't a very nice day,
5. I need a new coat,
6. I had a headache,
7. S/he isn't feeling well today,
8. I studied hard last night,
9. Jan didn't take good care of her house plants,
10. S/he likes to travel,
11. S/he's a very selfish person,
12. It was a very cold night,
13. It's going to be nice tomorrow,
14. S/he doesn't speak English,
15. I have no money,
16. S/he hates school/work,
17. I'm angry at him/her,
18. We love each other very much,

4.9

ABRIDGMENT OF SECOND MAIN CLAUSE

1. ABRIDGMENT means to shorten or to reduce in length; for example, in *She lives in Mexico, and her parents live in Mexico,* the second main clause reads and sounds repetitious. To avoid this unnecessary repetition, we may abridge the second clause through SUBSTITUTION.

2. There are several ways of substituting a second main clause:

   (a) An auxiliary can represent the omitted words in a clause of contrast: *He's not going to be there(,) but I **am**; They don't often go to the beach(,) but we **do**.*

   (b) An auxiliary plus the adverb *too* can substitute for a second main clause with an affirmative verb: *She studies very hard(,) and her roommate **does too**; My wife woke up early(,) and I **did too**.*

   (c) *So* plus an auxiliary may also act as an affirmative substitute. When this occurs, there is an inversion of the subject: *She's always studying hard(,) and **so am I**; He works very hard, and **so does his wife**.*
   Note: *So* (as an adverb) in this pattern has the meaning of *also. So* (as a coordinate conjunction) has the meaning of *therefore.*

   (d) An auxiliary plus *not* plus *either* may appear as a substitute for a second main clause with a negative verb: *We didn't enjoy ourselves(,) and the others **didn't either**; They're not going to take a vacation this year(,) and we **aren't either**.*

   (e) *Neither* plus an auxiliary also occurs as a negative substitute: *She doesn't like school(,) and **neither does** her brother; We didn't have a final examination(,) and **neither did** the other class.*

4.10

GRAMMAR EXERCISE
Name _____ Date _____

Focus: Substitution of a Main Clause with *But*

Fill in the blanks with appropriate auxiliaries (+ *not*).

EXAMPLES: a. Water doesn't contain any nitrogen, but air <u>does</u>.
b. The days in the Sahara are always hot, but the nights <u>aren't</u>.

1. A cat doesn't always respond to its name, but a dog _____.

2. The actors were wonderful, but the movie _____.

3. His dictionary cost a lot, but mine _____.

4. I'm not going to be here tomorrow, but everyone else _____.

5. Chinese is too difficult for me to learn, but English _____.

6. I got to the meeting on time, but nobody else _____.

7. He never does any homework, but all the other students _____.

8. My wife is going to be at the reception, but I _____.

9. The city has a lot of pollution, but the country _____.

10. It's not going to be nice today, but tomorrow _____.

4.11

GRAMMAR EXERCISE   Name _____ Date _____

Focus: Substitution of a Main Clause with *And*

Supply an appropriate auxiliary (affirmative or negative) plus *too* or *either* in the blank spaces.

EXAMPLES: a. That book cost a lot, and this one <u>did too</u>.
            b. They weren't at the last meeting, and we <u>weren't either</u>.

1. Cigarettes aren't good for you, and alcohol _____.

2. Time goes fast, and money _____.

3. She doesn't understand the explanation, and I _____.

4. His pronunciation is good, and his grammer _____.

5. I had a good time last night at the game, and s/he _____.

6. Love is important, and money _____.

7. Yesterday was a magnificent day, and the day before _____.

8. People in the East want peace, and people in the West _____.

9. He often gets into trouble in school, and his sister _____.

10. I didn't make the right decision, and you _____.

11. Women are usually afraid of snakes, and men _____.

12. She likes to practice yoga, and he _____.

13. He's often late to work, and everyone else _____.

14. They never travel abroad, and we _____.

15. Everyone wants to make a lot of money, and I _____.

16. I wasn't at the meeting last night, and a lot of others _____.

17. She never has time for recreation, and her brother _____.

18. The Japanese eat with chopsticks, and the Chinese _____.

19. English is difficult, and all other languages _____.

20. Tokyo is a very crowded city, and Hong Kong _____.

21. She never cheats on her income tax, and he _____.

22. Little girls are sometimes difficult, and little boys _____.

23. He never appreciates his parents, and his sister _____.

24. Diamonds are expensive, and pearls _____.

25. He's not completely satisfied with his life, and I _____.

26. Coffee is a stimulant, and tea _____.

27. Germans often have blonde hair, and Scandinavians _____.

28. China's population is extremely large, and India's _____.

29. She hurt herself on that machine, and I _____.

4.12

GRAMMAR EXERCISE   Name _____ Date _____

In the blanks, **supply** *so* or *neither* **plus an appropriate auxiliary. Note**: The use of *so* or *neither* causes inversion of the subject and verb.

EXAMPLES: a. Cleopatra killed herself, and <u>so did</u> Mark Antony.
               b. Yesterday wasn't nice, and <u>neither was</u> the day before.

1. Time goes incredibly fast, and _____ money.

2. I want to get a good grade in the course, and _____ everyone else.

3. Everyone in the class was wrong about the formula, and _____ the teacher.

4. Her husband didn't feel well on their vacation, and _____ she.

5. I didn't enjoy myself at the party, and _____ you.

6. John and Mary were absent yesterday, and _____ I.

7. She isn't a religious person, and _____ he.

8. A good radio costs a lot of money, and _____ a good TV.

9. This isn't appropriate for the occasion, and _____ that.

10. Our car cost a lot of money, and _____ our house.

11. The earth is circling around the sun, and _____ the other planets.

12. I'm eventually going to speak English well, and _____ everyone else in the group.

13. They're very unhappy with the political situation, and _____ we.

14. The French flag is red, white, and blue, and _____ the flag of the United States.

15. The East wants peace, and _____ the West.

16. Mr. and Mrs. Brown aren't here, and _____ the Smiths.

17. Venezuela has a lot of oil, and _____ Mexico.

18. An elephant is very large, and _____ a hippopotamus.

19. Jack is very happy with his job, and _____ I.

20. A donkey doesn't have much intelligence, and _____ a mule.

21. We don't want war, and _____ they.

22. The beach in the summer is nice, and _____ the mountains.

23. Tokyo has a lot of pollution, and _____ Los Angeles.

24. They never come late to the meetings, and _____ we.

25. You're going to have a successful life, and _____ I.

26. This exercise was easy, and _____ the last one.

4.13

GRAMMAR EXERCISE   Name _____ Date _____

Focus: Reviewing the Indefinite Article A, An or Zero Article

Supply *a*, *an*, or zero article in the blanks. First do this exercise as a quiz.

EXAMPLES: a. Rosemary is an herb. **Note**: *Herb* begins with a vowel sound; the *h* is silent.
b. I bought a new car yesterday.
c. 0 Deer are beautiful animals.

1. _____ university is _____ place of learning.

2. We're going to spend about _____ hour and _____ half at the park.

3. The Russian Revolution was _____ historical moment in history.

4. We saw _____ European film last night.

5. _____ meat is very expensive now. I baked _____ apple pie.

6. We're looking for _____ hotel in the middle of the city.

7. He does _____ half hour of exercise every morning.

8. Germany is not _____ united nation.

9. We had _____ unusual experience on our last vacation in China.

10. _____ women do not enjoy equality with _____ men in many places.

11. _____ ostrich thinks it is hidden when it buries its head.

12. _____ geese can be very vicious (cruel).

13. When we were at the reception, it was _____ honor to meet the King.

14. Our young son is quickly becoming _____ adult.

15. _____ children are _____ great responsibility.

16. _____ calculus was not _____ easy subject for me.

17. Pollution is _____ universal problem.

18. That young man is _____ heir to _____ great fortune.

19. _____ coffee is _____ stimulant.

20. Mary is _____ unusual woman.

21. _____ marriage is _____ union of two people.

22. _____ life is _____ mystery.

23. Do you have _____ aspirin? I have _____ headache.

24. _____ fish are fascinating to watch.

25. _____ octopus has many tentacles.

26. _____ house is not _____ home. (old saying)

27. _____ apple _____ day keeps the doctor away. (old saying)

28. _____ ounce of prevention is worth _____ pound of cure. (old saying)

4.14

GRAMMAR EXERCISE   Name _____ Date _____

Focus: Reviewing the Definite Article *The* or Zero Article

Supply *the* or zero article in the blanks. First do this exercise as a quiz.

EXAMPLES: a. <u>The</u> United States has a democratic government.
             b. <u>0</u> life is too short to worry about foolish things.

1. _____ Mt. Whitney (14,495 feet) is _____ highest mountain in California.

2. _____ Paris is often called _____ city of _____ light.

3. _____ Matterhorn is a beautiful mountain in _____ Switzerland.

4. _____ Hague is _____ capital of _____ Netherlands.

5. _____ fruit is good for your health. _____ fruit in the stores now isn't very good.

6. _____ air is composed of many gases.

7. _____ gas is an explosive.

8. _____ Amazon is _____ longest river in _____ South America.

9. _____ necessity is _____ mother of invention. (old saying)

10. _____ anthropology is the study of _____ man.

11. _____ water is not very plentiful in many parts of _____ world.

12. _____ love is stronger than _____ hate.

13. Everyone needs _____ sleep.

14. _____ air in the theater last night was bad.

15. _____ gas in the stove is leaking.

16. The Vikings were _____ first people to cross _____ Atlantic Ocean.

17. _____ money is a problem for most people. When you have it you don't need it, and when you need it you don't have it.

18. _____ money in this envelope is for Christmas presents.

19. _____ nature is a fascinating subject.

20. _____ nature of a mule is to be stubborn.

21. There are many political problems in _____ Union of South Africa.

22. _____ Soviet Union is _____ largest country in _____ world.

23. _____ rice is very good with _____ chicken.

24. _____ chicken in the refrigerator is for dinner.

25. _____ oil is an important natural resource of _____ Middle East.

26. _____ Hudson Bay is in _____ Canada.

27. Most of _____ South America is below _____ Equator.

28. _____ east coast of _____ Saudi Arabia is on _____ Persian Gulf.

29. _____ Asia is in _____ Eastern Hemisphere.

GRAMMAR EXERCISE   Name _____ Date _____

Supply an appropriate preposition in each blank. Do this exercise as a quiz.

at   between   down   during   from   in   on   through   up

EXAMPLES: a. Our son is graduating <u>from</u> the university in June.
            b. There is some bad news <u>in</u> the newspaper today.

1. I usually wake _____ early _____ the mornings.

2. We always have a big family picnic _____ July 4.

3. I fell asleep _____ the movie and didn't see the end.

4. The weather in California is wonderful _____ May.

5. The President of the United States lives _____ 1600 Pennsylvania Avenue.

6. Please put those tools _____ the bottom drawer of the cabinet.

7. Please wait for me _____ the corner _____ Broadway and Sixth Avenue.

8. The curtain is rising _____ seven o'clock.

9. There are a lot of good stores _____ Fifth Avenue.

10. What are you going to do _____ the Christmas holidays?

11. It's difficult for me to put thread _____ the eye of a needle.

12. We put our new TV set _____ the corner _____ our living room.

13. Bill is talking _____ the phone right now.

14. August is _____ July and September.

15. The climbers climbed _____ the mountain _____ the east side and climbed _____ _____ the west side.

16. Our plane is leaving _____ midnight.

17. What do you usually do _____ Sunday?

18. The rocket traveled _____ space at a fantastic speed.

19. There is a large fountain _____ front _____ our school.

20. My father's office is _____ the sixth floor of this building.

21. Are there any good programs _____ TV tonight?

22. Do you have your keys _____ your pocket?

23. The atlas is _____ the top shelf.

24. Who is your favorite actor _____ the movies?

25. Isn't that your wallet lying _____ the floor?

26. We keep a lot of old furniture _____ _____ the attic of our house.

27. We also keep some things _____ _____ the basement.

28. Look! There's a plane _____ _____ the sky.

GRAMMAR EXERCISE   Name _____ Date _____

Focus: Reviewing Prepositions

Supply an appropriate preposition in each blank.

at	for	from	in	into	of	on	out	to	up

EXAMPLES: a. I usually have my breakfast <u>on</u> my way <u>to</u> work.

b. I always stop at the store to buy groceries <u>on</u> my way home <u>from</u> work.

c. I came to school on the bus. I came <u>into</u> the room at ten o'clock.
Note: We come *to* a <u>place</u> (e.g., school, work), but we come *into* an <u>enclosure</u> (e.g., a room, a hall).

1. When are your friends leaving _____ South Africa?

2. What is the fastest way to get _____ _____ this city?

3. The astronauts conducted many scientific experiments _____ their way _____ the moon.

4. _____ my way home _____ the party, I had an accident.

5. What time did you come _____ this room today?

6. How do you come _____ school? How do you go home?
Reminder: With *come, go,* and *get,* no preposition precedes *home*.

7. When are we going to arrive _____ Peking?

8. What time does your boss usually arrive _____ the office?

9. Our son wants to get _____ Yale University.

10. Please stop _____ the store for some milk _____ your way home.

11. She left _____ school in a hurry. She left school at three o'clock.
Note: *To leave **for** a place* means *to leave one place for another; to leave a place* means *to exit*.

12. When are you going to get _____ _____ the meeting?

13. We always take our vacation _____ June.

14. The Queen came _____ the room, and everyone stood _____.

15. How did you come _____ that conclusion?

16. When I saw her _____ the party, she was _____ a fantastic dress.

17. Did you hear the news _____ the radio about the earthquake?

18. Is there anything interesting _____ the newspaper today?

19. You remind me _____ an old friend of mine.

20. _____ our way home _____ San Francisco, we stopped _____ Chicago for a few days.
Note: We stop *in* a city or a country, but we stop *at* a store, a bank, etc.

21. What time is the meeting going to come _____ an end?

22. This sentence is _____ the bottom _____ the page.

ADVERBIAL CLAUSES

5

5.1

SUBORDINATE CLAUSES

1. Unlike a main clause, a SUBORDINATE CLAUSE (dependent clause) cannot stand alone as a sentence; for example, the subordinate clause *because I didn't sleep well*, means nothing when it appears by itself; however, it has meaning when it is combined with a main clause: *I am very tired because I didn't sleep well*. A sentence containing both a main and subordinate clause is called a COMPLEX SENTENCE.

2. An ADVERBIAL CLAUSE is one type of subordinate clause. Some kinds of adverbial clauses are (a) time: *My grandfather is going to live in Florida **when he retires;*** (b) reason: *I don't want to go out **because it's too cold;*** and (c) contrast: ***Even though they're rich,*** *they're unhappy*.

3. SUBORDINATE CONJUNCTIONS connect a subordinate clause to a main clause. They are called introductory words (clause markers) because they introduce a subordinate clause to a sentence. A subordinate conjunction may appear as one word (*when*), two words (*even though*), or even three words (*as soon as*).

4. A TIME CLAUSE is a type of adverbial clause. Some time clauses and their special introductory words are (a) *when: I'm going to live in a warm climate **when I retire;*** (b) *before: We left the country **before the war began;*** (c) *after: She started crying **after she heard the news;*** (d) *until: He's going to love her **until the day he dies;*** and (e) *as soon as: I fell asleep **as soon as the movie began.***

5. A time clause most often occurs in the FINAL POSITION of a sentence: *I was tired **when I got home;** We were very happy **after we received the good news.*** No comma separates a main and time clause when the time clause is in final position.

6. A time clause sometimes occurs in the INITIAL POSITION of a sentence: ***Before I tell you the news,*** *please sit down;* ***After I got home last night,*** *I watched TV for a while*. In American English a comma usually separates a main and time clause when the time clause is in initial position.

5.2

Focus: Time Clauses with *When*

When a base form or an *-s* form follows *when, before,* and *after,* the meaning may be future time: ***I'm going to** get up when (before, after) the sun rises **tomorrow morning**.*

Supply *be going to* + a base form in the main clause, and a base form or an -s form in the time clause, in each of the following sentences.

EXAMPLES: a. (rise/be) When the sun rises, I'm going to be in my bed.
　　　　　　 b. (be/go) When the party is over (finished), I'm going to go home.

1. (take/have) They _____ a trip to Europe on a vacation when they _____ enough money and time.

2. (enter/finish) Mary _____ the University of Chicago when she _____ her English studies.

3. (watch/finish) I _____ TV for a while when I _____ my homework.

4. (wear/go) John _____ a tie and jacket when he _____ to the job interview.

5. (enter/stand) When the Queen _____ the reception hall, everyone _____ up.

6. (be/get) Nobody _____ in the house when I _____ home.

7. (have/be) When she finally _____ her baby, she _____ a very happy woman.

8. (wear/go) Barbara _____ her new dress when she _____ to her girl-friend's wedding next Saturday.

9. (go/end) I _____ home when this class _____.

10. (be/win) He _____ happy when he _____ the game.

11. (be/go) When the movie _____ over, I _____ straight home.

12. (be/get) The children _____ in bed when he _____ home.

13. (get/get) I _____ everything ready (to prepare things) for the party when I _____ back (return) to the house.

14. (have/end) Everyone _____ a big celebration when this century _____.

15. (speak/end) I _____ English better when this course _____.

16. (be/take) When the meeting _____ over, I _____ a walk.

17. (change/get) Bill _____ his clothes when he _____ home.

18. (serve/serve) She _____ wine when she _____ dinner.

19. (be/come) At his surprise birthday party, Jack _____ very surprised when all of his friends _____ into the house.

20. (study/enter) She _____ medicine when she _____ the university.

5.3

Focus: Time Clauses with *After* and *Before*

Supply *be going to* plus an appropriate base form in the main clause, and an appropriate base form or
-s form in the time clause, in each of the following sentences.

EXAMPLES: a. I'm <u>going to take</u> a vacation after this course <u>is</u> over.
             b. Before that mosquito <u>bites</u> me, <u>I'm going to kill</u> it.

1. He _____ to bed after he _____ his homework.

2. After I _____ breakfast, I _____ my teeth.

3. I _____ the ice in the refrigerator before it _____.

4. I _____ the dog for a walk before I _____ to bed.

5. She _____ the soup before she _____ the main course.

6. Before I _____ TV, I _____ those dirty dishes.

7. She _____ a new dress before she _____ out with that new fellow at
the office.

8. Before grandfather _____ dinner, he _____ a little nap.

9. Johnny _____ exercises on the piano before he _____ his homework.

10. I _____ dinner before I _____ to the movies.

11. We _____ a drive in the country in our new car before we _____
home.

12. After we _____ the game tomorrow, we _____ a victory celebration.

13. Everyone _____ English better before this course _____.

14. A lot of things _____ before this century _____.

15. After the class _____ over, everyone _____ lunch.

16. Before I _____ to the bank, I _____ some lunch.

17. I _____ everything ready before the guests _____.

18. He _____ a letter to the President before he _____ his taxes.

19. He _____ dinner before he _____ home from school.

20. Jack _____ a new car before he _____ out to California.

21. After I _____ up the apartment, I _____ it easy.

22. After this class _____, I _____ a little bit of an appetite.

23. I _____ a lot of things before today _____.

5.4

GRAMMAR EXERCISE   Name _____ Date _____

In information questions with time clauses, the main clause usually appears in the initial position of the sentence and the usual question forms are used: ***What are you going to do*** *when you get home?* ***Who is going to be home*** *when you get there?*
Note: The form of a time clause in a declarative sentence does not change when the sentence is transformed into an interrogative sentence: *He's going to get a job* ***when he graduates;*** *What is he going to do* ***when he graduates?***
A comma usually separates the main and time clauses of an information question when the time clause appears in the initial position of the sentence: *When you get home, who is going to be there?*

Supply appropriate base forms or -s forms in the blanks.

EXAMPLES: a. Where are you going to <u>be</u> when the sun <u>sets</u> this afternoon?
            b. What is the leader going to <u>do</u> when s/he <u>enters</u> the room tomorrow?

1. Where are you going to _____ when the sun _____ tomorrow morning? What are you going to _____ when your alarm _____?

2. When you _____ this course, what are you going to _____?

3. Who is going to _____ home when you _____ there this evening?

4. What are you going to _____ when you _____ a lot of money in the bank?

5. Who are you going to _____ with when you _____ back to your native country?

6. What are you going to _____ when summer _____?

7. What is going to _____ when spring _____?

8. When you _____ to the party, what color dress are you going to _____?

9. What are we going to _____ when we _____ this exercise?

10. What are you going to _____ on TV before you _____ to bed tonight?

11. What is your husband going to _____ before he _____ for work tomorrow morning?

12. Where are you going to _____ your school materials after you _____ your homework?

13. What are you going to _____ when the weather _____ warm/cold?

14. What am I going to _____ when I _____ into the room the next time?

15. What are you going to _____ when you _____ English well?

5.5

GRAMMAR EXERCISE   Name _____ Date _____

> Focus: Habitual Activity

> When we express an occasional or frequent activity, we use base forms or -s forms in both
> the main and time clauses of a sentence. When this occurs, frequency adverbs like *always,
> hardly ever, never, often, seldom, sometimes* and *usually* may appear in the main clause:
> *We **usually take** a picnic lunch when we go to the beach; I **never take** a lot of clothes when I
> go on a long trip.*
> **Reminder**: A comma usually separates a time clause and a main clause when the time
> clause occurs in the initial position of a sentence: *When the nice weather comes, we usually
> spend a lot of time in the mountains.*

Supply base forms or -s forms in the blanks.

EXAMPLES: a. In Mexico people often <u>take</u> a siesta (nap) after they <u>have</u> lunch.
            b. He seldom <u>has</u> Chinese food when he <u>goes</u> out to dinner.

1. When Mary _____ a trip to Europe, she usually _____ to Paris first.

2. I always _____ the phone when it _____.

3. After I _____ up in the morning, I usually _____ on the radio.

4. She usually _____ French food when she _____ out with Pierre on a date.

5. After I _____ breakfast, I always _____ my teeth.

6. He never _____ a cigarette when he _____ in an elevator; it's against the law
   (forbidden by law).

7. I never _____ on the radio when I _____ my homework.

8. My father always _____ his passport when he _____ on a business trip.

9. When we _____ on a long trip, we seldom _____ our children with us. My

   mother-in-law usually _____ care of them.

10. When my mother _____ cards, she hardly ever _____.

11. I always _____ the door when I _____ the house.

12. Our daughter usually _____ a good grade when she _____ a test.

13. When her husband _____ to Europe on business, she usually _____ with her
    mother.

14. My girlfriend usually _____ a bikini when she _____ to the beach.

15. My father always _____ an electric razor when he _____.

16. Our little boy sometimes _____ to wash his hands before he _____ down to
    dinner.

17. Maria always _____ -s forms when she _____ excited.

18. Barbara usually _____ worried when her husband _____ late.

19. We always _____ a lot of soda in the refrigerator when the weather _____ hot.

5.5 (Continued)

Now supply an adverb in the main clause as well.

20. I _____ a shower after I _____ tennis.

21. Bob _____ to the dentist when he _____ trouble with his teeth.

22. When they _____ a trip down to Mexico, they _____ their car.

23. When the President _____ a room, everyone _____ up.

24. When Jack _____ for a walk, he _____ his camera.

25. After my grandfather _____ lunch, he _____ a little walk.

26. Our teacher _____ a cigarette when we _____ a break.

27. We _____ to the beach when the weather _____ nice.

Now complete the sentences with appropriate clauses. Use commas when appropriate.

EXAMPLES: c. When I go to the beach, I usually take suntan lotion with me.
           d. I always have a good time when I go to their parties.

28. When I go on a vacation _____.

29. I usually take an aspirin_____.

30. When I have a birthday_____.

31. I usually take the bus _____.

32. When the teacher comes into the room _____.

33. I always say thank you _____.

34. My father always drinks a few cocktails _____.

35. My roommate always turns the radio on _____.

36. He always brushes his teeth _____.

37. My mother usually smokes a cigarette _____.

38. When the weather is nice _____.

39. When I take a trip _____.

40. After my father finishes dinner _____.

41. When the class is over_____.

42. When we take a break _____.

43. Before I come to school _____.

44. I sometimes take a nap _____.

45. I never go to bed late _____.

46. When I do my homework _____.

5.6

Focus: The Simple Past Tense in Main and Time Clauses

Supply appropriate past forms of the following regular and irregular verbs in the blanks.

arrive	come	fix	laugh	rise	turn
be	do	get	leave	sign	visit
become	eat	give	lock	smoke	walk
break	end	go	put	take	watch
brush	fall	have	read	tell	wear

EXAMPLES: a. I took off my coat after I walked into the room.

               b. He brushed his teeth after he had breakfast.

1. After I _____ my homework, I _____ quite tired.

2. I _____ up yesterday morning before the sun _____.

3. I _____ my school materials on my desk when I _____ home.

4. Everyone _____ here when I _____ into the room today.

5. I _____ the contract very carefully before I _____ it.

6. His parents _____ him a lovely present when he _____ twenty-one.

7. Their little boy _____ sick to his stomach after he _____ some green apples.

8. I _____ very excited when I _____ at the airport in Tokyo.

9. Everyone at the party _____ a lot when I _____ them the funny story about myself.

10. She _____ flowers with her when she _____ her friend in the hospital.

11. I _____ off the radio before I _____ to bed.

12. A mechanic _____ our car before we _____ on our trip.

13. She _____ a new dress when she _____ to the wedding.

14. I _____ on the radio after I _____ up this morning.

15. S/he _____ a cigarette when s/he _____ a break.

16. No one _____ there when I _____ into the room.

17. Everyone in the world _____ happy when the war in Vietnam _____.

18. When the electric power _____ off, I _____ in an elevator.

19. The kids _____ to bed after they _____ that program on TV.

20. He _____ his arm when he _____ down on a wet sidewalk.

21. He _____ the door before he _____ the house.

5.7

Focus: *As Soon As*

Supply appropriate past forms of the following regular and irregular verbs in the blanks. *As soon as* means *at the exact moment.*

arrive	eat	finish	lie	receive	spend	tell
be	end	get	meet	ring	stand	turn
begin	enter	go	open	rise	start	wake
buy	fall	hear	pay	send	take	write
drink	feed	leave				

EXAMPLES: a. I <u>fed</u> my dog his dinner as soon as I <u>got</u> home.
b. We <u>left</u> the theater as soon as the movie <u>ended</u>.

1. S/he _____ to cry as soon as I _____ him/her the news.

2. I _____ my return ticket as soon as I _____ at the airport.

3. I _____ the bill as soon as I _____ it in the mail.

4. I _____ the coat as soon as I _____ the money.

5. He _____ off his hat as soon as he _____ the church.

6. They _____ in love with each other as soon as they _____.

7. I _____ asleep as soon as I _____ into bed.

8. My headache _____ away as soon as I _____ an aspirin.

9. I _____ bored as soon as that terrible movie _____.

10. Everyone _____ up as soon as the President _____ the room.

11. I _____ a little nap as soon as I _____ home.

12. I _____ on the radio as soon as I _____ up.

13. The meeting _____ as soon as the leader _____.

14. I _____ all the windows as soon as I _____ home.

15. We _____ up yesterday morning as soon as the sun _____.

16. I _____ the house as soon as I _____ breakfast.

17. We _____ a reply to the government authorities as soon as we _____ their letter.

18. The class _____ as soon as the bell _____.

19. That young man/woman _____ drunk as soon as s/he _____ one cocktail.

20. I _____ most of my money as soon as I _____ my paycheck.

21. I _____ the clothes off the clothes line as soon as they _____ dry.

22. I _____ sick as soon as I _____ that greasy food.

23. Grandfather _____ down for a nap as soon as he _____ lunch.

5.8

GRAMMAR EXERCISE   Name _____ Date _____

Focus: Information Questions in the Simple Past Tense

Supply an appropriate base form in the main clause and an appropriate past form in the time clause.

EXAMPLES: a. What did you <u>do</u> as soon as you <u>got</u> home last night?
           b. What did you <u>put</u> on when you <u>left</u> the house this morning?

   1. What did you _____ after you _____ dinner last night?

   2. What did you _____ off after you _____ into this room today?

   3. Who did you _____ to first when you _____ home last night?

   4. How did you _____ when you _____ up this morning?

   5. What kind of cocktail did you _____ before you _____ dinner last night?

   6. What did you _____ yesterday after the meeting _____ over?

   7. Where did you _____ before you _____ to school today?

   8. Who did you _____ with before you _____ married?

   9. What did you _____ when you _____ to the store yesterday?

 10. What did I _____ when I _____ into this room today?

Now supply appropriate past forms in both main and time clauses. **Reminder**: *Did* does not occur in questions when an information word(s) is the subject of the sentence: *Who invented dynamite?* (but *When did Nobel invent it?*)

EXAMPLES: c. What countries in the world <u>became</u> independent after the Second World War <u>ended</u>?
           d. Who <u>was</u> here before I <u>came</u> into the class today?

 11. Who _____ the President of the United States after Richard Nixon _____? (Use *quit* or *resigned*.)

 12. Who _____ in this room when you _____ here today?

 13. What _____ to your life after you _____ married?

 14. How many people _____ down with the ship when the *S.S. Titanic* _____ in 1912?

 15. What _____ as soon as you _____ to the party?

 16. Who _____ in the house when you _____ up this morning?

 17. How many people _____ there in this room when you _____ in?
     Note: The preposition *into* does not appear at the end of an interrogative sentence.

 18. Who _____ to you first when you _____ into the house?

 19. What _____ to the aristocrats in France when the revolution _____ place?

5.9

Focus: Time Clauses with *Until*

In addition to the introductory words *when, before,* and *after,* we may also express an event in the future with *until* followed by a base form or an *-s* form: *I'm not going to tell you my secret **until you tell me yours**.*

Supply an appropriate negative form of *be going to* + a base form in the main clause, and an appropriate base form or -s form in the time clause.

EXAMPLES: a. The class isn't going to begin until the teacher comes.
              b. We're not going to leave the theater until the play is over.

1. They _____ happy until they _____ a lot of money in the bank.

2. S/he _____ a good job until s/he _____ and _____ English well.

3. This soup _____ any good until you _____ some more salt in it.

4. The class _____ until the bell _____.

5. I _____ dinner until the last guest _____.

6. They _____ married until they both _____ good jobs.

7. I _____ dinner until I _____ one more cocktail.

8. We _____ lunch until the chicken _____ ready.

9. I _____ the kitchen until I _____ the last dish.

10. I _____ up until the sun _____.

11. John _____ a new car until he _____ enough money to pay cash. (*To pay cash* means *to pay without credit.*)

12. We _____ the next exercise until we _____ this one.

13. We _____ satisfied until we _____ the top of the mountain.

14. Mary _____ anything else until she _____ her project.

15. I _____ satisfied with myself until I _____ this language well.

5.10

Focus: Clauses of Reason with *Because*

1. The subordinate conjunction *because* is used as an introductory word in a CLAUSE OF REASON: *She's a little unhappy **because her boyfriend forgot her birthday**.* A *because* clause answers *why: Why is he poor? . . . because he's lazy; Why is the male lion so lazy? . . . because the female does everything for him.*

2. A *because* clause usually occurs in the final position of a sentence; however, it sometimes appears in the initial position: ***Because I was angry at my boss**, I quit my job.*
   Reminder: When an adverbial clause is present in the initial position of a sentence, a comma usually separates it from the main clause.

Complete the following sentences with clauses of reason introduced by the subordinate conjunction *because*. Use the present or present continuous tense, the simple past tense, or *be going to* + a base form only.

EXAMPLES: a. I'm not tired because I slept very well last night.
               b. We're not going on a vacation because we don't have any money.

1. I'm very hungry _____.

2. I'm reading this book _____.

3. S/he's worried _____.

4. I'm pleased _____.

5. I'm in a good mood _____.

6. They're disappointed _____.

7. I don't like him/her _____.

8. John is an interesting person _____.

9. I'm very happy today _____.

10. The teacher is angry _____.

11. They're very excited _____.

12. I like (name of city) _____.

13. I like (name of person) _____.

14. I don't like (_____) _____.

15. I (don't) like American food _____.

16. She is angry at him _____.

17. I'm afraid of (_____) _____.

18. I'm learning English _____.

19. I am tired _____.

20. I am laughing _____.

21. S/he is popular _____.

22. I like (supply infinitive) _____.

5.11

NEGATIVE QUESTIONS

1. In negative *yes-no* questions, the adverb *not* contracted with the verb *be* or other auxiliary verbs precedes the subject: ***Isn't their little girl cute? Don't you want to go for a walk? Didn't you*** *sleep well?*

2. When we ask a negative *yes-no* question, we usually expect our listener to agree with us (say *yes*): *Isn't it a beautiful day?* ***Yes, it is;*** *Isn't he a nice person?* ***He certainly is.***

3. We also use a negative *yes-no* question to show great surprise or irritation (anger): *Didn't you pay your taxes? Aren't you making a foolish mistake?*

4. In very formal usage, the adverb *not* appears after the subject in a negative question: *Is the* ***government not*** *going to make a decision soon? Did the* ***Ambassador not*** *sign the document?*

5. When we are surprised, irritated, or wanting confirmation, the formal *Am I not?* is replaced by *Aren't I?* in informal usage: ***Aren't I*** *making a stupid mistake?* ***Aren't I*** *your friend?* ***Aren't I*** *being a little foolish?*

6. *Why* is the usual information word that occurs in a negative information question: ***Why don't you*** *relax?* ***Why didn't you*** *send any Christmas cards last year?*

7. A negative information question with *why* may also take the form of a polite request: *Why don't you take off your coat and visit me for a while? Why don't you make yourself more comfortable?*

   Pronunciation Note: (a) *Aren't you* sounds like *aren't-chew;* (b) *don't you* sounds like *don't-chew;* (c) *didn't you* sounds like *didn't-chew;* and (d) *weren't you* sounds like *weren't-chew.*

5.12

GRAMMAR EXERCISE   Name _____ Date _____

Focus: Negative Questions

Fill in the blanks with *aren't, isn't, wasn't, weren't, don't, doesn't,* or *didn't.*

EXAMPLES: a. <u>Didn't</u> you have a good time at the dance last night?
   b. <u>Don't</u> you like Paris? I am really surprised.

1. _____ your parents going to be at your graduation next week?

2. _____ I a good friend of yours? _____ you trust me?

3. _____ you at the meeting yesterday?

4. _____ your lawyer take care of the problem last week?

5. _____ you going to be here tomorrow? I am really disappointed.

6. _____ it raining outside? It sounds like it.

7. _____ you love your mother and father? I can't believe it.

8. _____ the movie last night good?

5.12 *(Continued)*

Name _____ Date _____

9. _____ I responsible for myself?

10. _____ you have enough money to eat lunch today?

11. _____ your husband come home last night?

12. _____ you believe in God?

13. _____ you sick? You look it.

14. Why _____ you go call the police when they robbed your house?

15. Why _____ I a millionaire? Why _____ I have more money?

16. Why _____ you want a Christmas present?

17. What _____ you understand?

18. Why _____ you put the ice cream in the refrigerator before it melted? Why _____ you more careful?

19. Why _____ the children in their beds?

20. Why _____ they have breakfast before they went to school today?

21. Why _____ there peace in the Middle East?

22. Why _____ I doing the right thing? How am I wrong?

23. Why _____ you going to enter the university next fall?

24. Why _____ you want to tell me about your problem?

25. Why _____ he get to the meeting on time yesterday?

26. Why _____ you going home when the class is over?

Now complete the sentences.

27. Why aren't _____?

28. Why isn't_____?

29. Why don't _____?

30. Why doesn't _____?

31. Why didn't _____?

32. Why wasn't _____?

33. Why weren't _____?

34. _____ to the party?

35. _____ your homework?

36. _____ tomorrow?

37. _____ yesterday?

38. _____ when you were sick?

39. _____ when you saw me?

5.13

GRAMMAR EXERCISE   Name _____ Date _____

Focus: Concessive Clauses with *Even Though*

The subordinate conjunction *even though* introduces a contrast clause of concession: ***Even though they have a lot of money***, *they are very selfish people*. The main clause in a sentence with an *even though* clause is called a clause of unexpected result because we are surprised; for example, in *Even though I was tired, I went to the party*, the main clause *I went to the party* surprises us. An *even though* clause most frequently appears in the initial position of a sentence.

Complete the following sentences with an appropriate main clause. Use the simple present and past tenses or *be going to* + a base form.

EXAMPLES: a. Even though they are a good football team, they never win a game.
              b. Even though it's cold, I'm going to take a walk in the park.

1. Even though he has an important job in the company, _____

_____

2. _____ even though I'm not very tired.

3. Even though I have little appetite, _____

_____

4. Even though they have everything they need, _____

_____

5. _____ even though it's raining.

6. Even though s/he's a very popular person _____

_____

7. Even though I'm extremely tired, _____

_____

8. Even though the material in the course is getting more difficult, _____

_____

9. Even though s/he is a little heavy, _____

_____

10. Even though s/he believes in God, _____

_____

11. Even though grandmother is taking medicine, _____

_____

12. Even though I sent a lot of cards last Christmas, _____

_____

THE PAST CONTINUOUS TENSE

6

6.1

EMPHASIZING PAST EVENTS

1. One use of the PAST CONTINUOUS TENSE is for emphasizing an event that took place at one point of time in the past: *Their plane **was taking** off for Rio at exactly this time yesterday afternoon; Everyone in the house **was sleeping** at the time of the fire; It **was raining** early this morning.*

2. To form the past continuous tense, *was* and *were* are used as auxiliaries, and a present participle serves as a main verb. *Not* is inserted between the auxiliary and the main verb in a negative verb phrase.

	Singular	Plural
First person	I was (not) working	we
Second person	you were (not) working	you } were (not) working
Third person	he she } was (not) working it	they

3. The subject of a sentence follows the auxiliary in *yes-no* and information questions: ***Was the General** receiving accurate information at the time of the attack? Who **were you** talking to on the phone a few minutes ago?*

4. Like information questions containing other verb tenses, the usual question form does not occur when an information word(s) is the subject of a sentence: ***How many people** were sitting in the theater when the fire started? **What** was happening in the world when you were born?*

SPELLING BEE (CONTEST) Name _____ Date _____

Make present participles (-*ing* forms) out of the base forms in the following list.

EXAMPLES: a. get getting
b. try trying

1. bring _____
2. set _____
3. lie _____
4. plan _____
5. turn _____
6. take _____
7. begin _____
8. die _____
9. copy _____
10. drive _____
11. stop _____
12. hit _____
13. rise _____
14. stay _____
15. swim _____
16. blow _____
17. tie _____
18. cut _____

163

6.2

Focus: One Point of Time in the Past

Fill in the blanks with appropriate affirmative or negative verb phrases in the past continuous tense.

EXAMPLES:
  a. I <u>was listening</u> to the news at 7:30 this morning.
  b. They <u>weren't sleeping</u> at the time of the earthquake, fortunately.

1. He _____ his homework around eleven last night.

2. Yesterday, I _____ home on the bus at three o'clock.

3. A beautiful woman _____ flowers in her hair at the dance last night, and everyone _____ at her.

4. My parents were in Lebanon in 1974, and the civil war _____.

5. They had wonderful food on the picnic, but, unfortunately, it _____ hard.

6. People _____ down at the reception because it was too crowded. Everyone _____ up.

7. Some boys _____ baseball in the street early this afternoon.

8. Fortunately, I _____ in my bed at the time of the fire.

9. A lot of women _____ long dresses at the cocktail party two nights ago.

10. Fortunately, people _____ in the factory at the time of the explosion, so nobody was hurt.

11. He _____ well yesterday morning, so he went home.

12. The wind _____ hard yesterday afternoon.

13. I _____ a letter at eight o'clock last night. I know because I gave my watch a quick look at the time.

14. Few people _____ in Siberia at the turn of the century.

15. I _____ for Christmas presents at lunchtime.

16. I _____ to the teacher about my homework before the class began. Nobody else _____ in the room at the time.

17. I got very wet yesterday morning because I didn't have my umbrella, and it _____ hard.

18. Everybody _____ at the monkeys in the cage when we were at the zoo. Everybody _____ them peanuts.

19. Unfortunately, the sun _____ when we were at the beach.

20. Everyone _____ about the past continuous tense at the beginning of this exercise.

21. I _____ anything in particular yesterday afternoon.

22. Nobody _____ about anything special at the meeting.

6.3

GRAMMAR EXERCISE   Name _____ Date _____

Focus: The Past Continuous Tense in Complex Sentences

The major use of the past continuous tense is in a main clause of a complex sentence that has a time clause in the past tense: *We **were living** in Saigon when the war in Vietnam **came** to an end.* In effect, the past action that is expressed in the time clause suddenly (sometimes by surprise) interrupts the past continuing action that is expressed in the main clause: *When we arrived at the ball* (interruption), *everyone was dancing; When I walked into the room* (interruption), *everyone was talking about me.*

Reminder: A comma usually separates a main and time clause when the time clause occurs in the initial position of a sentence: *When the earthquake occurred, most people were sleeping.*

Supply an appropriate past form in the time clause and an appropriate verb phrase in the past continuous tense in the main clause in each of the following sentences.

EXAMPLES: a. I was thinking about my girlfriend when the mailman delivered a letter from her.
             b. Hitler wasn't thinking when he made the decision to invade Russia.

1. She _____ dinner when she _____ her hand with a sharp knife.

2. Jack's father _____ his car to work when he suddenly _____ a heart attack.

3. When I _____ into the classroom yesterday morning, the janitor _____ the blackboard.

4. The little girl _____ any clothes when she _____ into the crowded room.

5. Unfortunately, I _____ an umbrella when it _____ to rain yesterday afternoon.

6. When we _____ at the concert hall, the orchestra _____ to play.

7. When I _____ to the party, a lovely girl with long hair _____ a guitar and _____ folk songs.

8. I _____ when I _____ that careless mistake.

9. Mom _____ dinner when I _____ home last night.

10. I _____ my breakfast when the phone _____ .

11. Birds _____ in the tree outside my bedroom window when I _____ up this morning. It was a lovely sound.

12. I _____ to the radio when the sensational news suddenly _____ on. (Use *came.*)

13. The thief _____ a gun when he _____ the elderly woman on the street.

14. I _____ about my last vacation when my alarm clock _____ this morning.

15. When I _____ Mary up last night on the phone, she _____ her homework.

16. Fortunately, people _____ in the factory when the explosion _____.

17. Unfortunately, my roommate _____ well when s/he _____ up yesterday morning.

18. When I _____ my parents at the airport, both of them _____.

19. What a surprise! I _____ about you when I _____ your letter.

20. My mother _____ a beautiful dress when she _____ married.

21. The mailman _____ the mail when I _____ the house for work this morning.

22. I _____ in the garden when it suddenly _____ to rain very hard.

23. All the students _____ at their desks when the bell _____.

24. When I _____ home last night, everyone in the family _____ TV.

25. The bride _____ a white dress when I _____ her at the wedding.

26. When I _____ to the corner of Fifth Avenue and 57th Street, my girlfriend/boyfriend _____ for me.

27. When I _____ Mary at the picnic, she _____ a blue dress with white polka dots.

28. The patient _____ when the doctor finally _____ at the hospital.

29. What a nice surprise! I _____ about a good friend of mine when I suddenly _____ a letter from her in my mailbox.

6.4

GRAMMAR EXERCISE   Name _____ Date _____

Focus: *Yes-No Questions*

Supply *was* or *were* in the first blank, an appropriate present participle in the second blank, and an appropriate past form in the third blank.

EXAMPLES: a. <u>Was</u> the curtain <u>rising</u> when you <u>entered</u> the theater last night?
          b. <u>Were</u> you <u>listening</u> to the radio when the news about the war <u>came</u> on?

1. _____ it _____ when you _____ up this morning?

2. _____ I _____ an umbrella when I _____ into the room today?

3. _____ you _____ in the theater when the concert _____?

4. _____ the sun _____ when you _____ on the picnic?

5. _____ you _____ about anything in particular when you _____ to bed last night?

6. _____ you _____ well when you _____ up yesterday morning?

7. _____ he _____ a cigarette when you _____ him outside in the hall?

8. _____ the wind _____ very hard when you _____ at the beach?

9. _____ the two of you _____ about me when I rudely _____ your conversation?

10. _____ anybody _____ here when you _____ into the room today?

11. _____ anyone _____ TV when you _____ home last night?

12. _____ I _____ an overcoat when I _____ the room yesterday?

13. _____ your mother _____ at school when she _____ your father?

14. _____ you _____ about anything in particular when we _____ this exercise?

15. _____ the sun _____ when you _____ school yesterday afternoon?

16. _____ you _____ about anything in particular when you _____ up this morning?

17. _____ the mailman _____ the mail when you _____ the house this morning?

18. _____ the orchestra _____ up when you _____ the theater?

19. _____ the children _____ outside when you _____ them to come in?

20. _____ your favorite team _____ its best when you _____ to the game last Saturday?

GRAMMAR EXERCISE   Name _____ Date _____

Focus: Information Questions

Supply appropriate words in the blanks.

EXAMPLES: a. <u>What was happening</u> when you <u>came</u> into the room today?
            b. <u>Why were you crying</u> when I <u>saw</u> you outside in the hall?
            c. <u>Where were</u> your mother and father <u>living</u> when you were born?

1. When you _____ into the room today, what _____?

2. What _____ you _____ when I _____ you up last night?

3. How _____ you _____ when you _____ up this morning?

4. _____ when you arrived at the game?

5. What color umbrella _____ I _____ when I _____ into the room?

6. Who _____ you _____ to when I _____ into the room?

7. What _____ you _____ when the phone _____?

8. Who _____ TV when you _____ home last night?

9. Who _____ you _____ lunch with when I _____ you in the cafeteria last Wednesday?

10. What _____ you _____ about when you _____ to school yesterday morning?

11. When you got to work yesterday, _____?

12. When you got to the swimming pool, _____?

13. What _____ in the world when you _____ born?

14. What _____ you wearing when you _____ your diploma at graduation?

15. Who _____ sitting in this room when you _____ in?

16. What kind of dress _____ when I _____ you at the party the other night?

17. What _____ when you arrived at the airport?

18. What kind of typewriter _____ when you _____ this letter?

19. How _____ the patient _____ when he _____ out of the hospital?

20. What kind of car _____ when he _____ the accident?

21. Where _____ your parents _____ when the war _____?

22. What _____ you _____ about when you _____ up yesterday morning?

23. When you got home last night, _____?

24. When you woke up yesterday morning, _____?

25. When you arrived at the meeting, _____?

6.6

Name _____ Date _____

Focus: Emphasizing the Duration of an Event in the Past

The past continuous tense is sometimes used to emphasize the duration of an event in past time that has a beginning and an end: *I was shopping for your present* **all day long**; *My phone was constantly ringing* **from the beginning to the end of the day**.
Note: For expressing duration in the past, the simple past and the past continuous are essentially interchangeable; the past continuous only gives greater emphasis: *Life was changing (changed) very quickly during the second half of the nineteenth century*.

Fill in the blanks with appropriate verb phrases in the past continuous tense. Do not use negative forms in this exercise.

EXAMPLES: a. The team <u>was celebrating</u> its victory at the Olympics all night long.
             b. Yesterday, <u>I was cleaning</u> my apartment from the time I got up to the time I went to bed.
             c. Dr. Johnson was very busy at the hospital yesterday. S/he <u>was delivering</u> babies all day long.

1. I _____ at the library from three o'clock in the afternoon to around ten at night.

2. His wife had a baby yesterday morning, and he _____ congratulations at the office all day long.

3. I _____ about only myself during the fire at the factory.

4. We _____ in the ocean every day all summer long.

5. Everyone in the theater _____ during the whole movie.

6. A lot of aristocrats _____ their heads during the French Revolution.

7. It _____ hard during our whole vacation in the mountains.

8. The wind _____ unbelievably hard during the hurricane. It _____ _____ very hard, too.

9. Unfortunately, I _____ bad dreams all night long.

10. We _____ TV all evening long.

11. They _____ with each other from the day they got married to the day they got a divorce.

12. Many people _____ a lot of money during the last war.

13. She _____ about many events in her past life during her serious illness.

14. They _____ champagne during the reception for the King.

15. I _____ a lot of problems with my boss all week long.

16. When I was in London, it _____ all the time.

17. We _____ about only the past continuous tense during this exercise.

6.7

Name _____ Date _____

Focus: The Past Continuous Tense with Expletive *There*

Supply an appropriate form of the verb *be* in the first blank and an appropriate present participle in the second blank.

cook	happen	participate	run	stand	vote	work
dance	have	perform	shop	take	wait	
eat	live	play	sit	travel	walk	

EXAMPLES: a. There <u>were</u> a few people <u>sitting</u> in the room when I came in.
            b. There <u>wasn't</u> anything <u>cooking</u> on the stove when I got home.

1. _____ there any good musicians _____ in the last concert?

2. How many people _____ there _____ in this room at the last meeting?

3. _____ there anyone _____ care of your children when you were at the store?

4. _____ there a lot of people _____ in line for tickets when you got to the theater?

5. There _____ any other people except me _____ in the grocery store yesterday afternoon.

6. There _____ a very important meeting _____ place yesterday at noon.

7. There _____ a lot of patients _____ for the doctor when I got to his office.

8. There _____ a lot of people _____ in the park yesterday.

9. How many people _____ there _____ in the last election?

10. How many horses _____ there _____ in the last race?

11. Besides you, how many people _____ there _____ in the debate?

12. How many people _____ there _____ in England at the time of Shakespeare?

13. There _____ only a few children _____ in the playground during the morning. But there _____ a lot of older people _____ on the benches.

14. There _____ a lot of people _____ a party next door last night.

15. There _____ no people _____ at the party on Saturday night, so it wasn't much fun.

16. There _____ anything _____ at the meeting, so we decided to leave.

17. There _____ many people _____ in the restaurant when we were there.

18. There _____ a lot of tourists _____ on the busses and trains when we were in Scandinavia on our last vacation.

19. There _____ much _____ in town last Sunday.

6.8

WHILE

1. The subordinate conjunction *while* appears in a complex sentence in which both the main and time clauses contain the past continuous tense: *While I was talking to that shy girl, she was blushing; His heart was beating fast while he was listening to the exciting news; While I was studying at the university at night, I was working during the day.*

2. When *while* occurs in a time clause, we are emphasizing the duration of two events taking place at the same time at a specific point of time in the past: *While I was talking to him* (at the same time), *he wasn't paying much attention to me; When they met each other at the airport, they were both crying while* (at the same time) *they were laughing.*

3. *While* emphasizes the duration of an event or the passage of time: *While they were climbing Mt. Everest* (during the climb), *a hard wind was blowing; While the patient was dying* (during that time), *everyone in the room was crying.*

4. *When* is used for an event that takes place at a specific moment, or for an event that has no duration: *When they reached the top of Mt. Everest* (at that moment), *the sun was rising over the Himalayas; When the patient died* (at that moment), *everyone in the room was crying.*
   Note: In current usage, we sometimes see and hear the past continuous tense in a *when* clause; however, the simple past tense is preferred.

6.9

GRAMMAR EXERCISE

Name _____ Date _____

Focus: *While*

Fill in the blanks with appropriate verbs in the past continuous tense; use present participles made from the base forms in the following list.

admire	discuss	explain	have	paint	think
blow	do	fly	laugh	play	wave
climb	draw	get	listen	take	write
dictate	eat	give	make	talk	

EXAMPLES:
a. While the artist was painting her portrait, she was admiring his handsome profile.
b. The little boy was laughing a lot while he was playing with the cat.

1. While we _____ the mountain, the wind _____ hard.

2. While he _____ the problem with his boss, he _____ about his girlfriend.

3. I _____ to the radio this morning while I _____ dressed.

4. While I _____ to the teacher's explanation, I _____ about the person next to me.

6.9 (Continued)

5. While the teacher _____ the complicated formula, she _____ a diagram on the blackboard.

6. The radio _____ while I _____ the crossword puzzle.

7. While he _____ the letter, his secretary _____ in short-hand.

8. He was going to night school for a couple of years. While he _____ money during the day, he _____ progress in his English at night.

9. While the traffic cop _____ his whistle, he _____ his hand to direct traffic.

10. While she _____ dinner ready, her husband _____ the children their baths.

11. He _____ her beautiful figure while he _____ to her about the homework for their class.

12. A lot of people _____ kites while I _____ a walk through the park.

13. We _____ delicious appetizers while we _____ cocktails.

6.10

GRAMMAR EXERCISE

Name _____ Date _____

Focus: *When* and *While*

Finish the following incomplete sentences with appropriate main clauses. Use the past continuous tense only.

EXAMPLES: a. When I heard on the radio that the President was dead, <u>I was driving my car to Florida.</u>
b. While I was coming to school, <u>I was thinking about you.</u>

1. While he was taking care of the children, _____.

2. When she walked into her husband's office, _____.

3. When the phone rang, _____.

4. When I was born, _____.

5. When the lights suddenly went off, _____.

6. While her husband was fighting in the war, _____.

6.10 *(Continued)*

7. When I woke/got up this morning, _____.

8. While I was doing my homework, _____.

9. When I last saw my mother/father at the airport, _____.

10. While he was talking about all of his problems, _____.

11. When I saw her at the store/the party/the beach, _____.

12. While I was getting ready to go to school/work, _____.

13. When I went to bed last night, _____.

14. When my father met my mother, _____.

15. While I was doing this exercise, _____.

6.11

GRAMMAR EXERCISE

Focus: *Because* Clauses

Complete the following sentences with appropriate clauses of reason introduced by *because*. Use the past continuous tense only.

EXAMPLES: a. He was blushing <u>because his girlfriend was teasing him</u>.
b. I lay down for a nap this afternoon around three <u>because I was feeling a little tired</u>.

1. There was a terrible smell in the kitchen _____.

2. I didn't sleep well last night _____.

3. I didn't understand him/her _____.

4. S/he took the bus to work yesterday morning _____.

5. There was a long line of people at the corner _____.

6. The sidewalks were very slippery _____.

7. We didn't go for a drive in the country last Sunday _____.

8. I was angry at myself _____.

9. I didn't know the time _____.

10. Our vacation at the beach wasn't very nice _____.

6.12

GRAMMAR EXERCISE   Name _____ Date _____

Focus: Reviewing Prepositions

Supply an appropriate preposition in each blank. Do this exercise as a quiz.

about	around	during	in	of	to
across	at	from	into	on	

EXAMPLES: a. Charles Lindbergh was the first person to fly <u>across</u> the Atlantic.
    b. He did it <u>in</u> 1927.

1. The Panama Canal connects the Pacific _____ the Atlantic.

2. What time is the President going to arrive _____ the reception?

3. What _____ the world is that strange-looking object?

4. Don't walk _____ the street when the light is red, children.

5. Please take care _____ this problem right away. Do it before the boss comes back _____ the office.

6. I got _____ work yesterday before everyone else.

7. When is the French Ambassador going to arrive _____ Washington?

8. What are you going to be doing _____ the spring vacation?

9. Children, be sure to look both ways when you walk _____ the Avenue.

10. Jack, would you please stop _____ the drugstore _____ your way home _____ work. Bobby is sick _____ bed with the flu.

11. Isn't your vacation going to begin _____ April 1?

12. Ferdinand Magellan was the first person to try to sail _____ the world.

13. What time are you coming _____ school tomorrow?

14. Everyone laughed when the little boy came _____ the room without any clothes on.

15. We usually pick the apples off our tree _____ September.

16. Betsy, please put your toys _____ the toy box.

17. I always keep my dictionary _____ the top drawer _____ my desk.

18. A lot of people were dancing _____ the party last night.

19. Why is he always worrying _____ his business?

20. Potatoes grow _____ the ground. Tomatoes grow _____ a vine. Apples grow _____ trees. Birds live _____ trees.

21. The bee stung our boy _____ his nose.

22. Listen! Isn't there someone knocking _____ the door?

23. She was working _____ her garden _____ early morning _____ late afternoon.

24. My dog doesn't like to wear a collar _____ his neck.

COMPARISON

7.1

COMPARISON OF ADJECTIVES

1. A SYLLABLE is a unit of spoken language; for example, the word *syllable* consists of three units: *syl-la-ble; few* contains one syllable; *easy* has two syllables: *eas-y; beautiful* has three syllables: *beau-ti-ful; intelligent* has four syllables: *in-tel-li-gent*. Any good dictionary gives the syllabic division of a word.

2. There are three degrees for the comparison of adjectives: (a) the COMPARATIVE DEGREE: *English is **easier than** many other languages;* (b) the SUPERLATIVE DEGREE: *French wine is* ***the best*** *in the world;* and (c) the POSITIVE DEGREE: *Work is **as important as** pleasure.*

3. The conjunction *than* always appears in the comparative degree: *Nothing is more important **than** love; Men are usually taller **than** women.*

Rules for Forming the Comparative Degree

(a) Adjectives of one syllable: Add *-er* to the adjective and add *than: old, older than; fast, faster than; few, fewer than.*

(b) One-syllable adjectives ending in a final single consonant preceded by a single vowel: Double the final consonant before adding *-er* and add *than: big, bigger than; thin, thinner than; hot, hotter than.*

(c) Two-syllable adjectives ending in *-y* preceded by a consonant: Change the *-y* to *-i* and add *-er* and *than: easy, easier than; tasty, tastier than; crazy, crazier than; happy, happier than.*

(d) Two-syllable adjectives ending in *-er:* Add *-er* plus *than: clever, cleverer than; tender, tenderer than.*

(e) Two-syllable adjectives ending in *-ble* and *-ple:* Add only *-r* plus *than: humble, humbler than; simple, simpler than.*

(f) Two-syllable adjectives ending in *-ous, -ish, -ful, -ing, -ed,* and *-less:* Place *more* before the adjective plus *than: famous, more famous than; childish, more childish than; useful, more useful than; interesting, more interesting than; relaxed, more relaxed than; careless, more careless than.*

(g) Two-syllable adjectives ending in *-ct, -nt,* and *-st:* Place *more* before the adjective and follow the adjective with *than: exact, more exact than; recent, more recent than; honest, more honest than.*

(h) Two-syllable adjectives ending in *-ow* and *-some* can occur with either *-er* or *more: narrow, narrower than* or *more narrow than; handsome, handsomer than* or *more handsome than.*

(i) Adjectives of three or more syllables: Place *more* before the adjective and follow the adjective with *than: beautiful, more beautiful than; intelligent, more intelligent than.*

7.1 (Continued)

(j) A few adjectives are compared irregularly.

Positive Degree	Comparative Degree
good	better than
bad	worse than
far	{ farther than { further than
little	{ less than { littler than (see note)
much many	more than

Note: Use *littler* when referring to size: *Our girl is littler than our boy.* Use *less* when referring to amount: *I have less (money) than you do.*

4. *Much* may be used to intensify an adjective in the comparative degree: *Mt. Everest is **much higher than** the Matterhorn.*

7.2

GRAMMAR EXERCISE   Name _____ Date _____

Focus: The Comparative Degree of Adjectives

Transform the adjectives in parentheses into adjectives in the comparative degree. Check the spelling rules carefully.

EXAMPLES: a. Athens is (old) <u>older than</u> Rome.
b. Algebra is (difficult) <u>more difficult than</u> arithmetic.

1. Life with money is (easy) _____ life without.

2. This kind of apple is (tasty) _____ that kind.

3. A lion in a jungle is (happy) _____ a lion in a cage.

4. I'm (thin) _____ my father.

5. Mexican food is (hot) _____ American food.

6. A fox is (clever) _____ a rabbit.

7. Veal is (tender) _____ beef.

8. Their home is (humble) _____ ours.

9. Your goals are (noble) _____ mine.

10. This formula is (simple) _____ that one.

11. Few people in history are (famous) _____ Christopher Columbus.

12. Sometimes adults are (childish) _____ children.

13. A dictionary is (useful) _____ a novel.

14. A biography is (interesting) _____ a novel.

7.2 (Continued)

15. I am (tired) _____ than you.

16. Your definition of the word is (exact) _____ mine.

17. This memorandum is (recent) _____ that one.

18. Children are usually (honest) _____ adults.

19. He is (handsome) _____ his father.

7.3

GRAMMAR EXERCISE   Name _____ Date _____

Focus: The Comparative Degree of Adjectives

Supply *is* or *are* plus an appropriate adjective in the comparative degree in the blanks. Use the adjectives in the following list.

ambitious	clean	emotional	friendly	lazy	sweet
bad	cool	expensive	good	light	tall
big	curious	far	high	neat	weak
cheap	dirty	fast	industrious	strong	

EXAMPLES: a. The Nile is longer than the Mississippi.
            b. Diamonds are harder than pearls.

1. S/he _____ s/he. (him/her = informal)

2. The sun _____ the moon.

3. Women/men _____ men/women.

4. A Rolls-Royce _____ a Ford.

5. Mt. Everest _____ Mt. Fuji.

6. Helium _____ air.

7. The night/the day _____ the day/the night.

8. Europeans _____ Asians.

9. Vodka _____ wine.

10. Cigarettes _____ alcohol.

11. An orange _____ a lemon.

12. Gold _____ silver.

13. Rice _____ potatoes in Asia.

14. I _____ the person next to me.

15. You _____ I. (me = informal)

16. Wool _____ cotton.

17. Love _____ money.

18. Life in the country _____ life in the city.

19. A rabbit _____ a turtle.

7.4

Focus: The Comparative Degree with *Less*

With adjectives of three or more syllables, *less* (the opposite of *more*) is often used in the comparative degree: *The Soviet Union is **less populated than** China; Money is **less important than** good health.* *Less* is not often used with adjectives of two syllables or less.

Supply the comparative degree of the adjectives in the following list in the appropriate blanks. Use *less*.

agricultural	developed	enthusiastic	industrial	romantic
comfortable	difficult	expensive	intelligent	sophisticated
complicated	discouraged	important	polluted	successful
crowded	emotional	independent	populated	

EXAMPLES: a. Money is less important than love.

           b. Life in the country is less complicated than life in the city.

1. The day is _____ the night.

2. South America is _____ North America.

3. Chicken is _____ beef.

4. Women in many countries are _____ women in the United States.

5. The southern part of Italy is _____ the northern part.

6. The beginning of this book is _____ the end.

7. The country is _____ the city.

8. The western part of the United States is _____ the eastern part.

9. Dinner at home is _____ dinner in a restaurant.

10. Men are usually _____ women.

11. Life in my grandmother's early days was _____ life is today.

12. An apartment is _____ a house.

13. S/he is _____ s/he.

14. Pearls are _____ diamonds.

15. This report is _____ the other report.

16. His parents are _____ her parents.

17. Last year I was _____ I am this year.

18. Spain is _____ Germany.

19. Primitive men were _____ modern men.

7.5

Focus: The Comparative Degree with *But* and *Even*

The adverb *even* is used to intensify an adjective in the comparative degree; sometimes it appears in a clause of contrast introduced by the conjunction *but*: *The earth is far from the sun,* **but Mars is even further;** *Alcohol is bad for your health,* **but cigarettes are even worse.**

In the blanks, supply *even* plus an appropriate adjective in the comparative degree.

EXAMPLES:
  a. He has little money, but I have even less.
  b. She's a beautiful woman, but her sister is even more beautiful.
  c. India is a large country, but China is even larger.

1. Yesterday was nice, but the day before was _____.

2. A horse has little intelligence, but a mule has _____.

3. He's rich, but his wife is _____.

4. Tokyo is large, but Shanghai is _____.

5. Our vacation is Hong Kong was fun, but our vacation in Taiwan was _____.
  Note: The adjective *fun* is an exception to the general rule for one-syllable adjectives in the comparative degree; it always takes *more*: *This game is* **more fun** *than that one.*

6. Fred is very tall, but his father is _____.

7. He's crazy, but his wife is _____.

8. I have few friends, but my brother has _____.

9. They're quite poor, but their neighbors are _____.

10. Guatemala is small, but Costa Rica is _____.

11. The wine at the dinner party last night was bad, but the food was _____.

12. Algebra is difficult, but calculus is _____.

13. This is a very funny book, but that one is _____.

14. His grandmother is very wise, but his grandfather is _____.

15. I have little money, but my roommate has _____.

16. This shirt is cheap, but that one is _____.

17. A hippo is large, but an elephant is _____.

18. This wine is good, but the other is _____.

19. Mexico City is very high in altitude, but La Paz, Bolivia, is _____.

20. Iron is very strong, but steel is _____.

7.6

THE SUPERLATIVE DEGREE

1. The definite article *the* always appears with an adjective in the superlative degree: *The Bible is **the** most famous book in the world; The Sequoias in California are **the** oldest trees in the world.*

Rules for Forming the Superlative Degree

2. (a) Adjectives of one syllable: Add *-est* to the adjective and place *the* before the adjective: *high, the highest; fast, the fastest; old, the oldest; odd, the oddest.*

(b) One-syllable adjectives ending in a final single consonant preceded by a single vowel: Double the final consonant before adding *-est: big, the biggest; hot, the hottest; thin, the thinnest.*

(c) Two-syllable adjectives ending in *-y* preceded by a consonant: Change the *-y* to *-i* before adding *-est: dirty, the dirtiest; easy, the easiest; lazy, the laziest; pretty, the prettiest.*

(d) Two-syllable adjectives ending in *-ble* and *-ple*: Add only *-st: humble, the humblest; noble, the noblest; simple, the simplest.*

(e) Two-syllable adjectives ending in *-ous, -ish, -ful, -ing, -ed,* and *-less.* Add *the most* before the adjective: *famous, the most famous; foolish, the most foolish; awful, the most awful; interesting, the most interesting; relaxed, the most relaxed; careless, the most careless.*

(f) Two-syllable adjectives ending in *-ct, -nt,* and *-st*: Add *the most* before the adjective: *exact, the most exact; recent, the most recent; honest, the most honest.*

(g) Two-syllable adjectives ending in *-ow* and *-some* can occur with *-est* or *most: handsome, the handsomest* or *the most handsome; narrow, the narrowest* or *the most narrow; shallow, the shallowest* or *the most shallow.*

(h) Adjectives of three or more syllables: Add *the most* before the adjective: *beautiful, the most beautiful; fabulous, the most fabulous; powerful, the most powerful; magnificent, the most magnificent.*

(i) A few adjectives are compared irregularly in the superlative degree.

Positive Degree	Superlative Degree
good	the best
bad	the worst
far	{ the farthest / the furthest
little	the least
much / many }	the most

Note: Use *littlest* when referring to size; *Our son is the littlest boy in the class.* Use *least* when referring to amount: *I have the least (money) of all my friends.*
Note: *Farther* and *farthest* are used in reference to distance (*the farthest planets*); *further* and *furthest* indicate additional degree (*further in debt*).

3. *Least* (the opposite of *most*) is sometimes used in the superlative degree: *My boss is the least difficult problem at my office; He is the least intelligent of all their children.*

7.7

Focus: The Superlative Degree of Adjectives

Transform the adjectives in parentheses into adjectives in the superlative degree and fill in the blanks. Check the spelling rules carefully.

EXAMPLES: a. This is (easy) the easiest sentence in the book.
           b. The last exercise in the book is (difficult) the most difficult one.

1. Mt. Everest is (high) _____ mountain in the world.

2. (fast) _____ trains in the world are in Japan.

3. Some of (old) _____ people in the world are in the Republic of Georgia in the Soviet Union.

4. She is (nice) _____ girl in my class.

5. The elephant is (big) _____ animal in Africa.

6. Death Valley, California, is one of (hot) _____ places in the United States.

7. Bob is (thin) _____ boy in the class.

8. The male lion is one of (lazy) _____ animals in the jungle.

9. Calcutta is probably one of (dirty) _____ cities in India.

10. (clever) _____ student in a class doesn't always get the best grades.

11. My graduation from school was (happy) _____ day of my life.

12. The elephant is (noble) _____ of all the animals in the jungle.

13. They live in (humble) _____ house in town, but they're happy.

14. Which exercise is (simple) _____ of all?

15. Who is (handsome) _____ man in your class?

16. He is (foolish) _____ man in town.

17. Who is (famous) _____ woman in the world?

18. She is (awful) _____ student in the class.

19. (interesting) _____ part of the movie was the beginning.

20. The most honest people often receive (bad) _____ treatment.

21. What medicine is (good) _____ for a bad cold?

22. The Vale of Kashmir is one of (beautiful) _____ places in India.

23. Jimmy, please wade in (shallow) _____ part of the pool.

7.8

Name _____ Date _____

   Focus: The Superlative Degree of Adjectives

Fill in the blanks with the superlative degree of the adjectives given in the parentheses.

EXAMPLES: a. (close) Mercury is <u>the closest</u> planet to the sun.
      b. (far) Pluto is <u>the farthest</u> planet from the sun. (3,670,000,000 miles)

1. (long) The Nile is _____ river in the world.

2. (famous) Shakespeare is one of _____ writers in the world. *Romeo and Juliet* is probably one of _____ plays in the world's literature.

3. (handsome) Her husband is one of _____ men in town.

4. (high) La Paz, Bolivia, is _____ city above sea level in South America.

5. (hard) What is _____ wood in the world?

6. (valuable) What is _____ mineral in the world?

7. (bad) What is one of _____ things for your health?

8. (shallow) Please swim in _____ part of the pool, children. (deep) _____ part of the pool is dangerous.

9. (long) What is _____ word in the English language?

10. (good) One of _____ foods with wine is cheese.

11. (important) The printing press was one of _____ inventions of the fifteenth century.

12. (much) What religion has _____ members in the world?

13. (little) For a very rich man, money is often _____ of his problems. (rich/happy) _____ people in the world are sometimes not _____.

14. (tall) The giraffe is _____ of existing animals.

15. (serious) Pollution and overpopulation are two of _____ problems in the world today.

16. (high) Lake Titicaca in South America is _____ large lake in the world.

17. (expensive) The Rolls-Royce is one of _____ automobiles in the world today.

18. (tall *or* high) At one time, the Empire State Building in New York was _____ building in the world.

19. (large) Tokyo is _____ city in the world.

20. (short) _____ distance between two points is a straight line.

21. (short) What is _____ way to get to school?

7.8 (Continued)

Name _____ Date _____

Now supply your own adjectives.

22. What is _____ language in the world today?

23. The Bible is _____ book in the world.

24. Who is _____ woman/man in the movies now?

25. What is one of _____ sports in Switzerland?

26. Who is _____ person in your family?

27. The Nile is _____ natural resource of Egypt.

28. What is _____ way to go around the world?

29. What is _____ kind of wine to serve with fish/beef?

30. What is _____ animal in the world?

31. What is one of _____ animals in the jungle?

32. The shark is one of _____ fish in the world's oceans.

33. The Pacific is _____ ocean in the world.

34. What is _____ river in Europe/your native country?

35. What is one of _____ problems in the world today?

36. What is _____ way to cook chicken?

37. What are _____ watches/cameras in the world?

Now complete the sentences.

38. Pollution is one of _____.

39. The Nile _____.

40. She _____ in her class.

41. Buddhism _____ in Asia.

42. (supply name) _____ man in the world.

43. Good health _____ thing in life.

44. China _____.

45. Rice _____.

46. Mt. Everest _____.

47. The United States _____.

48. The Queen of England _____.

49. I/you/s/he _____.

7.9
THE POSITIVE DEGREE

1. In the POSITIVE DEGREE OF ADJECTIVES (the comparison of equality), we are comparing two units (two people or things) to an equal degree: *The blue hat is **as attractive as** the brown one; Shanghai is almost **as large as** Tokyo; There is no place in the United States **as hot as** Death Valley, California.*

2. To form the positive degree of adjectives, the adverb *as* is put before and after a given adjective: *No other animal in the world is **as** tall **as** a giraffe; Sometimes, grapefruits are **as** sour **as** lemons; Adults are never **as** happy **as** children.*

3. Unlike the comparative and superlative degree of adjectives, the form of the adjective in the positive degree never changes: *We are as **young** as we feel; According to many religions, death is as **important** as life.*

4. When the positive degree occurs in negative comparisons, the first *as* of the phrase may be replaced by the adverb *so* in more formal usage: *England isn't **so** (as) powerful as she was in the nineteenth century; Frequently, people are not **so** (as) good as they appear; Natural resources are not **so** (as) plentiful as they were; Air isn't **so** (as) light as helium; Money isn't **so** (as) important as personal satisfaction.*

5. Certain figures of speech with *as . . . as* occur in informal speech (never in formal writing); here are a few:

   a. Their child is always *as quiet as a mouse.*
   b. My boss is always *as busy as a bee/beaver.*
   c. She is *as clever as a fox.*
   d. His grandfather is *as stubborn as a mule.*
   e. Their little boy is *as good as gold.*
   f. One of my teachers is always *as nervous as a cat.*
   g. For some unknown reason, I feel *as weak as a kitten.*
   h. My! Your hands are *as cold as ice.*
   i. I'm in a wonderful mood today! I feel *as free as a bird.*
   j. What an appetite I have! I am *as hungry as a wolf.*
   k. His father has been very sick; he's *as thin as a rail.*
   l. Our young son is *as strong as an ox.*
   m. Her voice is *as clear as a bell.*
   n. The fog last night was *as thick as pea soup.*
   o. My new sweater is *as soft as a pillow.*
   p. Why are you blushing? My! Your face is *as red as a beet.*

7.10

Name _____ Date _____

Focus: The Positive Degree of Adjectives

Fill in the blanks with appropriate adjectives.

EXAMPLES: a. Men are as <u>emotional</u> as women.
    b. The Atlantic Ocean isn't so <u>deep</u> as the Pacific.

1. Everyone in my office is always as _____ as a beaver.

2. My lawyer is as _____ as a fox. He can also be as _____ as a mule.

    Physically, he's as _____ as an ox.

3. My mother isn't so _____ as my father.

4. When I teased the little girl, her face got as _____ as a beet.

5. Gosh, I have an appetite! I'm as _____ as a wolf.

6. Listen children! I want you to be as _____ as a mouse.

Now supply *as (so)* + adjective + *as*.

7. A kilometer isn't _____ a mile.

8. India isn't _____ China.

9. Love is _____ money.

10. The Matterhorn isn't _____ Mt. Everest.

Now supply an appropriate form of the verb *be* as well.

11. European cars _____ American cars.

12. The Mississippi _____ the Nile.

13. A boy/girl _____ a girl/boy.

14. Men/women _____ women/men.

15. Europeans/Orientals _____ Orientals/Europeans.

16. The South/North _____ the North/South.

17. A cat/dog _____ a dog/cat.

18. A cow/horse _____ a horse/cow.

19. Silver/gold _____ gold/silver.

20. Life in the country _____ life in the city.

21. This (_____) _____ that one.

22. I _____ you are.

23. You _____ I am.

24. I _____ the person next to me

GRAMMAR EXERCISE   Name _____ Date _____

Focus: The Comparative and Positive Degrees

When we compare two things, persons, or conditions, an auxiliary sometimes follows the second item in the comparison: *A lion isn't as fast as a horse **is**; They have less money than I **do**; I have fewer friends than she **does**.*

Supply an appropriate form of an adjective in the first blank and an appropriate form of the verb *be* or an auxiliary in the second blank of each sentence.

EXAMPLES: a. The end of the movie wasn't as good as the beginning was.
             b. Male lions are lazier than females are.
             c. The Middle East has more oil than Venezuela does.

1. A telephone call is _____ than a telegram _____.

2. My right foot is _____ than my left foot _____.

3. Colombia has _____ coffee than Brazil _____.

4. Rome was _____ than Athens _____.

5. She had a _____ time at the party than her husband _____.

6. The Pacific Ocean is _____ than the Atlantic _____.

7. English is _____ than Chinese _____.

8. The earth isn't as _____ to the sun as Mercury _____.

9. Her hair isn't as _____ as mine _____.

10. The days in December aren't as _____ as the nights _____.

11. She drinks _____ coffee than her husband _____.

12. I have _____ time for my studies than the other students _____.

13. Yesterday was _____ than today _____.

14. Last night was _____ than this morning _____.

15. She isn't so _____ as he _____.

16. In the Sahara the nights aren't so _____ as the days _____.

17. Children don't have as _____ problems as adults _____.

18. He got a _____ grade in the course than she _____.

19. She has _____ pronunciation in English than I _____.

20. A cat eats _____ food than a dog _____.

21. Today isn't so _____ as yesterday _____.

22. My father has _____ free time than my mother _____.

23. The very rich have _____ problems than we _____.

24. The weather in Alaska is _____ than the weather in Canada _____.

25. Spanish wine isn't as _____ as French wine _____.

7.12

THE COMPARISON OF ADVERBS

1. Adverbs are compared in much the same way as adjectives. With the irregular adverbs of manner like *hard* and *fast*, we add *-er* or *-est*: *He works **harder than** I do; He works **the hardest** of anyone in the office; That horse runs **faster than** mine; It runs **the fastest** of all the horses in the stable.*

2. Adverbs of time like *early, late,* and *soon* also take *-er* or *-est* when they are compared: *Of all the students, she usually arrives **the earliest**; He arrived **later than** I did; I'm going to get to the party **sooner than** you.*

3. Adverbs of manner that end in *-ly* take *more . . . than* and *the most* when they are compared: *She dances **more beautifully than** her sister; He always works **more carefully than** his boss; She sings **the most beautifully** of all the women in the choir.*

4. A few adverbs of manner like *slowly, quickly,* and *loudly* sometimes occur without *-ly* ending: *Please drive slow(ly) through town; Would you please drive slower* (or *more slowly*) *than this.*

5. *Less . . . than* and *the least* are sometimes used in the comparison of adverbs (usually with long adverbs): *She dresses **less beautifully than** her mother; He works **the least efficiently** of the workers.*

6. A few adverbs are compared irregularly: (well) *He speaks **better than** his brother does; He speaks **the best** of all the students;* (far) *He can throw a ball **farther than** I can; He can throw a ball **the farthest** of all the players on the team.*

Positive Degree	Comparative Degree	Superlative Degree
well	better than	the best
badly	worse than	the worst
far	father than (*or* further)	the farthest (*or* the furthest)
much	more than	the most
little	less than	the least

7.13

Focus: The Comparison of Adverbs

Make appropriate adverbial forms out of the adjectives in the following list and supply them in the blanks.

bad	careless	fast	hard	little	reckless
careful	early	good	late	much	slow

EXAMPLES: a. John doesn't drive as <u>fast</u> as his Dad does.
b. Grandpa drives <u>faster</u> than grandma does.
c. Who drives the <u>fastest</u> in your family?

1. Bill writes compositions the _____ of all the students in his writing class.

2. Who in your family gets up the _____ in the morning?

3. Do you read _____ or _____ than you did when you were younger?

4. Do you speak English _____ now than you did before you started this course?

5. Does Bob play football as _____ as his brother does?

6. S/he types the _____ of all the secretaries in the office.

7. Do you speak English _____ than your father does?

8. Did you wake up _____ or _____ than your roommate this morning?

9. Who works the _____ in your family?

10. Do you read _____ or _____ than your roommate?

11. Does s/he read as _____ as you do?

12. Does your mother drive _____ than your father?

13. Who cooks the _____ in your family?

14. Do you spell _____ than the other students in this class?

15. Did you come to school _____ than the other students did?

16. Did you go to bed _____ or _____ than your roommate last night?

17. Who speaks English the _____ in your family?

18. Who sings the _____ in this group?

19. Do you sing _____ than your mother?

20. Do you dance as _____ as your father?

21. Do you read _____ than you did a year ago?

22. Does a cat eat _____ or _____ than a dog?

23. Does the female lion work _____ than the male?

24. Do you write as _____ as you speak?

25. Who eats the _____ in your family?

7.14

CONTRAST AND SIMILARITY

1. We may contrast two nouns with the expression *different from: Mary's personality is **different from** her sister's; Chinese food is very **different from** Japanese food; Boys are **different from** girls.*

2. *The same* + a noun + *as* is used to express a similarity: *My grandmother is **the same age as** my grandfather; She is **the same height as** her mother; My cat is about **the same age as** my dog.*

3. *The same* + a noun is another way to express a similarity: *Frank and John are **the same age**; This shirt and that shirt are **the same price**; All of the students have **the same book**; She and I have **the same ideas**.*

4. *The same as* is also used to express a similarity: *His problems are **the same as** mine; The price of this shirt is **the same as** the price of that one.*

5. Linking verbs like *be, seem, look, act, feel, sound,* and *taste* followed by *like* are also used to express a similarity: *She **looks like** her mother; Today **feels like** winter; S/he sometimes **acts like** a fool.*

Practice answering the following questions. Review the three degrees for the comparison of adjectives before going on to the next exercise.

1. How is the city different from the country?
2. How is English different from French/Spanish/Italian/Chinese?
3. How is your mother different from your father?
4. How is a cat different from a dog?
5. How are North American women/men different from South American women/men? How are boys different from girls?
6. How is Europe different from America (North, Central, and South)?
7. How is your personality different from mine?
8. How is your brother/sister different from you?
9. How are American movies different from European movies?
10. How are Easterners different from Westerners?
11. How are my looks (appearance) different from yours?
12. How is your life now different from your life a year ago?
13. How is your life different from mine?

GRAMMAR EXERCISE   Name _____ Date _____

Focus: *The Same . . . As*

Supply the nouns *age, color, height, length, price, size, weight,* or *width* in the appropriate blanks.

EXAMPLES: a. I'm almost the same height as my father.
            b. This classroom is about the same size as my other classroom.

1. Tokyo is about the same _____ as Shanghai.

2. My sister is about the same _____ as my mother.

3. My right foot is exactly the same _____ as my left foot.

4. My hair is about the same _____ as yours.

5. His father is exactly the same _____ as the President of the United States.

6. A Chevrolet is about the same _____ as a Ford.

7. His hair is about the same _____ as mine.

8. Our neighbors' house is about the same _____ as ours.

9. A nice vacation at the beach is about the same _____ as a nice vacation in the mountains.

10. Japan is about the same _____ as California.

11. She is about the same _____ as her husband.

12. This shirt is exactly the same _____ as that one.

13. Their garden is almost the same _____ as ours.

14. This book is about the same _____ as that one.

15. Her cat is about the same _____ as her dog.

16. He is almost the same _____ as his wife.

17. Dinner at that restaurant is about the same _____ as dinner at home.

18. My bedroom is exactly the same _____ as my living room.

19. Her eyes are the same _____ as her mother's.

20. The Chrysler Building in New York is about the same _____ as the Empire State Building.

21. Our little boy is about the same _____ as our little girl.

22. Chicago is about the same _____ as Philadelphia.

23. Her eyes are the same _____ as the sky on a clear day.

24. This book is exactly the same _____ as that one.

25. Her shoes are almost the same _____ as her sister's.

26. My algebra class is the same _____ as my chemistry class.

27. Their car is the same _____ as ours.

7.16

GRAMMAR EXERCISE   Name _____ Date _____

Focus: *The Same . . . As*

Fill in the blanks with appropriate words.

EXAMPLES: a. The length of her hair is the same as that of <u>mine</u>.
              b. The width of this room is the same as the <u>length</u>.

1. The color of our neighbors' house is the same as _____.

2. Your problems at work are the same as_____.

3. The price of a vacation at the beach is about the same as _____.

4. Our little boy's weight is about the same as _____.

5. My weight is the same as _____.

6. The price of a ticket in the first balcony is the same as _____.

7. Women's problems are not the same as_____.

8. The weather in Los Angeles is almost the same as _____.

9. My boss's problems at work are the same as_____.

10. The color of his eyes is the same as_____.

11. The size of my apartment is about the same as_____.

12. My best friend's age is the same as_____.

13. The nature of a female lion isn't the same as _____.

14. The weather in Florida is almost the same as _____.

15. The price of this blouse is the same as _____.

16. The color of her hair is the same as _____.

17. The price of a plane ticket to Los Angeles is almost the same as_____.

18. The size or our car is the same as _____.

19. The distance from my home to school is almost the same as _____.

20. The distance from London to New York is almost the same as _____.

21. Her height is about the same as_____.

22. Her interests are the same as _____.

23. Life in the United States is not the same as _____.

7.17

GRAMMAR EXERCISE   Name _____ Date _____

Focus: *Like*

In the appropriate blanks, supply -s forms made from the base forms in the following list: be, seem, look, act, feel, sound, taste.

EXAMPLES: a. The weather in Los Angeles is like the weather in southern Italy.
b. Her voice sounds like her mother's.

1. This fabric _____ like silk.

2. That _____ like Mexican music.

3. This _____ like Colombian coffee.

4. That man sometimes _____ like a little boy.

5. This powder _____ like sugar.

6. That bird _____ like a nightingale.

7. This bread _____ like French bread.

8. San Francisco _____ a little bit like Hong Kong.

9. His voice _____ very much like his father's.

10. S/he often _____ like a fool.

11. According to some people, life in San Francisco _____ a little bit like life in Europe.

12. Today _____ like Sunday.

13. This fabric _____ like wool.

14. That stone _____ like a diamond.

15. That music _____ like Chopin.

16. Because of his mistake, he _____ like a fool.

17. That man _____ like an old friend of mine.

18. His wife sometimes _____ like a little girl.

19. Her hair _____ like a wig.

20. He _____ like a rich man.

21. She _____ like a dream in that dress.

22. He _____ like a football player.

23. Because of her new job, she _____ like a new person.

24. That woman _____ like the Queen of England.

25. That man _____ like a movie star.

26. Spanish _____ a little bit like Italian.

27. Today _____ like spring.

28. Their house _____ like ours.

29. Danish _____ a little bit like English.

GRAMMAR EXERCISE   Name _____ Date _____

          Focus: More Prepositions of Place

Supply appropriate prepositions in the blanks.

EXAMPLES: a. The patient is <u>between</u> life and death.
             b. I divided the candy <u>among</u> the four children.
                (*Between* is used for a unit of two; *among* is used for a unit of three or more.)
             c. On our way to Lima, our plane flew <u>over</u> the Andes.
             d. My neighbors <u>above</u> me are very noisy.
                (*Over* is used for a point generally higher; *above* is used for a point directly higher.)
             e. I found my shoes <u>under</u> my bed.
             f. Most of South America is <u>below</u> the Equator.
                (*Under* is used for a point generally lower; *below* is used for a point directly lower.)
                Note: The distinction between *under* and *below* is not always made; they are frequently interchangeable.

1. Is there going to be an intermission _____ the first and second acts?

2. Our house is situated _____ some lovely maple trees.

3. My parents live in the apartment directly _____ mine.

4. The subways run _____ the ground.

5. Large ships cannot sail _____ that bridge.

6. Whose shoes are these _____ my chair?

7. Grandma keeps her purse _____ her pillow.

8. Mexico is directly _____ the United States; Canada is directly _____. The United States is _____ the two countries.

9. The thief hid the money _____ a large rock in the forest.

10. There are many layers of gasses _____ the surface of the earth.

11. There is a certain amount of honor _____ thieves.

12. When she entered the church, she put a veil _____ her head.

13. We have a house on the mountain _____ our town.

14. On the scientific expedition to the North Pole in a submarine, the scientists stayed _____ the surface of the water for almost two months.

15. The sky is _____ us; the earth is _____ us.

16. The Queen stood _____ the people at the reception with great majesty and dignity.

17. This is my sister _____ my mother and father in this photograph.

MODAL AUXILIARIES 8

8.1

EXPRESSING MOOD

1. Modal auxiliaries constitute a group of words which add a special meaning to the verbs that they precede. Because of the complexity of modals, most of their past forms will not be discussed in this chapter. A detailed discussion of modals and their past forms will be found in the chapter on modal auxiliaries in Book 2 of this work.

   The chart below contains a list of the modal auxiliaries.

	Noncontracted Negative Form	Contracted Negative Form
can	cannot, can not	can't
could	could not	couldn't
may	may not	mayn't (British)
might	might not	mightn't (British)
shall	shall not	shan't (British)
should (ought to)	should not (ought not to)	shouldn't (oughtn't to)
will('ll)	will not ('ll not)	won't
would ('d)	would not ('d not)	wouldn't
must	must not	mustn't
need	need not	needn't
dare	dare not	daren't (British)

Note: Because *have to* and *be able to* are idiomatic substitutes for *must* and *can,* they are discussed in this chapter along with the modals.

Special Note: Base forms, *never -s* forms, always follow modals.

8.2

CAN/COULD

1. The modal auxiliary *can* + a base form expresses (a) a physical ability: *He **can jump** the highest of all the boys; Our daughter **can run** fast;* (b) a learned ability: *My dog **can do** a lot of tricks; I **can type;*** and (c) a possibility: *You **can fly** across the Atlantic in about six hours; Our factory **can produce** thousands of bicycles a month.*

2. *Can't,* the contraction of *cannot,* occurs in informal usage: *A hippo **can't be** away from water for very long; My dog **can't swim.***

3. When expressing possibility, *can* may indicate future time: *I can take care of your children **tomorrow;** We can't visit the city **next week.***

4. In *yes-no* and information questions, *can* precedes the subject in all persons: *Can she be here tomorrow? How long can you stay under water?*

5. *Could,* the past form of *can,* expresses ability and possibility in past time. *Couldn't,* the contraction of *could not,* is used in informal usage: *Fortunately, they **could finish** the project on time; I **couldn't send** the letter because I had no stamps.*

YES-NO AND INFORMATION QUESTIONS WITH CAN/COULD

Information Words	Modal Auxiliary	Subject	Base Form	Prepositional Phrase/Time
	Can	you	go	with me?
Why	can't	I	stay	at your house?
For how many days	could	they	be	in London?
Why	couldn't	you	go	yesterday?
How high	can	he	jump?	

Special Note: A base form always appears with *can*. You will sometimes hear a student of English as a second language say something like: *I can **to speak** English*. An infinitive with *to* following *can* is wrong.

YES-NO ANSWERS WITH CAN/COULD

Yes, I you he she it we you they } can/could.

No, I you he she it we you they } can't/couldn't.

8.3

Focus: Learned and Physical Ability with *Can*

Pronunciation Note: The vowel in *can* is usually unstressed; for example, *I can* sounds like *I-kin; He can* sounds like *he-kin*. However, there is a stress on *can* when we want emphasis: *They can't speak English well, but I can* (not *I-kin*). The vowel in *can't* is given its full value. Listen to your instructor very carefully during this exercise and practice the pronunciation of *can* and *can't* (*cannot*).

Supply *can* or *can't* in the blanks.

EXAMPLES: a. He can't eat spicy food because he has an ulcer.
              b. An elephant can pull a very heavy load.

1. She _____ cook well, but her husband _____.

2. I _____ figure out this problem because I don't have a calculator.

3. Very few people _____ play the piano well.

4. An elephant _____ run very fast, but it _____ eat a lot.

5. A cat _____ eat as much as a dog.

6. I _____ sing at all. (*At all* means *in absolutely no way*. The expression occurs in negative statements only: *I can't swim at all; I didn't make any money at all.*).

7. A good diver _____ hold his breath for a long time.

8. Grandma _____ walk well because she has a serious arthritis condition.

9. My mother _____ drive well, but my father _____.

10. How many words a minute _____ you type?

11. Usually, a chicken _____ lay only one egg a day.

12. What kind of sport _____ you play well?

13. Jim _____ play basketball very well, but his brother _____.

14. No one _____ do everything well.

15. He _____ play sports at all because of his bad leg.
    Pronunciation Note: *At all* often sounds like *a-tall*.

16. He _____ run a mile under four minutes.

17. Johnny _____ run faster than all the other boys.

18. You _____ lift that heavy chair without assistance.

19. He _____ walk very well because of his sore toe.

20. A rabbit _____ run fast, but a turtle _____.

21. He _____ get out of bed because he's very ill.

22. He _____ speak French well, but his sister _____.

23. I _____ remember all of the irregular verbs.

24. How many languages _____ you speak? _____ you speak Russian?

8.4

Name _____ Date _____

Focus: Possibility with *Can*

Fill in the blanks with *can* or *can't*. Focus on pronunciation; for example, *you can* (= *you-kin*), *we can* (= *we-kin*), *s/he can* (= *s/he-kin*), and *I can* (= *I-kin*).

EXAMPLES: a. We <u>can</u> reach the top of the mountain before noon.
             b. I'm a little disappointed because I <u>can't</u> go out with my friends tomorrow night, since I have another date.

1. In Southern California in February, one _____ swim in the Pacific, but it's cold. (*One* means *you in general,* more common in British usage.)

2. One _____ find many different kinds of people in Hong Kong.

3. Because of fire regulations, you _____ smoke in movie theaters.

4. I _____ develop this film myself because I don't have a dark room.

5. Life in many parts of the world _____ be very hard.

6. Unfortunately, I _____ go with you to the party tonight.

7. The world _____ provide enough food for its people.

8. Most plants and flowers _____ grow without good sunlight.

9. General Motors _____ produce thousands of cars a day.

10. In many cities in the United States, one _____ buy alcohol on Sundays; it's against the law.

11. We _____ make progress toward a better world.

12. You _____ find a list of irregular verbs at the back of this book.

13. One _____ fly from New York to Los Angeles in about five hours.

14. I _____ be at your house within an hour.

15. I _____ go to the meeting because I have a dentist appointment.

16. I _____ appreciate that kind of art because I don't know anything about it.

17. The government _____ build new highways because it doesn't have enough funds (money).

18. Because of production problems at the factory, we _____ fill your orders for more parts. We apologize for this inconvenience.

19. One _____ find much water in the Sahara.

20. All of us _____ be selfish at times.

21. You _____ find almost everything in New York stores.

22. He's difficult to talk to because I _____ understand his ideas.

23. Our factory _____ produce enough to fill its orders.

24. No one _____ be perfect. However, we _____ try.

25. You _____ find everything you need up in the mountains.

8.5

Focus: Ability and Possibility in Past Time with *Could*

Fill in the blanks with *could* or *couldn't* (*could not*).

EXAMPLES: a. I <u>could</u> understand his explanation easily because he was using excellent examples.
          b. She <u>couldn't</u> speak English well when she first arrived in England.

1. Because the report was in Chinese, I _____ read it.

2. I _____ bake a cake because I didn't have any sugar.

3. We _____ go to California last week because all of the airlines were on strike.

4. I _____ get into the theater free because I knew the owner.

5. She _____ go to work yesterday for only a couple of hours.

6. I _____ understand him because he was speaking with a thick (heavy) foreign accent.

7. I _____ carry the package home because it wasn't heavy.

8. He _____ drink any alcohol while he was taking penicillin.

9. I _____ call anyone last weekend because my phone was out of order. (*Out of order* means *not working*. The expression is most often used in reference to telephones, elevators, and doors.)

10. He _____ go to the party yesterday because he wasn't working.

11. Our daughter _____ vote in the last election because she wasn't old enough.

12. Even though she _____ go to the party, she decided to stay home.

13. I _____ believe myself when I made that foolish mistake.

14. He _____ lift anything heavy while he was having trouble with his back. He _____ carry anything, either.

15. My parents _____ stay with me on their visit to New York because I have a very large apartment.

16. We _____ take the elevator because it was out of order.

17. We _____ buy any alcohol for the party because it was Sunday. We _____ buy only soda.

18. Our little boy _____ speak well until he was about four.

19. Because he speaks English very well, he _____ get a job right away when he arrived in London.

20. We _____ drive out to the desert last weekend because our car wasn't working.

21. I _____ cook dinner because my stove wasn't working.

22. When he arrived in the United States, Pierre _____ enter the university right away because his score on the entrance examination was very high.

8.6

ASKING FOR PERMISSION WITH MAY AND CAN

1. Even though many textbooks say that only the modal *may* should be used for asking permission, *can* is heard in informal speech: *May (can) I close the door? May (can) I ask you a personal question?*

2. A request for permission takes the form of a *yes-no* question, and a *yes-no* answer grants (gives) or denies the permission. <u>Second person (singular or plural) does not occur in a request for permission.</u>

First person	May (can) I go?	Yes, you may (can).
	May (can) we go?	No, you may not (can't).
Third person	May (can) she go?	Yes, she may (can).
	May (can) they go?	No, they may not (can't).

   May and *can* are also used to mean *be permitted: You cannot smoke* (you are not permitted to smoke) *in the elevators; You may not walk* (you are not permitted to walk) *on the grass; You may use* (you are permitted to use) *your dictionary during the test.*
   Note: *Mayn't,* the contraction of *may not,* occurs only in British English, where it is rare.

3. The polite word *please* is best used in a request for permission; it follows the subject: *May **I please** have another piece of chicken? May **I please** leave the table? May **I please** go out and play, Mommy?*

4. *Could* sometimes occurs in requests; however, *can* or *may* usually appears in the answer: ***Could** I borrow your car for the weekend? Yes, you **may**; No, you **cannot** (can't).*

5. *Might,* another form of *may,* occasionally appears in a request, but it is very formal and is rarely used in informal speech: ***Might** I make a request? **Might** I speak to the president herself?*

6. Both *may* and *can* occur in requests that are not asking for permission. This kind of request is similar in meaning to requests in the imperative mood: *Waiter, may I please have another glass of water? Excuse me, could you please tell me the time? Can you please give me an answer by tomorrow? Could you please give me change for a ten-dollar bill?*
   Note: Second person occurs in this form.

GRAMMAR EXERCISE   Name _____ Date _____

    Focus: Asking for Permission with *May* and *Can*

Fill in the blanks with appropriate base forms from the following list: ask, be, borrow, close, have, help, leave, open, tell.

EXAMPLES: a. Are you looking for something? May I help you?
             b. Can I <u>be</u> the first to congratulate you on your most recent success?

1. Isn't it a little cold in here? May I please _____ the window?

2. I don't have a token for the bus. Can I _____ one from you?

3. Isn't there a draft in here? May I please _____ the door?

4. Isn't it hot in here? May I please _____ the window?

5. May I _____ you a personal question?

6. May we please _____ the office a little early today?

7. I understand your version of the story. May I now _____ you mine?

8. I don't feel well. May I please _____ the room?

9. I'm still a little hungry. May I please _____ another piece of chicken? May I _____ some more wine, too?

10. Mommy, may I please _____ the table?

11. Dad, may I _____ your car tonight? I want to take my girlfriend to the high school dance. Also, may I _____ a few bucks? (*A buck* is very informal for *a dollar*.)

12. Children, may I _____ you to be quiet?

Now write appropriate *yes-no* questions with *may* (*can*) that might follow the remarks and questions stated below.

EXAMPLE: c. I'm so happy to hear about your promotion. <u>May I congratulate you?</u>

13. I don't have enough money to go to the movies. _____

14. I'm curious about your new girlfriend. _____

15. My typewriter isn't working. _____

16. Mother, I'm finished with my dinner. _____

17. I'm very much in love with you. _____
    Reminder: Second person does not occur in polite requests.

18. I have some wonderful news from my family. _____

19. Aren't you happy in your marriage? _____

20. Are you having a problem with your homework? _____

8.8

BE ABLE TO

1. The idiom *be able to* and the modal *can* have the same meaning: *I am able to* (can) *understand everything in the class; They're able to* (can) *make a lot of money in their small business.*

2. A negative verb phrase is formed by inserting *not* between *be* and *able to: Because of the bad weather, we **are not able to** (cannot) *plant anything in the garden.*

3. Besides present time, *be able to* may occur in past time before a base form: *We **weren't able to** (couldn't) go for a drive because our car wasn't working; We **were able to** (could) pass through the barricades.*

4. *Be able to* (alone) appears less frequently than *can* for events in future time. However, *be able to* is often combined with *be going to* to express a coming event: *He **isn't going to be able to enter** the university until his English improves; Fortunately, we **are going to be able to move** into our new house next month.*

5. *Be able to* may also occur with a few modals: *We **may be able to** attend the graduation ceremonies; He's a smart student and **should be able to** get better grades; He **must be able to** do better.*

6. We form *yes-no* and information questions by inserting a subject between *be* and *able: **Are you able to** come to school tomorrow? What time **were you able to** get to the meeting last night?*

8.9

GRAMMAR EXERCISE   Name _____ Date _____

Focus: Ability with *Be Able to*

Fill in each blank with an appropriate form of *be able to* + base form.

EXAMPLES: a. (take) I'm not <u>able to take</u> a vacation this year because I can't afford it. (*I can't afford it* means *I don't have enough money to do it.*)
   b. (attend) Fortunately, I <u>was able to attend</u> the important meeting.
   c. (take) I'm not <u>going to be able to take</u> another course next semester because I can't afford it.

1. (get) She _____ to work yesterday because of the bad storm.

2. (buy) We _____ a new car last year because we couldn't afford it.

3. (call) I _____ you last night because my phone was out of order.

4. (be) Fortunately, I _____ with my family next Christmas because I can afford the plane ticket.

5. (help) I'm sorry, but I _____ you with the job now.

6. (grow) We _____ plants in our apartment because we don't have very much sunlight.

7. (take) We _____ a vacation next year.

8. (find) He _____ a good job because he isn't a dependable person.

9. (enter) She _____ the university until she speaks and writes English better.

8.9 (Continued)

10. (understand) I _____ the teacher's explanation because he explained everything very carefully.

11. (watch) We _____ our favorite program last night because our TV wasn't working.

12. (get) When she speaks English well, she _____ a good job because she's a clever woman.

13. (go) Because they can afford it, their children _____ to the best schools in the city.

14. (get) He's a very good student, but he _____ good grades because he doesn't study hard enough.

15. (take) We have a little extra money this year, so we _____ a vacation in Europe next summer.

16. (go) He's not feeling very well, so he _____ to the dance tomorrow night unfortunately.

17. (run) A lion _____ as fast as a horse.

18. (eat) A cat _____ as much as a dog.

19. (buy) We _____ a house until we have more money in our savings account.

20. (give) Luckily, they _____ their children the best of everything because they can afford it.

21. (find) She _____ a good job because she doesn't try hard enough.

22. (make) The General _____ the right decision because he had the wrong information about the enemy's position.

23. (attend) We _____ our son's graduation next Saturday because we're both sick in bed with the flu.

PROBABILITY WITH *MAY*

1. Besides asking for permission and making requests, *may,* and its other form *might,* are used to mean slight (little) probability. Essentially, *may* and *might* have the same meaning: *We may (might) have a victory celebration tonight.* A base form always follows *may (might)* for present time.

2. A statement with *may* or *might* is made in response to some kind of evidence (information) that is known by the speaker. Compare:

Evidence	Slight Probability
I feel a little warm.	*I **may have** a fever.*
My feet hurt a little.	*My shoes **might be** too small.*
He didn't say hello to me.	*He **might be** angry at me.*

3. A negative verb phrase is formed by inserting *not* between the modal and the base form.

This soup tastes bland.	*It **might not have** any salt in it.*
She doesn't get good grades.	*She **might not study** hard enough.*
I can't start the engine.	*I **may not have** any gas.*

4. *Could* may replace *may* or *might* in a statement of probability (but only in an affirmative verb phrase).

Why isn't she here today?	*She **could be** sick.*
The patient feels warm and sweaty.	*He **could have** a slight fever.*

   Special Note: *Could not* does not mean slight probability; it means impossibility: *He **couldn't be** at work today; he's in the hospital! This letter **couldn't be** from John Smith; he's dead!*

5. *May* does not occur in questions of slight probability. *Could* is the modal we use for questions; it also occurs in a *yes-no* answer, always accompanied by a base form.

***Could** Mary be sick today?*	*She **could** (may, might) **be**.*
***Could** I have the wrong formula?*	*You **could** (may, might) **have**.*

6. Do not confuse the adverb *maybe,* a synonym for perhaps, with *may be. Maybe* occurs at the beginning of a sentence: ***Maybe she is** sick;* and *may be* always follows the subject: *She **may be** sick.*

8.11

Focus: Slight Probability with *May/Might*

Fill in the blanks with *may* (*might*) or *may* (*might*) *not*.

EXAMPLES: a. I feel a little strange today. I <u>may</u> be sick.
b. He doesn't seem to enjoy his class. He <u>might not</u> like his teacher.

1. Why is this soup bland? There _____ be any salt in it.

2. Why are my eyes bothering me? I _____ have the right prescription in my glasses.

   They _____ be too strong.

3. She doesn't usually like to play with my cat. She _____ like cats, or she _____
   be allergic to them. I really don't know.

4. I'm worried about the next test. I _____ make a few mistakes.

5. The dog refuses its food. He _____ be hungry.

6. I always get a busy signal when I call him. His phone _____ be out of order, or the

   receiver _____ be off the hook.

7. She doesn't want to go to the dance with him. She _____ like him, or she

   _____ have a better invitation.

8. He doesn't want to go to the movies with me. He _____ have enough money, or he

   just _____ want to go with me.

9. That technical word isn't in my dictionary. The book _____ be out of date. (*Out
   of date* means *old, not modern.*)

10. I can't find that African country on my map. My map _____ be up to date. (*Up
    to date* means *new, modern.*)

11. She _____ be able to come to school because of her bad cold.

12. My radio doesn't always come on right away. It _____ be broken, or I _____
    have the right kind of antenna.

13. These statistics seem wrong. They _____ be out of date.

14. I don't want to discuss this problem with my boss. He _____ like it, or he _____
    understand my position.

15. John isn't acting his usual self. He _____ be in love.

16. He has a constant cough. He _____ smoke too much, or he _____ be
    sensitive to the city's pollution.

17. My plants are dying. They _____ get enough sunlight.

18. I can't understand this explanation. It _____ be correct.

8.12

STRONG PROBABILITY WITH MUST

1. The modal auxiliary *must* is most frequently used to mean necessity; however, it may also mean strong probability (deduction): *A Rolls-Royce **must be** very expensive to operate; The President's job **must be** extremely difficult.* A base form always follows *must* in present time.

2. Like *may,* a statement with *must* is made in response to some kind of evidence that is known by the speaker. But *must* shows a stronger sense of certainty and probability than *may;* there is no conjecture.

Evidence	Strong Probability (Deduction)
They have twenty oil wells.	*They **must be** rich.*
India has millions of people.	*Life **must be** hard for the poor.*
It's the best restaurant in town.	*A dinner there **must cost** a lot.*
That writer was born in 1890.	*He **must be** dead by now.*

3. *Not* is inserted between *must* and the base form in negative verb phrases.

They're always fighting with each other.	*They **must not be** happy together.*
His I. Q. (intelligence quotient) is around 160, but he never gets good grades in school.	*He **must not study** much.*
My house plants are dying.	*They **must not have** enough sunlight.*

4. We use *mustn't,* the contraction of *must not,* in informal usage: *The dog **mustn't be** hungry because he doesn't touch his food; She **mustn't be** happy with her husband because she's leaving him.* However, *must not* occurs more frequently for probability, even in informal speaking. *Mustn't* is most often used for prohibition.
   Note: No question form occurs when we use *must* for strong probability.

GRAMMAR EXERCISE   Name _____ Date _____

Fill in the blanks with *must* or *mustn't* (*must not*).

EXAMPLES: a. Her hair is a very unusual color. Yes, she <u>must</u> dye it.
            b. I <u>must not</u> have on the right kind of shoes because my feet hurt.

1. He's always telling everyone he's George Washington. He _____ be crazy. He _____ have no sense of reality.

2. She's always counting her money and worrying about it. She _____ be a stingy (selfish) person. Because of her stinginess, she _____ have many friends. She _____ be an unhappy person.

3. This chocolate is bitter. There _____ be any sugar in it.

4. Chinese _____ be a difficult language. It _____ be easy to learn. It _____ be difficult for the Chinese themselves to learn. It _____ be one of the most difficult languages in the world.

5. He _____ have much money because he's always wearing very old clothes.

6. I get only a buzz when I dial John's number. His phone _____ be out of order.

7. He always gets very high grades in school. He _____ study very hard because it's a difficult school. He _____ be smart.

8. The windows of my apartment face north, and all of my house plants are dying. They _____ have enough sunlight.

9. He _____ like his job because he never talks about it.

10. Look at the way he's staggering! He _____ be drunk.

Now supply an appropriate base form as well.

11. The life of a successful movie star _____ exciting.

12. It _____ a lot to take a trip around the world.

13. Life on an island in the South Pacific _____ wonderful.

14. They have an oil well on their farm. They _____ rich.

15. She always gets bad grades at school. She _____ hard enough.

16. I have a temperature, I'm perspiring heavily and I feel quite dizzy. Something _____ wrong with me.

17. Look at her expensive rings and clothes. She _____ a lot of money.

18. Why isn't this experiment working? I _____ the right formula.

19. Her name isn't in the phone book. She _____ a phone.

20. Life in India _____ easy for the poor.

8.14

NECESSITY, PROHIBITION, AND RECOMMENDATION WITH *MUST*

1. *Must* most frequently occurs with a base form to mean necessity: *We **must be** good; We **must** take** care of our health.* Compare:

Situation	Necessity
He is coughing all the time.	*He **must go** to the doctor.*
I cannot tell the secret.	*I **must keep** my promise.*
They were very kind to me.	*I **must thank** them.*

2. We also use *must* to make a strong recommendation: *It is a wonderful movie, you **must see** it; Hong Kong is an exciting place, you **must go** there; This wine is excellent, you **must try** some.*

3. *Must* may express necessity in future time: *I **must get up** early tomorrow morning; We **must go** to our lawyer next week.*

4. A subject is inserted between *must* and the base form in questions: ***Must I do** all of this homework? **What must we do** about this problem?*

5. Not is inserted between *must* and the base form in negative verb phrases. *Must not* has a completely different meaning from *must*. *Must* means necessity, but *must not* means prohibition. Compare:

Necessity	Prohibition
*We **must eat** to live.*	*We **must not live** to eat.*
*We **must believe** in God.*	*We **must not believe** in the devil.*
*We **must protect** our allies.*	*We **must not protect** our enemies.*
*We **must do** right.*	*We **must not do** wrong.*

6. *Must* follows the subject in *yes-no* answers: *Must I take this medicine every day? Yes, **you must**; Must I walk home late at night? No, **you must not**.*

7. *Mustn't*, the contraction of *must not*, occurs in informal usage: *You **mustn't play** with your food, Timmy; We **mustn't cheat** on our income tax; You **mustn't smoke** in a gas station.*
   Note: *Must*, when it means necessity, has no past form. When we want to express necessity in past time, we use *had to*, the past form of the idiom *have to*.

8.15

Focus: Necessity, Prohibition and Recommendation with *Must*

Fill in the blanks with appropriate base forms of words in the following list.

do	eat	leave	put	sit	take	waste
drink	forget	listen	read	solve	talk	water
duplicate	have	obey	see	sweep	try	

EXAMPLES: a. You must <u>listen</u> to your lawyer's advice. (necessity)
             b. Children, you must never <u>tell</u> a lie. (prohibition)
             c. You really must <u>read</u> this book. (recommendation)

1. You must _____ your house plants right away, or they are going to die. (_____)

2. You mustn't _____ about your friends behind their backs. (_____)

3. You must _____ that movie; it's wonderful. (_____)

4. You must _____ this letter to the President as soon as possible.

5. The patient has high blood pressure. He mustn't _____ any salt on his food.

6. Sh! We mustn't _____ during the movie. It disturbs other people.

7. This candy is delicious. You must _____ some of it.

8. I mustn't _____ to defrost the refrigerator; it isn't working right. I must _____ it
at once. (*At once* means *immediately*.)

9. It's a beautiful day. We must _____ a drive out in the country.

Now fill in the blanks with *must* or *mustn't* as well.

10. The floor is very dirty. I _____ it.

11. He has very poor teeth. He _____ too much sugar.

12. I feel a little dizzy. I _____ any more alcohol.

13. You aren't an adult, Terry. You _____ your parents.

14. I _____ the lawn (grass) today. It looks dry.

15. Listen, Billy, you _____ your time at school.

16. I _____ to send a birthday card to my father.

17. War is foolish and destructive. We _____ peace.

18. We _____ the problem of pollution.

19. We _____ our natural resources.

20. Listen young man, you _____ your money on foolish things.

21. We _____ the law.

22. I _____ to thank my parents for my birthday present.

23. I _____ to use *-s* forms when I am speaking and writing.

24. My boss wants a copy of this report. I _____ it at once.

8.16

NECESSITY WITH *HAVE TO*

1. Like *must,* the idiom *have to* + a base form expresses necessity: *I **have to eat** lunch early today; I **have to go** home.*
   Pronunciation Note: *Have to* sounds like *half to.* The idiom has a different pronunciation from *have* meaning possession.

2. *Have to* appears as an *-s* form in the third person singular: *Everyone **has to pay** taxes; No one in my family **has to work** on Sundays.*

3. *Have to* does not express necessity as strongly as *must.* We use *must* to express a strong sense of duty, obligation, or loyalty: *You must obey the law; We must not lie; We must protect our freedom at all costs; We must unite against the tyranny of the dictatorship.*

4. *Have to* is most often related to the problems of daily living: *I have to go to the store for some sugar; I have to feed my dog twice a day.*

5. Like *be able to, have to* can be used in all the verb tenses: *I have to work every day; I had to work yesterday; I'm going to have to work tomorrow. Have to* alone can express future time: *I have to go tomorrow.*

YES-NO AND INFORMATION QUESTIONS WITH *HAVE TO*

Information Words	Auxiliary	Subject	Idiom	Base Form	Prepositional Phrase/ Time/Object
	Does	she		be	at school tomorrow?
	Do	you		eat	at home?
How often	do	you		do	homework?
What time	did	they	have to	go	to the doctor's?
Who	do	you		see	this afternoon?
How much	does	she		pay	for materials?
When	did	you		go	to the police?

NEGATIVE SENTENCES WITH *HAVE TO*

Subject	Do + Not	Idiom	Base Form	Prepositional Phrase/ Time/Object
I	don't		work	tomorrow.
She	doesn't		do	very much homework.
They	didn't	have to	take	another course.
He	doesn't		get	a haircut.
She	didn't		take	the children to school.
We	don't		buy	a new car.

6. In affirmative verb phrases, *have to* and *must* are very similar in meaning; however, the negative form of *have to* has a completely different meaning from the negative form of *must*. *Must not* means prohibition, but *do not have to* means lack of necessity. Compare:

Prohibition with Must not

You must not drink that water because it's polluted.
You mustn't tell the secret because you promised not to [tell].
You really mustn't rent that apartment because you can't afford it.

Lack of Necessity with Do not have to

I don't have to drink any water because I'm not thirsty.
I don't have to tell the secret because everybody already knows about it.
I don't have to rent that apartment because I have a home with my family.

7. Always respond to *yes-no* questions containing *have to* in the present and past tenses with *yes-no* answers containing *do, does,* or *did.* **Do** *you have to be here every day? Yes, I* **do;** **Does** *she have to be here tomorrow? No, she* **doesn't;** **Did** *you have to be at the meeting yesterday? Yes, I* **did.**
Special Note: The auxiliary *do* occurs in questions and negatives containing *have to* in both American and British usage.

8.17

Focus: *Have to* in Affirmative Verb Phrases

Fill in the blanks with *have to* + appropriate base forms or appropriate forms of *be going to* + *have to* + base form. **Reminder**: *I have to go tomorrow* and *I'm going to have to go tomorrow* mean the same thing.

be	call	come	eat	find	go	pay	take	write
buy	clean	do	enter	get	make	study	work	

EXAMPLES: a. I had to take my umbrella yesterday because it was raining.
b. She has to work because her husband doesn't have a job.
c. I'm going to have to take my car to work tomorrow.

1. Fortunately, no one in my family _____ on Sundays.

2. My sister _____ to the doctor yesterday.

3. I usually _____ the house on Saturdays.

4. I _____ a new job because I'm not making enough money.

5. The government _____ something about unemployment.

6. We _____ rice all the time on our trip to China last year.

7. The patient _____ the medicine three times a day.

8. Would you please excuse me. I _____ a telephone call.

9. He _____ his wife's car to work because his wasn't working.

10. Our son _____ a physical examination before he enters the university.

11. He was angry because he _____ a lot of taxes.

12. I _____ a smallpox vaccination before I go to India.

13. I _____ to the bank before it closes.

14. We _____ very careful with the water while we were traveling in the tropical zone.

15. I _____ a taxi to work yesterday because I was in a hurry.

16. I _____ my car to the garage because the radiator is leaking.

17. The children _____ home from the playground before it gets dark.

18. Our daughter _____ at the university for three more years.

19. A person _____ for a long time to become a medical doctor.

20. I _____ a lot of letters yesterday afternoon.

21. Unfortunately, his wife _____ the hospital for an operation.

22. I _____ at an important meeting tomorrow afternoon.

23. Frank _____ a job when he goes back to Chicago.

24. I _____ the police last night because of my noisy neighbors.

25. She _____ a course in composition next semester.

8.18

Focus: *Have to* in Negative Verb Phrases (Lack of Necessity)

Fill in the blanks with appropriate base forms.

buy	do	go	put	take	walk
cook	fix	operate	repair	tell	wear
defrost	get	pay	stay	use	worry

EXAMPLES: a. Fortunately, the surgeon doesn't have to operate on my father.
              b. I didn't have to get up early yesterday morning.

1. I didn't have to _____ a lie to the police, but I did.

2. You're not going to have to _____ anything about the problem.

3. She doesn't have to _____ care of the children today because her mother's doing it.

   She doesn't have to _____ about them.

4. What a relief! I don't have to _____ this letter over. (*To do over* means *to do again with corrections.*)

5. Because tomorrow is Saturday, I'm not going to have to _____ to school. I don't have

   to _____ about any homework, either.

6. I don't have to _____ my refrigerator because it's automatic.

7. We don't have to _____ water in the radiator of our car because it's air-cooled. We

   don't have to _____ much gas, either.

Now supply complete negative verb phrases with *have to.*

8. We _____ a lot of taxes last year.

8. He _____ another English course next semester.

10. The children _____ inside today because it's not raining. They

   _____ their raincoats.

11. She _____ dinner tonight because her husband is taking her out. She

   _____ about the children either, because her mother is taking care

   of them.

12. Fortunately, our son _____ to the dentist often.

13. You _____ this TV set often because it's solid state. You _____

   _____ about big repair bills.

14. I _____ the elevator much because my office is on the second floor.

15. You _____ about the problem because I'm going to take care of it.

16. I _____ any homework last night.

17. I _____ this letter over because there are no mistakes.

18. I _____ to church every Sunday, but I enjoy it.

8.19

GRAMMAR EXERCISE   Name _____ Date _____

Focus: *Yes-No* Questions with *Have to*

Fill in the blanks with appropriate base forms.

EXAMPLES: a. Didn't you have to <u>speak</u> to your lawyer about the problem?
b. Do you have to <u>do</u> a lot of homework for your chemistry class?

1. Are you going to have to _____ care of your little sister?

2. Do you have to _____ this composition over?

3. Don't you have to _____ up early every morning?

4. Does Bill have to _____ a suit and tie when he goes to work?

5. Did they have to _____ a visa before they went to India?

6. Aren't you going to have to _____ to work tomorrow?

Now supply *do, does, did, are,* or *is* in the blanks as well.

7. _____ everyone have to _____ _____ at the meeting on Tuesday?

8. _____ your sister going to have to _____ care of the problem?

9. _____ you yourself have to _____ your parents the bad news?

10. _____ you have to _____ up early yesterday morning?

11. _____ your lawyer going to have to _____ this problem to court?

Now supply *don't, doesn't, didn't, aren't,* or *isn't* in the blanks.

12. _____ you have to pay any taxes last year?

13. _____ you going to have to do something about this problem?

14. _____ everyone going to have to take the final examination?

15. _____ everyone on your team have to practice a lot?

16. _____ you have to work very hard at your office?

17. _____ we going to have to do something about this situation?

Now complete the sentences.

18. Don't you have to _____?

19. Does your teacher have to _____?

20. Do I have to _____?

21. Are you going to have to _____?

22. _____ when you were sick?

23. _____ when you go to school?

24. _____ last year/today?

8.20

Focus: Information Questions with *Have to*

Fill in the blanks with appropriate base forms.

EXAMPLES: a. What time did you have to get up yesterday morning?
b. Why didn't you have to take the final examination?

1. Why did you have to _____ to the police about the matter?

2. What do I have to _____ to make a million dollars?

3. Why aren't you going to have to _____ any taxes next year?

4. How much rent do you have to _____ for your house?

5. How long does the turkey have to _____ in the oven?

6. What time are you going to have to _____ at tomorrow's meeting?

7. How many hours does your father have to _____ every day?

8. How many courses are you going to have to _____ next semester?

9. How much did you have to _____ for your ticket last night?

10. Why didn't you have to _____ to work yesterday?

Now supply appropriate auxiliaries (+ *not*) in the blanks.

EXAMPLES: c. What do you have to do tomorrow?
d. Why don't you have to take care of this problem yourself?

11. What time _____ you have to get to work?

12. Why _____ you going to have to talk to the police about this?

13. What time _____ everyone have to be there?

14. Why _____ you have to do any homework tonight?

15. What kind of clothes _____ you have to take with you on your last vacation?

16. What time _____ you have to get to work yesterday?

Now complete the sentences.

17. What time did you have to _____?

18. Why don't you have to _____?

19. Why aren't you going to have to _____?

20. What do you have to _____?

21. _____ when the class is over?

22. _____ when you go to the store?

23. _____ when you were a child?

24. _____ tomorrow/last night?

8.21

> Focus: *Have to* in Main and Subordinate Clauses

Complete the following sentences with appropriate main or subordinate clauses. Use *have to* + an appropriate base form.

EXAMPLES: a. I had to go to the store because I didn't have any sugar.
  b. He's going to have to stay at the university until he speaks English well.
       Note: We could also say *He has to stay* . . . in example b.)
  c. When he was sick, he had to take medicine three times a day.
  d. I didn't have to go to the doctor because I wasn't sick.

1. While he was a student at the university, _____

    _____

2. When I finish this course, _____

    _____

3. _____
    because I have enough money in my wallet for the weekend.

4. _____
    because I was tired after I finished dinner.

5. _____
    because there was nobody on the beach when we went swimming.

6. _____
    because it wasn't dirty.

7. _____
    when we take our trip around the world.

8. Because a maid is expensive, _____

    _____

9. _____
    because I am feeling much better now.

10. While he was working for that company, _____

    _____

11. I couldn't go to school yesterday morning _____

    _____

12. I was worried/angry/nervous _____

    _____

13. Because they are very rich/poor, _____

    _____

14. Since it rained all week, _____

    _____

8.22

GRAMMAR EXERCISE   Name _____ Date _____

  Focus: Lack of Necessity versus Prohibition

Supply an appropriate negative form of *have to* or *must* in each blank, using the base forms given in the parentheses.

EXAMPLES: a. (take) He <u>doesn't have to take</u> another English course because he speaks and writes well.
   b. (cheat) You <u>mustn't cheat</u> on your income taxes because you might get into trouble with the government.
   c. (go) I <u>didn't have to go</u> to the doctor because I wasn't sick.

1. (smoke) You _____ cigarettes because they're bad for your health.

2. (pay) Fortunately, he _____ a lot of rent for his house.

3. (waste) You _____ your time while you're at school.

4. (lie) He _____ to the police because he wasn't guilty of any crime.

5. (tell) You _____ the secret to anyone because you swore on the Bible (made an oath in God's name).

6. (do) You _____ your homework, but it's a good idea to try your best.

7. (trust) You _____ that person because s/he never tells the truth.

8. (work) His father _____ because he has a lot of money, but he enjoys the spirit of competition.

9. (keep) You _____ the fish out of the refrigerator for very long, or it will spoil.

10. (pay) They _____ a lot of taxes last year because they didn't make very much money.

11. (go) You _____ out in the rain without a jacket because you might catch cold.

12. (work) She _____ hard because she has an easy job, and her boss is never there.

13. (be) You _____ at the meeting because nobody expects you to be there.

14. (play) Children, you _____ with matches.

15. (lie) I _____ down for a nap because I'm not tired.

16. (get) The patient _____ out of bed until he is better.

17. (serve) You _____ white wine with chicken, but it's best.

18. (order) We _____ any cheese yet because there is enough for several weeks.

8.23

EXPECTATION WITH *SHOULD* AND *OUGHT TO*

1. The modal *should* may be used to show expectation: *Everyone **should be** good; These shoes **should be** more comfortable than they are.*

2. The modal *ought to* has exactly the same meaning as *should,* and the two modals are interchangeable: *They **ought to** (**should**) **be** happy, but they're not; He's an intelligent person and **ought to** (**should**) **have** a better job than he does.* As with the other modals, a base form always follows *should* (*ought to*).
   Note: In American English, *should* occurs more frequently than *ought to*.

3. The expectation expressed with *should* or *ought to* is very weak; for example, *My typewriter should (ought to) be much better than it is because it cost a lot of money; She's a beautiful and intelligent woman and should (ought to) have a lot of admirers, but for some reason she doesn't have any.*

4. We insert *not* between *should* and a base form; however, *not* is inserted between *ought* and *to: There **should not be** so much crime in the city, but there is; We **ought not to have** so many problems with our car, but we do.*
   Note: *Ought not to* occurs less frequently than *should not* in American English.

5. We use *shouldn't,* the contraction of *should not,* in informal usage: *Because she's so nice, you **shouldn't** have any problems with your boss, but you do; There **shouldn't** be unhappiness in his life, but there is.*

6. A subject is put between *should* and a base form in questions: ***Should he make** more money than he does? How **should the patient feel** after he takes the medicine?*
   Note: Questions with *ought to—Ought she to be here?*—almost never occur in American English.

7. Should follows the subject in *yes-no* answers: *Should it cost a lot? Yes, **it should;** No, **it shouldn't.***

8. When *be* is the base form in a question, it may be repeated in a *yes-no* answer: *Yes, it should* (***be***); *No, it shouldn't* (***be***).

GRAMMAR EXERCISE　　　　　　　　　Name _____ Date _____

Focus: Expectation with *Should* and *Ought to*

Fill in each blank with *should* or *ought to* + an appropriate base form. Do not use negative forms in this exercise. **Pronunciation Note**: <u>When spoken quickly</u>, *ought to* sounds like *oughta*.

EXAMPLES:　a. The best director in Europe directed the movie, so it <u>should be</u> good.
　　　　　　　b. I <u>ought to get</u> a good grade in the exam, because I studied very hard.

1. I paid a lot of money for these shoes. They _____ much more comfortable than they are.

2. After eating such a big meal, he _____ full.

3. My favorite actor is in the movie. It _____ good.

4. You _____ nice weather when you're in Paris next May.

5. I invited my guests to come at seven o'clock, but it's almost 8:30. They _____ here by now.

6. He's a smart and capable person, so he _____ a much better job than he does.

7. She's the best student in the class. She _____ better compositions than she does.

8. Our hotel room _____ nice; it's costing a hundred dollars a day.

9. The best student in the class _____ the best grade.

10. I used the best ingredients in this cake, so it _____ good, but it's terrible.

11. There _____ peace everywhere in the world, but there isn't.

12. With all of her abilities, she _____ the president of the company, but she's not.

13. This is an important scientific word and it _____ in the dictionary, but it isn't.

14. That place is the most expensive restaurant in town, so the food _____ good.

15. I have beautiful sunlight in my apartment, so my plants _____ well, but they don't.

16. He's a native speaker, so he _____ the language well.

17. When you go to the Riviera in August, the weather _____ very nice.

18. Our little boy _____ better grades at school, but he's more interested in baseball.

8.25

ADVISABILITY, RECOMMENDATION, AND OBLIGATION WITH *SHOULD/OUGHT TO*

1. *Should* and *ought to* may also be used to mean advisability and recommendation: *You should sit down and rest for a short while; I ought to serve white wine with the fish tonight.*

2. Like *must, should* and *ought to* are used to show a kind of obligation or sense of necessity, but there is a difference in meaning. Compare:

Should (ought to)	Must
People shouldn't smoke in elevators, but some people do.	*You must not smoke in elevators.*
I ought to be nice to my noisy neighbor, but I'm not.	*I must be nice to my boss.*
I should take care of this problem, but I'm not going to.	*One must take care of one's health.*

3. Recommendations with *should* and *ought to* also have less force than those made with *must.* Compare:

When you have time, you ought to see that movie.	*You must see that movie; it's about your native country.*
You should serve white wine with chicken, but I prefer red.	*You must serve soy sauce with Chinese food; everyone expects it.*

4. Information questions with *should* are questions asking for recommendation or advice for a course of action that is best.

Read the following sentences aloud.

1. What should I do about the cockroaches in my kitchen?
2. What airline should I take on my trip around the world?
3. How should we solve the problem of pollution and overpopulation?
4. Where should my friends go on their honeymoon?
5. What movie should I see this weekend?
6. What should I take with me when I go to the beach tomorrow?
7. What new books should I read?
8. What courses should we take next semester?
9. Where should I go this weekend?
10. How much money should I save every month?

Note: As in *yes-no* questions and negative verb phrases, information questions with *ought to—Where ought we to go?*—rarely occur.

8.26

Focus: Recommendation and Advisability with *Should/Ought to*

Fill in the blanks with *should* (*not*) or *ought* (*not*) *to*. When a negative verb phrase is appropriate, remember that *ought not to* occurs less frequently than *should not* in American English.

EXAMPLES: a. You should take a good raincoat with you when you go to London.
           b. You shouldn't miss that film; it's about the future.
           c. He ought to go on a diet before he gets too heavy.

1. You _____ cry over spilled milk (worry about past mistakes).

2. When you don't know the meaning of a word, you _____ look it up.

3. You _____ drink too much coffee; it's not good for you.

4. When you don't feel well, you _____ go to your doctor right away.

5. When you visit France, you _____ spend all your time in Paris.

6. We _____ talk about our friends behind their backs.

7. When you go to Japan, you _____ go to Kyoto.

8. We _____ spend our money on unnecessary things.

9. You _____ take medicine when you don't need it.

10. You _____ play your radio too loud after midnight.

11. You _____ take an umbrella today; the radio predicted rain.

12. When you take any kind of medicine, you _____ read the directions on the label carefully.

13. You _____ feed your baby girl more than she wants.

14. Children, you _____ walk across the street when the light is red.

15. Listen Billy! You _____ tease the dog.

16. You _____ never cheat at school, Jimmy.

17. In the next election, you _____ vote for the Democrats/Republicans/Liberals/Socialists/Communists/Nationalists/Fascists.

18. _____ I vote for nationalization of the steel industry?

19. Where _____ we go for our next vacation?

20. What _____ we do about the problem of overpopulation?

21. When you go to a tropical country, you _____ be extremely careful of the water.

22. How _____ I address an Ambassador/the President/the Pope?

23. Why _____ I use a pencil in my homework?

24. What _____ I do about my problem?

25. What _____ we do next? _____ we take a break?

8.27

GRAMMAR EXERCISE   Name _____ Date _____

Focus: Information Questions with Modal Auxiliaries

Complete the following information questions. Use the modal and base form given in the parentheses preceding each sentence, but supply your own subject and any other necessary words.

EXAMPLES: a. (can/stay) How long <u>can you stay under water?</u>
            b. (should/tip) How much <u>should I tip the waiter?</u>

1. (can/speak) How many languages _____?

2. (must/do) What _____?

3. (should/serve) What _____?

4. (can/find) Where _____?

5. (should/buy) What kind of _____?

6. (can/get) Where _____?

7. (should/go) Why _____?

8. (must/buy) What kind of _____?

9. (should/be) What time _____?

10. (must/take) What train _____?

11. (should/speak) Who(m) _____?

12. (must/arrive) What time _____?

13. (can't/be) Why _____?

14. (shouldn't/go) Why _____?

15. (mustn't/smoke) Why _____?

16. (may/put) Where _____?

17. (must/pay) How much _____?

18. (should/invite) Who(m) _____?

19. (can/play) What kind of _____?

20. (should/put) How much _____?

21. (shouldn't/eat) Why _____?

22. (should/go) How often _____?

23. (can/deposit) How much money _____?

24. (should/put) Where _____?

25. (may/borrow) Which typewriter _____?

26. (can/get) How _____?

27. (must/take) What _____?

28. (can/stay) How long _____?

8.28

GRAMMAR EXERCISE   Name _____ Date _____

Focus: Reviewing Prepositions

Supply appropriate prepositions in the blanks. Do this exercise as a quiz—test yourself.

about	between	from	into	off	out	up
at	down	in	of	on	to	with

EXAMPLES: a. What time did you get <u>to</u> school yesterday morning?
b. Everyone stood <u>up</u> when the Pope came <u>into</u> the room.

1. You remind me _____ an old friend _____ mine.

2. Our office is _____ 430 Washington Avenue.

3. Our house is _____ Main Street _____ Fifth and Sixth Avenues.

4. The shortest distance _____ two points is a straight line.

5. How did you get _____ such terrible trouble _____ the police?

6. When we got _____ the airport, our plane was taking _____.

7. The weather in Mexico City is always nice _____ April.

8. This is a secret _____ you and me.

9. There is a mailbox _____ the corner _____ First Avenue and 53rd Street.

10. Don't forget to put stamps _____ that letter.

11. What is the best way to get _____ _____ this city?

12. The doctor arrived _____ the hospital too late to save the patient.

13. What are you worrying _____?

14. What time are you coming _____ school tomorrow?

15. Our son was born _____ Christmas Day.

16. Why don't you take _____ your coat and sit _____?

17. You may find those letters _____ the bottom drawer _____ my desk.

18. What kind of perfume do you have _____?

19. Would you please listen _____ me. This news is important!

20. Aren't those your gloves lying _____ the floor?

21. Why don't you lie _____ and take a little nap?

22. Children, please keep your hands _____ the walls.

23. Our daughter wants to get _____ the University of California.

24. Please put those books _____ the top shelf.

25. We breathe _____ our lungs, see _____ our eyes, and hear _____ our ears.

26. It is very hot _____ _____ the middle _____ the earth.

27. We keep a lot _____ old things _____ _____ the attic _____ our house.

THE FUTURE TENSE

9.1

FUTURE EVENTS

1. To form the future tense, we use the modals *will* (and *shall*, in the first person) and a base form as the main verb in a verb phrase: *The world's population **will get** larger and larger; I **shall return***.

	Singular	Plural
First person	I will (shall) go	we will (shall) go
Second person	you ⎫	you ⎫
Third person	he ⎬ will go	they ⎭ will go
	she ⎪	
	it ⎭	

Note: *Will* may be used in all persons in American English: *I **will** remember you always; We **will** be together forever*. The use of *shall* for the first person is most often used in British English.

2. *Not* is inserted between the modal and the base form in negative verb phrases: *We **will not** surrender to the enemy; Our side **will not** lose*.

I ⎫	we ⎫
you ⎪	you ⎬ will not go
he ⎬ will not go	they ⎭
she ⎪	
it ⎭	

3. Contraction of *will* and subject pronouns occur in informal usage: ***I'll** see you in a few days; **We'll** win the game*.

I ⎫	we ⎫
you ⎪	you ⎬ 'll
he ⎬ 'll	they ⎭
she ⎪	
it ⎭	

Pronunciation Note: In writing, such contractions of *will* and noun subjects do not appear; however, they occur in speaking: (a) *Mary will* sounds like *mary-ill;* (b) *Mr. and Mrs. Brown will* sounds like *Mr. and Mrs. brown-ill;* (c) *The food will* sounds like *the food-ill*.

4. *Won't*, the contraction of *will not*, occurs in less formal usage: *We **won't** give up the fort; I **won't** fight in the war*.
   Note: *Shan't*, the contraction of *shall not*, is chiefly British.

5. The subject follows *will* in *yes-no* and information questions: **Will she** *help us with the project? When* **will the enemy** *give up?*

6. *Will* follows the subject in *yes-no* answers: *Will you stop smoking? Yes,* **I will;** *No,* **I won't.**

7. Adverbs are very often used in the future tense and precede the base form: *I'll* **always be** *faithful to my wife; Man will* **eventually travel** *to outer space; I'll* **never break** *my promise; They will* **never give** *their young son to the army; Where will you* **eventually live?** *What will* **probably happen** *at the next meeting? How will you* **ever finish** *the project on time?*

8. *Be going to* and *will* are more or less interchangeable: *They are going to (will) get married in June; It's going to (will) snow tomorrow.* However, *will* gives much greater force to a statement, and it also means more than just an event in future time. In this respect, *will* functions in a way similar to the other modals like *may, can, must,* and *should. Will* expresses:

   (a) **Promise:** *I will love you forever; I will never tell our secret; I will be good; I will never tell a lie again.*

   (b) **Determination:** *I will protect my property with my life; We will fight our enemy until our last man falls; If necessary, we will defend our city with bricks; They will fight for their freedom.*

   (c) **Inevitability:** *The world will eventually come to an end; Women will eventually have equal opportunities with men; We will eventually have peace in the world.*

   (d) **Prediction:** *It will rain tomorrow; According to the prophet, the world will come to an end tomorrow; You will speak English well.*

9. *Will* also occurs in very polite requests: *Will you please give me your hand? Will you please go to the dance with me? Bonnie, will you please be a good girl at school? Class, will you please not forget to bring your dictionaries?*

9.2

GRAMMAR EXERCISE   Name _____ Date _____

        Focus: The Future Tense

Fill in the blanks with appropriate base forms from the following list:

be	come	fall	keep	melt	rise	try
become	cry	fly	love	need	solve	want
begin	explore	forget	make	remember	tell	

EXAMPLES: a. It'll probably <u>rain</u> when we go to the beach.
           b. I'll always <u>keep</u> my word. This is a promise. (*To keep one's word* means *to keep one's promise.*)

  1. I'll never _____ our secret to anyone.

  2. The birds in the north will always _____ south when winter comes; it's inevitable.

  3. The class will probably _____ as soon as the teacher comes.

  4. The rich will always _____ more than they have.

  5. We will eventually _____ the problem of pollution.

  6. The sun will probably _____ before this party is over.

  7. I will always _____ to be good.

  8. There will always _____ hope for a better world.

  9. The baby will probably _____ as soon as she gets hungry.

10. The world will eventually _____ to an end.

11. Our children will eventually _____ adults.

12. I will never _____ a serious lie to my parents.

Now supply an adverb + base form. Use *always, probably, eventually,* or *never*.

13. When we go to Moscow next March, it will _____ cold.

14. The leaves will _____ around the end of September.

15. Man will _____ other parts of our solar system.

16. I will _____ a few mistakes in the next test.

17. We will _____ perfect.

Now supply *will* + adverb + base form.

18. This course _____ to an end.

19. Love _____ stronger than hate.

20. I _____ my word.

21. According to some scientists, all of the ice on earth _____.

22. The world _____ a better place.

GRAMMAR EXERCISE   Name _____ Date _____

Focus: The Future Tense in Main Clauses of Complex Sentences

Supply appropriate base forms or -s forms in the blanks. Practice the pronunciation of 'll. **Reminder:** (a) A base form always follows *will;* (b) a base form or -s form following *when, until, before,* etc., may mean future time.

be	feel	give	make	speak	wait
begin	find	graduate	move	start	work
come	finish	have	retire	take	
die	get	love	sit	try	

EXAMPLES: a. She'll <u>love</u> him until the day she <u>dies</u>.
            b. You'll <u>have</u> fewer problems when you <u>move</u> out of the city.

1. They'll _____ married when the right time _____.

2. I'll _____ proud of you when you _____ from the university.

3. He'll _____ a very happy person when he _____ his promotion.

4. She'll _____ for her company until she _____ a better job.

5. They'll _____ a new business as soon as they _____ enough money.

6. It'll _____ wonderful when spring _____.

7. I'll _____ very tired by the time today _____ over. (*By the time* means *when.*)

8. We'll _____ glad to help you when you _____ your move to your new house.

9. I'll _____ to do my best when I _____ the final examination.

10. It'll _____ to rain in a few minutes, so _____ your umbrella.

11. I'll _____ the furniture to the bedroom when I _____ the party.

12. You'll _____ much better after you _____ your shower.

13. I'll _____ for you until you're ready to go.

14. We'll _____ English much better when we _____ this course.

Now complete the sentence with main clauses containing verb phrases in the future tense. Use no negative forms.

15. When summer comes, _____.

16. When I speak English well, _____.

17. When they get married, _____.

18. When we finish this exercise, _____.

19. After I do my homework, _____.

20. Before I go to bed, _____.

9.4

GRAMMAR EXERCISE   Name _____ Date _____

Focus: Negative Verb Phrases with *Will*

Supply negative verb phrases with *will* in the blanks.

announce	break	do	have	promise	ring	tell
be	choose	feel	make	retire	taste	

EXAMPLES: a. He <u>won't retire</u> until he reaches the age of sixty-five.
             b. The government <u>will not announce</u> its decision until the elections are over.

1. When I go to London for only a week, there _____ enough time to see everything.

2. S/he _____ happy until s/he finds romance.

3. We _____ the next exercise until we finish this one.

4. There _____ many people at the beach today because it's not a very nice day.

5. My phone _____ much this weekend because most of my friends are out of town.

6. The team _____ a new captain until the new season begins.

7. This soup _____ any good until you add some more salt.

8. I _____ you my secret until you tell me yours.

9. I'm a little worried because I _____ with anybody when I go home late tonight.

10. The committee _____ a decision until it has all of the important facts.

11. There _____ anyone in the house when I get home.

12. When I am in San Francisco, I _____ much time to see the city because I'll be too busy at the conference.

13. You _____ better until you stop smoking.

14. They _____ happy until they have a lot of money in the bank.

15. The world _____ progress until it solves the problem of overpopulation.

16. I _____ anything about this problem until I discuss it with my lawyer.

17. I _____ anybody about this scandal in your family.

18. I _____ anything to that company until they give me a contract.

19. Everyone in the business world likes him because he _____ a promise.

20. I _____ the call tonight; it is nearly 11 o'clock.

9.5

GRAMMAR EXERCISE   Name _____ Date _____

Focus: *Yes-No Questions with Will*

Supply a base form in the main clause and a base form or -s form in the time clause.

arrive	die	get	hear	promise	return	think
be	eat	go	inherit	receive	stay	visit
come	end	have	live	retire	take	wear

EXAMPLES: a. Will he <u>inherit</u> a lot of money when his father <u>dies</u>?
b. Will you <u>be</u> able to use your dictionary when you <u>take</u> the final examination?
c. Will the time ever <u>come</u> when there <u>is</u> no war?

1. Will the world _____ to an end before this century _____ over?

2. Will the time ever _____ when there _____ enough food for everybody?

3. Will the time ever _____ when the world _____ peace?

4. Will the company _____ his resumé before he _____ to the job interview? (A *resumé* is *a record of one's past history.*)

5. Will your father _____ unhappy when he _____?

6. Will you _____ to tell me the news as soon as you _____ it?

7. When today _____ over, will you _____ tired?

8. Will the day ever _____ when people _____ forever?

9. When winter _____, will your grandparents _____ south?

10. Will she _____ at this university until she _____ her degree?

11. Will you usually _____ out in restaurants while your family _____ away?

12. When she _____ her divorce, will she _____ a happier woman?

13. Will he _____ a different schedule when he _____ his promotion?

14. While you're away on your vacation, will you _____ about me?

15. When she _____ her operation, will she _____ in the hospital for a long time?

Now complete the following sentences with main clauses.

EXAMPLES: d. When you are older, <u>will you have a different attitude?</u>
e. When you finish this course, <u>will you take another one?</u>

16. When you get home tonight, _____?

17. When summer/winter comes, _____?

18. When you leave this room today, _____?

19. When we finish this exercise, _____?

20. When you get up tomorrow morning, _____?

9.6

GRAMMAR EXERCISE   Name _____ Date _____

Focus: Information Questions with *Will*

Supply appropriate base forms or -s forms in the blanks.

EXAMPLES: a. When will the earth <u>come</u> to an end?
            b. Who will <u>be</u> the King when the Queen <u>dies</u>?
            c. How long will the movie <u>last</u>?

   1. Where will you _____ when the sun _____ tomorrow morning?

   2. When this course _____ to an end, how will you _____?

   3. How much longer will this class _____?

   4. When you _____ and _____ English well, what will you _____?

   5. When you _____ back to your native country, whom will you _____ with?

   6. How will the patient _____ after she _____ her medicine?

   7. Who will _____ in the next election? Who will _____ the President?

   8. What will you _____ when you _____ a lot of money in the bank?

   9. How warm will tomorrow _____? Will it _____?

  10. What will we _____ when we _____ this exercise?

Now complete the sentences with appropriate time clauses.

EXAMPLES: d. What will happen <u>when your birthday comes</u>?
            e. Who will be here <u>when you arrive tomorrow morning</u>?

  11. What will you do _____?

  12. How will you feel _____?

  13. What kind of job will you get _____?

  14. Who will take care of your house _____?

  15. How much money will he make_____?

  16. What will you serve _____?

Now complete the sentences with appropriate main clauses.

EXAMPLES: f. When he gets his promotion, <u>what kind of schedule will he have</u>?
           g. When his father dies, <u>how much money will he inherit</u>?

  17. When you get home tonight,_____?

  18. When you go to the bank, _____?

  19. After she takes her medicine, _____?

  20. When you become a millionaire, _____?

9.7

GRAMMAR EXERCISE   Name _____ Date _____

Focus: *Shall* in Requests

1. The use of *shall* in requests is similar in meaning to *do you want me (us) to: Shall I turn on the radio? Shall we dance?*
   Note: Second person does not appear in requests with *shall*.

2. *Please do* or *please don't* is the common response to a *yes-no* request with *shall I: Shall I open the window?* **Please do;** *Shall I turn off the heat?* **Please don't.**

3. *Let's* or *let's not* is the response to a *yes-no* request with *shall we: Shall we dance?* **Let's;** *Shall we go to a movie tonight?* **Let's not.**

Supply appropriate base forms in the blanks.

EXAMPLES: a. Shall we <u>take</u> a drive in the country today?
             b. Shall I <u>arrive</u> at the party early or late?

1. Shall I _____ you about my plans for your birthday?

2. Shall we _____ another cocktail before we have dinner?

3. Shall I _____ this information to the police?

4. Shall I _____ off the TV?

5. Shall we _____ a little break?

6. Shall I _____ this letter over?

7. Shall we _____ for a walk in the park?

8. Shall we _____ some cards after dinner?

9. Shall we _____ our neighbors to the party?

10. Shall we _____ this boring party?

11. Shall I _____ my job?

12. Shall I _____ their invitation?

13. Shall we _____ longer or leave?

14. Shall we _____ a toast to the Queen? (Use *make.*)

15. Shall we _____ another exercise or take a break?

16. Shall we _____ a taxi or a bus to school today?

17. Shall we _____ in or out tonight? (*To eat in* means *to eat at home; to eat out* means *to eat at a restaurant.*)

18. There's our favorite song. Shall we _____?

19. Shall we _____ married?

9.8

THE FUTURE CONTINUOUS TENSE

1. We use the FUTURE CONTINUOUS TENSE to emphasize an event at a definite point of time in the future: *Our plane **will be taking** off for Rio at exactly this time tomorrow afternoon; All my friends **will be saying** good-bye to me.*

2. To form the future continuous tense, use *will* (*shall*) and the verb *be* as auxiliaries and a present participle as the main verb of a verb phrase. *Not* follows *will* in negative verb phrases.

   I will (shall) not be going

   you
   he } will not be going
   she
   it

   We will (shall) not be going

   you
   they } will not be going

   Reminder: Except for making polite requests, the use of *shall* in the future tense is chiefly British.

3. Besides being used to emphasize an event in future time, the future continuous tense is used to emphasize the duration of an event: *I'll be thinking of you **during my whole vacation**; He'll be working hard **from the beginning to the end of next week**.*

4. The form also occurs in the main clause of a complex sentence that contains a time clause with a base or -s form (or *am* or *are*). The action expressed in the time clause, in effect, interrupts the action expressed in the main clause: ***I'll be carrying** a large red book and wearing a white carnation in my lapel **when you come to meet me at the station**; A lot of things **will be changing while he is away from his native country**.*

5. A subject follows *will* in yes-no and information questions: ***Will you be working** tomorrow morning? What time **will you be** getting up?*

6. In *yes-no* answers, *be* may follow *will*, but its use is optional: *Will you be studying in the library this afternoon? Yes, I **will** (**be**); No, I **won't** (**be**).*

7. Like *not*, other adverbs follow *will*: *He **will probably be** having dinner around six tonight; The sun **will probably be** shining tomorrow.*

9.9

Name _____ Date _____

Focus: Emphasizing the Duration of an Event in Future Time

Fill in the blanks with appropriate verb phrases in the future continuous tense; use present participles made out of the base forms in the following list. Do not use negative forms.

clean	dance	discuss	live	revolve	take	use
convalesce	dig	edit	practice	ride	think	wait

EXAMPLES:
    a. The editor <u>will be editing</u> the manuscript for the book for several months.
    b. He'll <u>be convalescing</u> for several months after he gets out of the hospital.

1. I _____ my air conditioner a lot until this heat wave is over. (A *heat wave* is a period of very hot weather.)

2. I _____ right here until you return. (*Right here* means *exactly here.*)

3. They _____ in a hotel while they are looking for a house.

4. When we travel from Paris to Istanbul, we _____ on the train for about seventy hours.

5. I _____ my apartment for the better part of the day. (*The better part of the day* [or *night*] means *most of the day.*)

6. The earth _____ around the sun for millions of more years.

7. I _____ this sonata a long time before I am able to perform it in public.

8. We _____ a very serious problem during tomorrow's meeting.

9. I _____ a lot of pictures during my vacation in North Africa.

10. The phone repairmen _____ a hole in the street for the rest of the day.

11. The professor _____ the theory of evolution during his next lecture.

12. Everyone _____ at the party from the beginning to the end.

13. He _____ about his girlfriend a lot while she's away on her vacation.

9.10

GRAMMAR EXERCISE   Name _____ Date _____

Focus: Negative Verb Phrases in Main Clauses

Supply appropriate negative verb phrases in the future continuous tense in the main clause, and an appropriate base form or -s form in the subordinate clause in the following sentences.

be	end	get	learn	make	set	think
come	enter	go	leave	move	shine	use
develop	feel	have	listen	reach	speak	
eat	find	know	live	retire	take	

EXAMPLES: a. He won't be making much money until he learns a skill.
          b. You will not be feeling better until you take your medicine.

1. She _____ important decisions in her job until she _____ more about the business.

2. We _____ any other language except English until this meeting _____.

3. Fortunately, I _____ about my problems at work when I _____ on my vacation.

4. I _____ anything today until I _____ dinner because I'm on a diet.

5. We _____ to the radio when we _____ for our drive in the country because it's broken.

6. We _____ dinner until the last guest _____.

7. They _____ into a larger apartment until they _____ a little bit more money in the bank.

8. I _____ out of bed until I _____ better.

9. He _____ his dictionary when he _____ the final examination because it's not permitted.

10. The sun _____ when I _____ out of work today.

11. The country _____ much progress in pollution control until the government _____ new programs.

12. They _____ a divorce until s/he _____ the final decision.

13. They _____ married until they both _____ good jobs.

14. He _____ his job until he _____ a better one.

15. His father _____ in New York when he _____.

16. Our child _____ school until he _____ the age of six.

9.11

Name _____ Date _____

Focus: *Yes-No* Questions with Complex Sentences

Supply *be* + a present participle in the main clause, a base form or an *-s* form, or *is* or *are*, in the subordinate clause in each of the following sentences. Practice *yes-no* answers.

arrive	deliver	finish	live	rise	stay	travel
be	do	get	make	sleep	take	wait
come	feel	happen	retire	snow	think	wear

EXAMPLES: a. Will you be thinking about her while she is away?
b. Will the baby be taking a nap after she finishes her lunch?

1. Will it _____ when we _____ out of the meeting?

2. Will the children _____ their homework when Dad _____ home from work?

3. Will the two of you _____ in the same room when you _____ at the hotel during the conference?

4. Will you _____ anything in particular when I _____ to the station to pick you up? (How will I recognize you?)

5. Will anyone _____ for you when you _____ home?

6. Will you parents _____ here when they _____ from their jobs?

7. Will you _____ when this century _____ to an end?

8. Will your sister _____ much better when she _____ out of the hospital?

9. Will she _____ better after she _____ this medicine?

10. Will you _____ when the sun _____ tomorrow morning?

11. Will you _____ at a hotel or with friends while you _____ on your vacation in San Francisco?

12. Will you _____ in this city after you _____ your studies?

13. Will anything in particular _____ when you _____ to work tomorrow morning?

14. Will Bob _____ a lot of money when he _____ his new job?

15. Will the President _____ an important speech when he _____ at the convention in Chicago?

16. Will Bill's wife _____ with him while he _____ on his next business trip?

17. Will everyone in your family _____ for you when you _____ at the airport?

9.12

GRAMMAR EXERCISE

Focus: *Probably*

On a separate piece of paper, compose an appropriate main clause containing a verb phrase with *will* + *probably* + *be* + present participle for each of the following sentences.

EXAMPLES: a. *The sun will probably be shining* when we reach the top of the mountain.
b. *Grandpa will probably be feeling better* after he gets out of the hospital.

1. . . . when this course is over.
2. . . . when we arrive at the airport.
3. . . . before we have dinner.
4. . . . when I get home/to school.
5. . . . when I get up tomorrow.
6. . . . when we go to the beach.
7. . . . while the sun is setting.

8. . . . while I'm in Paris.
9. . . . when we take the exam.
10. . . . after I graduate.
11. . . . when I enter the room.
12. . . . when my alarm rings.
13. . . . when the teacher comes.
14. . . . after I take my nap.

9.13

GRAMMAR EXERCISE

Focus: *Because* Clauses

On a separate piece of paper, compose appropriate clauses of reason introduced by *because*. Use the future continuous tense only. **Note**: The adverb *probably* precedes *won't*: *When we go to the beach tomorrow, the sun **probably won't** be shining*. In more formal usage *probably* is inserted between *will* and *not*: *The President **will probably not** be delivering a speech at the banquet*.

EXAMPLES: a. I should take my umbrella *because it will probably be raining*.
b. We're not going sailing *because the wind won't be blowing*.

1. S/he's very excited . . .
2. I can't go with you to the fair tomorrow . . .
3. Please don't call me after lunch . . .
4. Please don't make any noise when you get home tonight . . .
5. Please don't call between seven and eight this evening . . .
6. I don't want to go to school tomorrow . . .
7. We're not going to the beach tomorrow . . .
8. I don't want to go to work tomorrow . . .
9. I have to take the bus to work tomorrow . . .
10. Bob should wear a shirt and tie to the party . . .
11. Please try to get to the station before nine o'clock . . .
12. I'll probably take my snowshoes tomorrow morning . . .

9.14

GRAMMAR EXERCISE   Name _____ Date _____

For the very immediate future (almost right after we speak), *be about to* + a base form may occur: *Hurry up! The movie **is about to begin**; Listen! The TV announcer **is about to tell** of the government's decision.*

Fill in the blanks with appropriate forms of *be about to* + a base form.

arrive	close	die	finish	go	land	rain	sneeze
begin	come	enter	get	have	leave	serve	take

EXAMPLES:
  a. Do you happen to have a tissue? I'm about to sneeze.
  b. Let's hurry up. It's about to rain, and we don't want to get wet.

1. Hurry up! Our plane _____ off, and we want to be on it.

2. Please let's not go now. The best part of the party _____.

3. Everyone is excited because the President _____.

4. Please hurry up! The bank _____, and I need to get some money for the weekend.

5. He's worried because his wife _____ the hospital for a serious operation.

6. I'm a little nervous because my guests _____.

7. I don't want to go shopping because it _____.

8. I don't want to go to bed now because a good movie _____ on TV, and I don't want to miss it.

9. The students are all excited because they _____ the final examination for the course.

10. Unfortunately, the patient _____.

11. Please turn off the radio because I _____ to bed.

12. I must tell my boss when I _____ for the meeting because he wants to go with me.

13. I'm making some sandwiches for the children because they _____ home from school, and they'll be a little hungry.

14. I'm going to leave this meeting because I _____ angry.

15. My favorite TV program _____ on.

16. Will everyone please stand up because the King _____ the room?

17. Children, please come to the table because we _____ dinner.

18. Fasten your seat belts because we _____.

19. We _____ this exercise.

20. We _____ on to another exercise.

9.15

DURATION WITH *TAKE*

1. When we want to express the length of an event, we use the following pattern: *it + take + stated duration + infinitive + balance of sentence*: **It takes about an hour to fly** to *Washington from New York;* **It's going to take an hour to do** *that exercise;* **It will take a couple of years to write** the book.

2. An object can occur after *take,* but its use is optional: *According to the Bible, it took (God) six days to create the world; It took (the astronauts) three days to get to the moon; It took (the speaker) three hours to deliver the speech.*

3. *How long* usually occurs in information questions with *take* expressing duration: **How long** *does it take to get to Bombay by ship?* **How long** *did it take Beethoven to compose the Ninth Symphony?* **How long** *will it take us to learn English well?*

4. *How many* + seconds, minutes, hours, etc., is also frequently used in information questions: **How many minutes** *does it take to cook an egg?* **How many years** *did it take scientists to develop the first atomic bomb?*

9.16

GRAMMAR EXERCISE   Name _____ Date _____

      Focus: *Take*

Supply appropriate infinitives in the blanks.

EXAMPLES: a. How much longer will it take <u>to finish</u> this book?
           b. How long does it usually take you <u>to do</u> your homework?

1. How long did it take you _____ home yesterday?

2. How long did it take the Egyptians _____ the pyramids?

3. How long did it take the author _____ this book?

4. How long does it usually take you _____ your house/apartment?

5. How long does it take _____ from New York to London by air?

6. How long does it take _____ from New York to Los Angeles by plane/by train/by bus/by car/by ship/by hitchhiking?

7. How long does it usually take a student _____ English as a second language well?

8. How long did it take the police _____ the criminal?

9. How long does it take _____ a movie?

10. How long did it take scientists _____ the atomic bomb?

11. How long did it take the astronauts _____ to the Moon?

12. How long does it take _____ a medium-sized chicken/potato ?

13. How long is it going to take you _____ your homework tonight?

14. How long does it usually take a man _____ in the mornings?

15. How long did it take you _____ to the United States/England?

16. How long did it take you _____ to school today?

9.16 (*Continued*)

Now complete the sentences with your own words.

17. How long does _____ ?

18. How long did _____ ?

19. How long will _____ ?

20. How long should_____ ?

21. How many hours/days/weeks/years_____ ?

9.17

GRAMMAR EXERCISE   Name _____ Date _____

Focus: Information Questions with *Take*

Transform the following sentences into information questions.

EXAMPLES: a. It took *millions of years* for the earth to evolve. How long did it take for the earth to evolve?
           b. It took *a long time* to write the Bible. How long did it take to write the Bible?

1. It took *hundreds of years* to build Rome. _____

2. It should take *about a week* to drive from New York to Los Angeles. _____

   _____

3. It will take *about three days* to climb to the top of the mountain. _____

   _____

4. It's going to take *only a few minutes* to walk to the store. _____

   _____

5. It will take *at least a year* to finish the next project. _____

   _____

6. It took John *three years* to learn French well. _____

7. It took the surgeon *three hours* to complete the operation. _____

   _____

8. It usually takes *ten or fifteen minutes* to do an exercise. _____

   _____

9. It should take *about an hour* to bake a potato. _____

10. It usually takes her *about a month* to knit a sweater. _____

    _____

11. It took *three weeks* to drive from Casablanca to Cairo. _____

    _____

12. It should take *about seven hours* to cook the turkey._____

    _____

13. It takes him *about fifteen minutes* to shave. _____

9.18

TAG QUESTIONS

1. When we ask a simple *yes-no* question, we do not ordinarily know the answer until we have received the reply. With a TAG QUESTION, however, we usually know the answer, or we are just seeking confirmation of something we already know. For example, in *Life is difficult, isn't it?* we know that most people will agree with us; we are only confirming a well-known fact.

2. The first part of a tag question is a statement—for example, *You're not a native speaker*—and the second part of the question is called a TAG ENDING: *You're not a native speaker, **are you?*** A comma separates the statement from the tag ending.

3. When the statement is positive, the tag ending is negative: *You're an American, **aren't** you?* When the statement is negative, the tag ending is positive: *You're **not** an American, **are** you?*

4. When a noun subject occurs as the subject in the statement, it is always replaced by a pronoun in the tag ending: ***Mary** is a nice person, isn't **she?** **Algebra and calculus** are difficult, aren't **they?***

5. When *there* and *it* appear in the statement, they are repeated in the tag ending: ***There** isn't enough time in a day, is **there?** **It's** not going to take a long time to learn English, is **it?***

6. In the simple present and past tenses (except for the verb *be*) and in the idiom *have to,* a form of the auxiliary *do* always occurs in the tag ending: *Jack **likes** to play baseball, **doesn't** he? Napoleon **crowned** himself, **didn't** he? We **have to** try our best, **don't** we?*

7. When *I* appears with the verb *be* in a negative tag ending, *am I not?* appears in formal usage—*I am your Ambassador, **am I not?**—*and *aren't I?* appears in informal usage: *I'm a good friend of yours, **aren't I?***

8. When *never* and *seldom* occur in the statement, the tag endings are positive: *I'll **never** be rich, **will I?** They're **seldom** here, **are they?***

9. When we are sure of the answer, the final intonation of the tag ending is down: *You love your children, don't you?* When we are not sure of the answer, the intonation is up: *You won't be here, will you?*

9.19

GRAMMAR EXERCISE   Name _____ Date _____

                        Focus: Tag Questions

Supply appropriate tag endings in the blanks.

EXAMPLES: a. Everyone in the class studies hard, <u>doesn't he?</u>
                 Note: We may hear *don't they?* in informal usage.
           b. She has to take another course, <u>doesn't she?</u>
           c. I'm going to get a good grade in the course, <u>aren't I?</u>

1. They were never happy together in their mariage, _____?

2. Your mother has to work hard in the house, _____?

3. You'll always be a good friend of mind, _____?

4. Barbara should take the next course, _____?

5. This exercise is fun, _____?

6. The class is about to finish this book, _____?

7. A male lion seldom hunts for food, _____?

8. Marconi invented the wireless, _____?

9. You were born in a hospital, _____?

10. A clause always has a subject and a verb, _____?

11. You'll never tell our secret, _____?

12. Tokyo is the largest city in the world, _____?

13. The formula for water is H_2O, _____?

14. The earth revolves around the sun, _____?

15. The beginning of this book wasn't difficult, _____?

16. We had to study hard during the course, _____?

17. I'm eventually going to speak English well, _____?

18. Students often forget -*s* forms, _____?

19. You didn't study English when you were a child, _____?

20. There are a lot of problems in the world, _____?

21. The Nile is the longest river in the world, _____?

22. The shortest distance between two points is a straight line, _____?

23. There isn't any nitrogen in water, _____?

24. It's not always easy to be good, _____?

25. You couldn't lift a thousand pounds, _____?

26. Alexander Graham Bell invented the telephone, _____?

27. Prepositions are sometimes difficult, _____?

28. You have to take another course, _____?

29. You're going to be able to continue your studies, _____?

NUMBERS, DATES, AND ARITHMETIC

Appendix 1

1.1

CARDINAL AND ORDINAL NUMBERS

Cardinal	Ordinal
1 one	1st first
2 two	2nd second
3 three	3rd third
4 four	4th fourth
5 five	5th fifth
6 six	6th sixth
7 seven	7th seventh
8 eight	8th eighth
9 nine	9th ninth
10 ten	10th tenth
11 eleven	11th eleventh
12 twelve	12th twelfth
13 thirteen	13th thirteenth
14 fourteen	14th fourteenth
15 fifteen	15th fifteenth
16 sixteen	16th sixteenth
17 seventeen	17th seventeenth
18 eighteen	18th eighteenth
19 nineteen	19th nineteenth
20 twenty	20th twentieth
21 twenty-one	21st twenty-first
22 twenty-two	22nd twenty-second
23 twenty-three	23rd twenty-third
30 thirty	30th thirtieth
40 forty	40th fortieth
50 fifty	50th fiftieth
60 sixty	60th sixtieth
70 seventy	70th seventieth
80 eighty	80th eightieth
90 ninety	90th ninetieth
100 a/one hundred	100th a/one hundredth
1,000 a/one thousand	1,000th a/one thousandth
1,000,000 a/one million	1,000,000th a/one millionth
1,000,000,000 a/one billion	1,000,000,000th a/one billionth

241

1.2

SPELLING EXERCISE   Name _____ Date _____

   Focus: Ordinal Numbers

   In writing, ordinal numbers are usually spelled out: *The end of the **twentieth** century is rapidly approaching.*

Spell out the ordinals given in parentheses in the blank spaces.

EXAMPLES: a. Shakespeare was born in the (16th) <u>sixteenth</u> century.
       b. The (18th) <u>eighteenth</u> century was a century of great change.

1. Columbus landed in America at the end of the (15th) _____ century.

2. Neil Armstrong was the (1st) _____ man on the moon.

3. A friend of mine's (40th) _____ birthday is coming soon.

4. My grandparents just celebrated their (50th) _____ wedding anniversary.

5. January is the (1st) _____ month of the year, February is the (2nd) _____,
   March is the (3rd) _____, April is the (4th) _____, May is the (5th)
   _____, June is the (6th) _____, July is the (7th) _____,
   August is the (8)th _____, September is the (9th) _____, October is the
   (10th) _____, November is the (11th) _____, and December is the
   (12th) _____.

6. I got a watch on my (21st) _____ birthday.

7. This is the (7th) _____ sentence of this exercise.

8. Our daughter is in the (8th) _____ grade.

9. Silver is an appropriate gift for a (25th) _____ wedding anniversary.

10. They have an (18th) _____-century house on West (9th) _____ Street.

11. (5th) _____ Avenue is a famous street in New York.

12. My father's (50th) _____ birthday is just around the corner (very near).

13. Friday the (13th) _____ is an unlucky day.

14. My grandmother is approaching her (100th) _____ birthday. She was born in the
    (19th) _____ century.

15. In many buildings in New York there is no (13th) _____ floor.

1.3

TELLING THE TIME

Note: *To tell the time* is idiomatic for *to give the time*.

1. Usually, the hours of the day in the United States are not numbered beyond twelve. To indicate day or night we use the abbreviations from Latin A.M., *ante meridiem* (before noon) and P.M., *post meridiem* (after noon); for example, *The plane arrived at exactly 9:00 A.M.* (in the morning); *The class ends at 1:00 P.M.* (in the afternoon).

2. Never use A.M. with *in the morning* or P.M. with *in the evening,* and never use the expression *o'clock* (of the clock) with either A.M. or P.M., or figures: *We left at 5:00 A.M.* (but, *We left at five o'clock in the morning*); *We arrived at 6:00 P.M.* (but, *We arrived at six o'clock in the evening*).
   Pronunciation Note: *O'clock* sounds like *a clock*.

3. *What time is it? It's . . .*

7:00 seven	7:35 seven thirty-five
seven o'clock	twenty-five (minutes) to eight
7:05 seven 0 five	twenty-five (minutes) of eight
five (minutes) after seven	7:45 seven forty-five
7:10 ten (minutes) after seven	a quarter to eight
7:15 seven fifteen	a quarter of eight
a quarter after seven	7:55 seven fifty-five
a quarter past seven	five (minutes) to eight
7:30 seven thirty	five (minutes) of eight
half past seven	12:00 noon
	midnight

Note: The word *minutes* is often omitted.

Read the following times aloud.

12:03	6:50
12:18	8:57 (almost nine o'clock)
3:00	8:03 (a little bit after eight)
4:29 (almost four thirty)	8:57 (a little bit before nine)
1:20	9:00 (nine o'clock sharp)

1.4

DATES AND YEARS

1. Two forms for writing a date are (a) *June 1, 1977* or (b) *1 June 1977*. Note that a comma follows the day in example a, but no comma appears in example b.

2. In less formal usage (in the United States), abbreviated dates are written with the month first: *10/12/1492* means *October 12, 1492; 7/4/1776* means *July 4, 1776.*

3. Dates are usually spoken or read aloud as ordinal numbers, and years are expressed in groups of ten: (December 25, 1955) *December* (the) *twenty-fifth, nineteen fifty-five;* (March 17, 1940) *March* (the) *seventeenth, nineteen forty.*
   Note: The article *the* is optional.

4. In answer to the question *What day is it?* we say *It's the twenty-sixth of February* or *It's February twenty-sixth.*

Read the following sentences aloud.

1. Christopher Columbus landed in the New World on October 12, 1492.
2. On March 15, 44 B.C. (before Christ) Julius Caesar was stabbed to death.
3. The S.S. *Titanic* sank on the night of April 14, 1912.
4. Marie Antoinette died at the guillotine on October 16, 1793.
5. Cleopatra lived from 69 to 30 B.C.
6. Shakespeare lived from 1564 to 1616.
7. The United States won its independence on July 4, 1776.
8. The Batista government in Cuba fell on January 1, 1959.
9. Joseph Stalin died on March 5, 1953.
10. Mohammed lived from 570? to 623.
11. The Second World War began in 1939 and ended in 1945.
12. Buddha lived from 563 to 483 B.C.
13. Napoleon Bonaparte was born in 1769 and died on the island of Saint Helena on May 5, 1821.
14. The San Francisco earthquake occurred in 1906 (nineteen 0 six).
15. His mother was born on February 7, 1932.
16. Her mother was born on April 16, 1928.
17. His grandmother was born on August 22, 1887, and died on December 3, 1970.

1.5

UNITED STATES MONEY

1. a penny = one cent   a quarter = twenty-five cents
    a nickel = five cents   a half dollar = fifty cents
    a dime = ten cents   a dollar = one hundred cents

2. In written amounts of money the cent sign follows the number, but the dollar sign precedes it.

5¢	$.05	$1.59 a dollar fifty-nine or one fifty-nine
10¢	$.10	$7.35 seven dollars and thirty-five cents
25¢	$.25	$69.95 sixty-nine ninety-five

Note: We frequently omit the words *dollars* and *cents*. They appear only when we wish to give an exact amount: *Exactly how much did the United States pay Russia for Alaska?* $7,200,000 (seven million two hundred thousand dollars).

Read the following sentences aloud.

Exactly how much did you pay for it?
1. I paid $12.95 (twelve dollars and ninety-five cents).
2. I paid $135.65 (one hundred thirty-five dollars and sixty-five cents).
3. I paid $1,600.00 (sixteen hundred dollars).
4. I paid $3,837.48 (three thousand eight hundred thirty-seven dollars and forty-eight cents).

Exactly how much did it cost?
1. It cost $27,927.22 (twenty-seven thousand nine hundred twenty-seven dollars and twenty-two cents).
2. It cost $32,000.00 (thirty-two thousand dollars).
3. It cost $1,936,000 (one million nine hundred thirty-six thousand dollars).
4. It cost $1,232.16 (one thousand two hundred thirty-two dollars and sixteen cents).

Read the following amounts aloud.

$27.38	$47.28	$22,000.	$483.00	$1,000,000,000.
$137.98	$198.98	$5,927.38	$358.00	$10.00
$12.98	$238.05	$52.78	$1,000,000.	$00.01

SIMPLE MATHEMATICAL TERMS

+ plus	= equals
− minus	¼ one-fourth
÷ divided by	½ one-half
×{times, multiplied by}	⅓ one-third
	⅔ two-thirds

1. $5 + 5 = 10$ (five plus five is [equals] ten)
2. $8 - 2 = 6$ (eight minus two is six)
3. $8 \div 2 = 4$ (eight divided by two is four)
4. $10 \times 10 = 100$ (ten multiplied by 10 is [*or* are] a hundred)
5. $3 \times 3 = 9$ (three times three is [*or* are] nine)

1. How much is (are) 8 and 2?
   8 and 2 is (are) 10.
2. How much is 12 from 20?
   12 from 20 is 8.
3. How much is 5 times 5?
   5 times 5 is 25.
4. How much is 7 multiplied by 3?
   7 multiplied by 3 is 21.
5. How much is 5 into 20?
   5 into 20 is 4.
6. How much is 100 divided by 2?
   100 divided by 2 is 50.

Do the following problems aloud.

1. $7 + 2$		9. $122 + 18$
2. 5×7		10. $250 \div 2$
3. $7 - 3$		11. 2×75
4. $33 \div 3$		12. $3 - 2$
5. $12 + 18$		13. 3×8
6. 7×7		14. 10×100
7. $10 \div 2$		15. 100×100
8. 6×3		16. 100×1000

LIST OF COMMONLY USED IRREGULAR VERBS

Note: Past participles are not discussed in Book 1.

Base Form	Past Form	Base Form	Past Form
arise	arose	grind	ground
awake	awoke	grow	grew
be	was	hang	hung
beat	beat		hanged (*meaning* being
become	became		hanged by the neck
begin	began		until dead)
bend	bent	have	had
bet	bet	hear	heard
bite	bit	hide	hid
bleed	bled	hit	hit
blow	blew	hold	held
break	broke	hurt	hurt
bring	brought	keep	kept
broadcast	broadcast, broadcasted	kneel	knelt, kneeled
build	built	knit	knit, knitted
burst	burst	know	knew
buy	bought	lay	laid
cast	cast	lead	led
catch	caught	leap	leaped, leapt
choose	chose	leave	left
come	came	lend	lent
cost	cost	let	let
deal	dealt	lie (to recline)	lay
dig	dug	(not to tell the truth)	lied
do	did	light	lit, lighted
draw	drew	lose	lost
dream	dreamed, dreamt	make	made
drink	drank	mean	meant
drive	drove	meet	met
eat	ate	mistake	mistook
fall	fell	overcome	overcame
feed	fed	pay	paid
feel	felt	put	put
fight	fought	quit	quit
find	found	read	read (*pronounced* "red")
flee	fled	ride	rode
fly	flew	ring	rang
forbid	forbade	rise	rose
forget	forgot	run	ran
freeze	froze	say	said
get	got	see	saw
give	gave	seek	sought
go	went	sell	sold

LIST (CONTINUED)

Base Form	Past Form	Base Form	Past Form
send	sent	sting	stung
set	set	stink	stank
shake	shook	strike	struck
shine (intransitive)	shone	swear	swore
(transitive)	shined	sweep	swept
shoot	shot	swim	swam
shrink	shrank, shrunk	swing	swung
shut	shut	take	took
sing	sang	teach	taught
sink	sank, sunk	tear	tore
sit	sat	tell	told
sleep	slept	think	thought
slide	slid	throw	threw
speak	spoke	understand	understood
speed	sped, speeded	wake	woke, waked
spend	spent	wear	wore
spin	spun	weave	wove
spit	spit, spat	weep	wept
split	split	win	won
stand	stood	wind	wound
steal	stole	withdraw	withdrew
stick	stuck	write	wrote